D0416793

EVERYMAN,
I WILL GO WITH THEE,
AND BE THY GUIDE,
IN THY MOST NEED
TO GO BY THY SIDE

ANDREW MARVELL

The Complete Poems

Edited by George deF. Lord
with an Introduction by A. Alvarez

EVERYMAN'S LIBRARY

153

This book is one of 250 volumes in Everyman's Library
which have been distributed to 4500 state schools
throughout the United Kingdom.
The project has been supported by a grant of £4 million
from the Millennium Commission.

First included in Everyman's Library, 1984
Introduction, Bibliography and Chronology © David Campbell
Publishers Ltd., 1993
Typography by Peter B. Willberg

ISBN 1-85715-153-4

A CIP catalogue record for this book is available from the
British Library

Published by David Campbell Publishers Ltd.,
Gloucester Mansions, 140A Shaftesbury Avenue,
London WC2H 8HD

Distributed by Random House (UK) Ltd.,
20 Vauxhall Bridge Road, London SW1V 2SA

CONTENTS

CONTENTS

INTRODUCTION

Marvell had a reputation during his lifetime, but not as a lyric poet. He was renowned as a political insider and combative parliamentary backbencher, as a satirist and pamphleteer. Early in Marvell's career, Milton, who was his friend, recommended him for a government post as a man 'of singular desert for the State to make use of'; a Frenchman who met him later in Saumur described him, less sympathetically, as 'a notable English Italo-Machiavellian'. Margaret Thatcher would have called him 'one of us'.

Marvell's credentials for a place in the political establishment were impeccable. His father was a Church of England minister, MA Cantab., Master of Hull Grammar School, lecturer at Holy Trinity Church, and famous enough to be included in the contemporary guide book to the great and good, Fuller's *Worthies of England*, where he is described as 'Most *facetious* in his *discourse*, yet *grave* in his *carriage*, a most excellent preacher.'

Andrew Marvell, the poet, was born in 1621, went up to Trinity College, Cambridge, in 1633 and published his first verses, in Latin and Greek, in 1637, when he was sixteen. A year later, his mother died and his father remarried. Marvell's response was to leave Cambridge and convert briefly to Catholicism. But his clerical father found him in London and bustled him back to university and that, effectively, was the end of his unconventionality. He stayed at Cambridge until his father died in 1641, then went down without taking his MA and spent five years – 1642-7 – travelling on the continent, possibly as tutor to a rich young Englishman, Edward Skinner.

By 1653, when Milton wrote his recommendation, Marvell was attached to the household of one of the most powerful men in England: he was tutor to the daughter of General Fairfax, who had recently retired as commander-in-chief of the Parliamentary forces. Lord Fairfax was an enlightened and liberal man and he had resigned his command because he refused to invade Scotland. His post was then taken by his less forgiving lieutenant-general, Oliver Cromwell, and in due course Marvell went on to tutor Cromwell's ward and prospective son-in-law, William Dutton. This apprenticeship to the great and good of his own generation was eventually rewarded in 1657 when Marvell landed the government job he wanted; he joined Milton as Latin Secretary to the Council of State. Two years later, he was elected MP for Hull and he held the seat until he died in 1678. By then, his fame as a political pamphleteer and satirist was established; a generation after his death, Swift wrote admiringly of *The Rehearsal Transprosed* and called Marvell a 'great genius'.

For Swift, Marvell's genius was in his satires, but he also had a considerable reputation as a Latin poet. According to Aubrey, 'He was a great master of the Latin tongue; an excellent poet in Latin and English; for Latin verses there was no man could come into competition with him.' Some of those Latin poems were published in Marvell's lifetime, as were his political satires in English (most of them anonymously), but the poems that eventually made him famous were not printed until 1681, three years after his death, and it took another two and a half centuries for his real achievement as a poet to be recognized. Dr Johnson ignored him, except for a passing reference in his life of Milton; the two Romantics who noticed him – Hazlitt and Lamb – thought him quaint and whimsical; the late Victorian scholars edited him in the same archaeological spirit as they edited Suckling or Aurelian Townshend. It was not until 1921 that Marvell properly entered the pantheon. Grierson began the process in the introduction to his famous anthology of *Metaphysical Lyrics and Poems*, where he wrote, 'Apart from Milton, he is the most interesting personality between Donne and Dryden, and at his best a finer poet than either', and T. S. Eliot completed the job with his marvellous essay celebrating the three hundredth anniversary of Marvell's birth.

In that tercentenary essay Eliot wrote, 'To bring the poet back to life [is] the great, the perennial, task of criticism', and he performed the miracle for Marvell brilliantly in the space of a couple of thousand words. Even so, three hundred years seems a long wait in oblivion for the author of some of the most formally perfect poems in the language. Indeed, oblivion seems to have set in almost before the ink was dry: very few of the poems on which his reputation now rests were published in Marvell's lifetime and they seem not even to have circulated widely among his friends, since very few manuscripts survived.

There is nothing unusual about this. In the sixteenth and seventeenth centuries, gentlemen – members of the professional classes as well as courtiers – did not write verse for the general public – not even for that small section of the general public that could read. For Marvell and the Caroline courtly poets, as for Donne and his followers, poetry was not a profession, it was a social grace, like singing or swordsmanship, an accomplishment friends might appreciate and admire but not something to be flaunted before strangers. They passed their poems in manuscript to their friends, who, in turn, made copies for their friends, and occasionally they allowed their verse to appear in courtly anthologies, depending on the occasion and the other contributors. But printed collections were mostly published posthumously. Posterity, or even a poetic reputation outside their immediate circle, was not their concern. What Thomas Sprat, the historian of the Royal Society, wrote in praise of Abraham Cowley, was also true of Marvell: 'he never willingly recited any of his Writings. None but his intimate friends ever discovered he was a great Poet by his discourse.' Marvell published his satires because they were a function of his public career as a politician. The rest of his poetry was a private pleasure written for his own enjoyment and for that of a few friends.

Whence Marvell's confidence in his sophistication. He was writing for people who shared his interests and education, who would pick up his references, appreciate his wit and elegance, and were equally attuned to the Latin and Greek classical tradition that deeply permeated everything he wrote.

This shared sophistication gave Marvell a certain freedom as well as a certain strength. He needed an intimate audience because, despite his public career, he was an intensely private person and his poems mostly reflect that privacy:

Two Paradises 'twere in one
To live in Paradise alone.

Philip Larkin, Hull's other poet and also unmarried, once remarked, 'Sex is much too wonderful an experience to share with anyone else.' Marvell's couplet expresses more elegantly the same bachelor yearning for the uncluttered life. He was always a fastidious poet, detached and reserved, but sometimes the line is blurred between critical distance and plain distaste for the heat and muddle of the ordinary human condition.

The greatest of his poems depend on this fastidiousness. Although he became a staunch republican, until 1650 his sympathies had been with the Royalists, and the 'Horatian Ode', which was probably written in June 1650, is far from a celebration of Cromwell's martial triumphs. It is, instead, a reluctant tribute to the necessity of force from a man who had no taste for it:

> So restless *Cromwel* could not cease
> In the inglorious Arts of Peace,
> > But through adventrous War
> > Urged his active Star ...
> 'Tis Madness to resist or blame
> The force of angry Heavens flame:
> > And, if we would speak true,
> > Much to the Man is due:
> Who, from his private Gardens, where
> He liv'd reserved and austere,
> > As if his highest plot
> > To plant the Bergamot,
> Could by industrious Valour climbe
> To ruine the great Work of Time,
> > And cast the Kingdoms old
> > Into another Mold.

Marvell's own preference was for the private garden and his distaste for restlessness was as great as his disdain for go-getting industrious valour. He was a political liberal in an illiberal time, but he understood the realities of political power. That did not prevent him from being shocked by the sacrilege of regicide or from admiring the nobility with which the king went to his death. Although Marvell was a Puritan and a devoted Parliamentarian, he was never a religious fanatic and his particular style of highly civilized sophistication did not take willingly to violence. Hence his famous comment on the Civil War:

Whether it be a war of religion or liberty it is not worth the labour to enquire. Whatsoever was at the top, the other was at the bottom; but upon considering all, I think the cause was too good to have been fought for. Men ought to have trusted God – they ought to have trusted the King with the whole matter.

He was evidently a man not taken in by propaganda and the triumph of the 'Horatian Ode' is in its even-handedness in the teeth of his own natural aversion to the butchery perpetrated in the name of religious and political principles. He balances Cromwell's zeal and ruthlessness against the king's grace and dignity, admires the loser and judges the winner without ever compromising his own standards.

Fastidiousness, alas, is as rare in political poetry as it is in politics itself – which is why the 'Horatian Ode' is such an extraordinary achievement. But there is another side to Marvell's particular style of fastidiousness which prevents some of his great poems from being quite as great as they first appear. 'To his Coy Mistress' seems like a perfect love poem until you compare it with 'The Good Morrow' or 'The Anniversary' or 'A Valediction: of weeping' or any of a dozen of Donne's other finest poems, and then Marvell seems oddly impersonal, almost disembodied. The difference is that Donne writes as though he were talking, urgently and directly, to someone standing right in front of him; the poems are as swift and immediate as an overheard conversation. Marvell, in comparison, is celebrating not love or a living woman but what Eliot called 'one of the great traditional commonplaces of literature. It is the theme of *O mistress mine*, of *Gather ye rosebuds*, of *Go, lovely rose*; it is in the savage austerity of Lucretius and the intense levity of Catullus.' That commonplace is the theme of *carpe diem*, and Marvell plays skilled and beautiful variations on it, but I am not convinced he had anyone particular in mind when he was writing.

Anyone, that is, apart from himself. The first half of the poem is less concerned with passion than with absurdity: the absurdity of the rituals of courtship, of false modesty, of his own inadequacy as a lover:

> Thou by the *Indian Ganges* side
> Should'st Rubies find: I by the Tide
> Of *Humber* would complain . . .

The coy mistress gathers exotic treasures in exotic places while he is left to grumble in the dour northern town he was brought up in. The joke is clearly at his own expense. So is the 'vegetable love', given the passion he expresses elsewhere for fruits and flowers and gardens. The sudden quickening of pace and feeling, the 'surprise' both Eliot and Grierson rightly admired – 'But at my back I alwaies hear/ Times winged Charriot hurrying near . . .' – has nothing to do with his mistress's charms; it is provoked by the prospect of his own mortality and it leads him into accepting images of violence – the cannonball tearing 'with rough strife,/ Thorough the Iron gates of Life' – that go flatly against his own peaceful predilections. As I have written elsewhere, 'the real and moving poem is about time, death, waste and the *need* to love, rather than about love itself.'[1] The poem starts as variations on a literary theme, as a brilliant and inventive exercise, then gets swept up into a passionate, private but quite different concern.

Marvell did write love poems – poems, that is, full of delight, excitement and surprise – but all of them, in their different ways, were inspired by innocence rather than passion. His real love poems are about gardens and unspoiled nature, about young girls in bud, about mowers, shepherds and shepherdesses. In a word, they are about Eden and, like Milton's, Marvell's Eden was a garden enclosed by untamed nature. For Marvell, however, Eden had an English name and an English location. It was, I think, Lord Fairfax's estate at Nun Appleton House, where Marvell lived during the turmoil of the Civil War, with his charming young pupil and her sympathetic father, who had just retired from public life on a matter of principle. Fairfax's principles seem to have been much the same as Marvell's and that congeniality, combined with Nun Appleton's gardens, woods and spreading fields, seems to have inspired most of his best poems.

The Elizabethans resurrected the pastoral tradition as part of their rediscovery of Greek and Latin poetry and Shakespeare – above all in *The Winter's Tale* – then adapted it to the English landscape. Marvell brought these two elements together in a unique and special way. Since his own poetry was rooted in the classics, he naturally followed the classical conventions – shepherds and shepherdesses courting, spurning, languishing – but he used them as an excuse for a Shakespearian relish in detail:

> Oh what unusual Heats are here,
> Which thus our Sun-burn'd Meadows fear!
> The Grass-hopper its pipe gives ore;
> And hamstring'd Frogs can dance no more.
> But in the brook the green Frog wades;
> And Grass-hoppers seek out the shades.
> Only the Snake, that kept within,
> Now glitters in its second skin.

His poems are full of this kind of loving and precise observation: 'The hatching *Thrastle's* shining Eye', 'the Fountains sliding foot', 'Grass, with moister colour dasht,/ Seems as green Silks but newly washt'; or this extraordinary description of the woodpecker:

> He walks still upright from the Root,
> Meas'ring the Timber with his Foot;
> And all the way, to keep it clean,
> Doth from the Bark the Wood-moths glean.

This is nature poetry *avant la lettre*, but nature poetry written by someone who loved the subject for its own sake and without the pressure of Wordsworth's unrelenting egocentricity.

Marvell and Milton were two of the foremost classicists of their day and I think the sweet and pure simplicity of Marvell's pastorals – many of the dialogues sound as though they were written to be set to music – were deliberate attempts to re-create in English the lucid calm of Virgil's *Eclogues*, just

xv

as Milton's clangorous blank verse was a re-creation of Virgil's epic beat.

The pastoral, in its various forms, was also high fashion in the seventeenth century, in much the same way as working-class culture was fashionable in our time. This was a period when courtiers dressed up as shepherds and shepherdesses, artful formal gardens were a source of great pride to their owners and people paid fortunes for tulip bulbs. Marvell duly paid homage to 'skilful gardeners' and floral clocks, but his real passion was for the 'wild and fragrant innocence' of the natural world before its fall into art and worldliness.

It is a critical commonplace that his favourite adjective was 'green'. In his not very large body of work, excluding the satires, he used the word two dozen times – so often that it almost seems a stylistic tic. According to William Empson, 'it is connected ... with grass, buds, children, an as yet virginal prospect of sexuality, and the peasant stock from which the great families emerge'.[2] It is also connected with strong feeling. Whenever Marvell needed to imply special approval, a special intensity of feeling, a special kind of beauty, he used 'green'. At times, the word seems so right and so simple that only genius could have chosen it:

> He hangs in shades the Orange bright,
> Like golden Lamps in a green Night.

But the habit was so deep-rooted in him that he also used 'green' at moments when, to anyone else, it might have seemed obvious and flat:

> So Architects do square and hew
> Green Trees that in the Forest grew.

That is the final couplet of one of his most complex and subtle poems, 'A Dialogue between the Soul and Body', and the line-break ensures that 'green' gets all the emphasis. For Marvell, it implies the unviolated innocence of nature; for the un-initiated, it seems self-evident and a little feeble.

'Green', I think, was Marvell's shorthand for paradise and happiness, a word so soaked in private allusions that it generated its own mystery. Just what that mystery was is the subject of 'The Garden', the strange poem in which he described, ironically and with all sorts of jokes at the expense of classical myth and conventional love poetry, a condition the Book of Common Prayer calls 'the peace that passes all understanding'.

'The Garden' was probably written when Marvell was with the Fairfaxes in Yorkshire – there are jaunty variations on the same theme in stanzas 71–7 of 'Upon Appleton House' – and it reads like an answer to his 'Horatian Ode'. It starts with a farewell to arms, Oliver Cromwell-style – 'How vainly men themselves amaze/ To win the Palm, the Oke, or Bayes' – but its real subject is paradise and true happiness. Paradise is lonely and asexual – it begins with 'delicious Solitude,' 'When we have run our Passions heat' – and true happiness is a transcendental state achieved by what was, for Marvell, a kind of magical thinking through which his favourite word formed what mathematicians call a 'strange loop' with itself:

> Annihilating all that's made
> To a green Thought in a green Shade.

In 'The Extasie', John Donne and his mistress achieved a similar mystical revelation, eye to eye and sweaty palm to sweaty palm; but to make it perfect, 'Else a great Prince in prison lies', they had to come back down into their bodies and make love. In contrast, Marvell's mystical ecstasy is a solitary experience and at its climax his soul takes flight into the landscape:

> Casting the Bodies Vest aside,
> My Soul into the boughs does glide:
> There like a Bird it sits, and sings,
> Then whets, and combs its silver Wings ...

For Marvell, perfect bliss, the *raptus* of passion, was an out-of-body experience.

The nearest his poems ever came to sensuality was in the strange panegyric to murdered innocence, 'The Nymph complaining for the death of her Faun'. Like the 'Coy Mistress', this, too, starts out as variations on a conventional theme; there is an ancient and honoured literary tradition of poems

xvii

lamenting the death of a favourite pet: Catullus on Lesbia's sparrow, Ovid on Corinna's parrot, Skelton on Philip Sparrow. But none of them carries the curious sensual charge of Marvell's poem:

> Upon the Roses it would feed,
> Until its Lips ev'n seemed to bleed:
> And then to me 'twould boldly trip,
> And print those Roses on my Lip.
> But all its chief delight was still
> On Roses thus its self to fill:
> And its pure virgin Limbs to fold
> In whitest sheets of Lillies cold.
> Had it liv'd long, it would have been
> Lillies without, Roses within.

To me, that sounds closer in spirit to Freud on polymorphous perversion than to Catullus or Ovid. In her trance of blood and virginity, Marvell's Nymph has less in common with Lesbia or Corinna than with Count Dracula.

The poem may have begun as a sidelong reaction to the violence of the Civil War – scholars have suggested that 'the wanton Troopers' are the Scottish Covenanting Army which invaded England in 1640 – and it segues into a conventional story of pastoral seduction and betrayal, complete with all the usual puns on 'dears' and 'hearts'. But once the nymph is left alone with her faun it becomes a panegyric on the eroticism of innocence. For all its grace and tenderness, it seems a great deal more aroused than any of Marvell's other love poems.

It is also more moving. The poem is, of course, a lament and Marvell seems always to have been irresistibly stirred by feminine grief. Even 'Mourning', one of his most glib and cynical poems, deepens when confronting the strangeness and grandeur of a weeping woman:

> How wide they dream! The *Indian* Slaves,
> That sink for Pearl through Seas profound,
> Would find her Tears yet deeper Waves
> And not of one the bottom sound.

In 'The Nymph complaining ...' grief and innocence come together to create something even richer and stranger:

See how it weeps. The Tears do come
Sad, slowly dropping like a Gumme.
So weeps the wounded Balsome: so
The holy Frankincense doth flow.
The brotherless *Heliades*
Melt in such Amber Tears as these.

The lines are some of the most beautiful Marvell ever wrote
and they compress into a kind of solemn, slow-motion halluci-
nation of grief all the elements that spoke to him most
eloquently: man-ravaged nature – 'the wounded Balsome' – as
well as Christian and classical myth – 'the holy Frankincense'
and 'the brotherless *Heliades*'.

As I said earlier, gentleman poets wrote, at most, for an
intimate audience of friends. When Marvell was a young man
and writing his finest poems, he was living a secluded pastoral
life deep in the Yorkshire countryside and his only audience
was General Fairfax and his little daughter Mary. One way of
amusing them was the game of wit, as played both by Donne
and by late, decadent but at that time highly fashionable
Metaphysical poets like Cleveland and Cowley. It was a game
Marvell was supremely adept at and he brought to it his own
peculiar brand of perfection.

'The Definition of Love', for example, is an extended
scientific-mathematical conceit in the manner of Donne and
Lord Herbert of Cherbury, but Marvell handles it with a
difference. Instead of using his cleverness as a means of
seduction and blinding the lady with science, he takes the title
literally and produces an extended essay in abstraction in
which the imagery and the argument work cunningly together
to prove the impossibility of love. He starts with solid allegori-
cal figures, with tinsel wings, iron wedges and decrees of steel,
then gradually flattens them out and refines them away; the
round globe of 'Loves whole World' loses a dimension and is
'cramp'd into a *Planisphere*', which is then reduced to the lines
of a geometrical figure. The result is rueful and charming, but
it is not a love poem; it is what the poet says it is, the definition
of a love too refined to exist.

In its own terms, it is an elegantly logical performance, but
Marvell's logic was altogether different from Donne's. Donne

was always arguing fiercely, trying to prove a point or make an outrageous case or get a girl into bed. His poems are full of logical copulas – 'therefore', 'thus', 'and so'. His followers admired and imitated this mannerism; it was part of what Donne himself called his 'masculine perswasive force'. But those outside the select circle were less impressed. When Donne and his followers were labelled 'Metaphysical' – the word was applied to them long before Dr Johnson wrote his famous essay on Cowley – it was a derogatory term, an accusation. It implied that he sounded like the schoolmen, the mediaeval neo-Aristotelian philosophers who wasted their time in pointless casuistry, debating endlessly about how many angels could dance on the head of a pin. It implied that he was old-fashioned, out of key with the new scientific spirit of the Royal Society or the burgeoning rationality of the Enlightenment.

In comparison, Marvell's logic seems measured, Roman and far less aggressive. He uses the classical syllogism – thesis, antithesis, synthesis – less because he has anything urgent to prove than because it imposes on the poems a perfect formal shape. The result is a kind of Platonic ideal of the Metaphysical poem – polished, smoothed over, made abstract and fixed for all time, as though in amber.

Marvell's other way of amusing his captive audience at Appleton House was to take the Metaphysical conceit and push it into absurdity. This had already been done unwittingly by John Cleveland, a Cambridge don whose dreadful verse was briefly but hugely popular. (His 1647 *Poems* went through twenty editions, thirteen of them in two years, compared with two editions of Milton's 1645 *Poems*.) For Dryden, 'Clevelandism' meant punning, 'wresting and torturing a word into another meaning'. It also meant outlandish conceits by which, as Dr Johnson said, 'the most heterogeneous ideas are yoked by violence together'. The motive behind both processes was the donnish desire to show off the author's learning and ingenuity at whatever cost:

> I like not tears in tune, nor do I prize
> His artificial grief who scans his eyes.

Mine weep down pious beads, but why should I
Confine them to the Muse's rosary?
I am no poet here; my pen's the spout
Where the rain-water of mine eyes run out
In pity of that name, whose fate we see
Thus copied out in grief's hydrography.

This has all Cleveland's dotty faults and pretentions: the bad pun ('scan'), the ridiculous comparison (weeping eyes and rain-spouts), the knowing polysyllabic reference to an arcane science (hydrography). Above all, it has the prime distinguishing mark of Clevelandism: an utter inappropriateness to the occasion, which in this instance was the death by drowning of Edward King, Milton's friend and the subject of 'Lycidas'.

Marvell took this crass formula and transformed it into high art. He had always been a master of the subtle pun ('Deaf with the drumming of an Ear') and the elegant conceit ('A Soul hung up, as 'twere, in Chains/ Of Nerves, and Arteries, and Veins'). But he was also a master of the absurd. Whence the notorious figure of 'the Antipodes in Shoes', which Eliot accused of being one of those 'images which are over-developed or distracting; which support nothing but their own misshapen bodies'. In context, however, it seems altogether less offensive:

But now the *Salmon-Fishers* moist
Their *Leathern Boats* begin to hoist;
And, like *Antipodes* in Shoes,
Have shod theyr *Heads* in their *Canoos.*
How Tortoise like, but not so slow,
These rational *Amphibii* go?
Let's in: for the dark *Hemisphere*
Does now like one of them appear.

This is the last stanza, the ninety-seventh, of a very long poem and I do not believe that Marvell, a supremely self-confident craftsman, has let the Metaphysical style run away with him at this crucial moment. He is not going over the top with a far-fetched image, he is merely being playful.

He had, in fact, stolen the conceit from 'Square Cap', one of Cleveland's most popular poems: 'The antipodes wear their shoes on their heads.' Marvell then shows what can be done with it: he prepares the way with a pun – '*Leathern Boats*' suggests 'boots' – expands it into the solemn pedantry of the following couplet – 'How Tortoise like, but not so slow ...' – and ends with absurdity – the comparison of the dark coming down over the hemisphere with the coracles over the heads of the fishermen. It is ridiculous, of course, but that is precisely the point of the exercise. Cleveland, as a university wit, used the Metaphysical conceit to show off his cleverness and his learning. Marvell, a classicist and perfectionist, saw the conceit for what it mostly was, a literary joke in not very good taste, and used it accordingly: with mock seriousness at conventional occasions for conventionally exaggerated praise of his patron, and playfully when his patron's daughter makes her entry. The last stanza of the poem is the climax of this playfulness, the moment when it moves over into what was, at that point, an entirely new form: comic verse. Marvell may have been the finest inheritor of the line of wit that descended from Donne and Jonson, but he was also the initiator of another tradition entirely, a tradition that reached its peak two centuries later with Thomas Hood, Lewis Carroll and Edward Lear. There is a direct line from 'Upon *Appleton* House' to 'The Hunting of the Snark' and 'The Dong with the Luminous Nose'.

There is a portrait of Marvell in the National Portrait Gallery: a cupid's bow mouth with a full lower lip, a pencil moustache so carefully trimmed that it might almost be a shadow, the eyebrows long and fine and arched, the expression disdainful and withheld. 'He was of middling stature,' wrote Aubrey, 'pretty strong sett, roundish face, cherry cheek't, hazel eie, browne haire. He was in conversation very modest, and of very few words: and though he loved wine he would never drinke hard in company, and was wont to say that *he would not play the good-fellow in any man's company in whose hands he would not trust his life*. He kept bottles of wine at his lodgeing, and many times he would drinke liberally to refresh his spirits, and exalt his muse'.

It sounds like a peculiarly English combination: a public servant fastidious in his art and his politics, a bachelor with a gift for amusing children, a lover of nature and gardens, Latin and Greek poetry, innocence and privacy, a man who was obscurely vulnerable to women's grief but never vulnerable enough to marry, who wrote like an angel when he was young, then settled into a middle age of politics and controversy and solitary drinking. A couple of centuries later, all this would have been a recipe for eccentricity and unhappiness. But Marvell was writing at a time when people seemed to have been less at the mercy of their private inadequacies and he used his to produce some of the most classically perfect poems in the language. They are classical in the true, Latinate sense: chaste and musical, lucid and restrained, long on invention and elegance, short on appetite, monuments to a style of civilization that is now as remote and foreign as that of classical Rome and Greece themselves.

A. Alvarez

NOTES

[1] A. Alvarez, *The School of Donne*, 1961.
[2] William Empson, 'Marvell's Garden', *Some Versions of Pastoral*, 1950, p.127.

A NOTE ON THE TEXT

Very few of Marvell's poems were published during his lifetime. Of those few only two pieces in Greek and Latin on Charles I and the poems on Lovelace, Hastings, Witty, and Milton carried his name or initials. For the remaining poems written before 1660 – including all the lyrics on which Marvell's present reputation chiefly depends – the *Miscellaneous Poems* of 1681 (the first edition or Folio) provides in almost every case the only text. The three poems on Cromwell were cancelled from all copies of that edition except for one now in the British Museum which, however, omits ll. 185–324 of the elegy on Cromwell. The Folio of 1681 was published by 'Mary Marvell', an imposter who was trying to lay claim to the poet's estate by posing as his widow.

In 1776 an edition of the poems and letters edited by Capt. Edward Thompson appeared. Thompson claimed to base his edition on two MSS., one compiled by the poet's nephew and intimate friend, William Popple. Thompson added many poems to those printed in the Folio of 1681, most of them spurious. Since that time – the MSS. having meanwhile vanished – all editions have been based on the 1681 *Miscellaneous Poems* with the uncancelled portions in the British Museum copy, on Thompson's edition, and, for the later satires, on various printed and manuscript texts of doubtful authority.

In 1946 the Bodleian Library acquired a copy of the 1681 *Miscellaneous Poems* with extensive manuscript additions, including the three poems on Cromwell and seventeen verse satires of the reign of Charles II. A comparison of the texts of these poems with Thompson's versions proves beyond question that the MS. described by Thompson as 'written by Mr. Popple' had been recovered. Although Thompson was wrong about the hand (which is probably a commercial scribe's) the painstakingly prepared collection was undoubtedly compiled under Popple's direction for a projected Complete Poems of Marvell which never went to press.

Not only was the Bodleian MS. originally compiled and written with great care but it was subsequently checked against some other unidentified authority. Accordingly seven of the seventeen poems added to the canon are regarded as spurious. Two of these Thompson correctly identified as the work of John Ayloffe, a close associate of Marvell's from 1672, but he included four of the remaining five in his edition.

The Bodleian MS. (catalogued as Eng. poet. d. 49) indicates the authentic additions with crosses next to the titles. The seven poems lacking such crossmarks are:

'Upon the Cutting Sir John Coventry's nose'
'The Checker-Inn'
'Scaevola Scoto-Britannus'
'The Doctor turn'd Justice'
'On the Monument'
'Advice to a Painter to Draw the Duke' (by Ayloffe)
'Britannia and Rawleigh' (by Ayloffe)

Thompson added the first four poems on this list but excluded 'On the Monument', perhaps because he may have regarded it wrongly as an early version of another poem on the same topic, 'Hodge's Vision from the Monument', which he included in his edition. Subsequent editors have printed the poems with various degrees of doubt as to their authenticity, but the late great Marvell scholar, H. M. Margoliouth (*The Poems and Letters of Andrew Marvell* [1927]), questioned all of them except for *Scaevola Scoto-Britannus*. Their inferior quality and radical difference in style and viewpoint from Marvell's authentic work provide abundant internal evidence against Marvell's authorship. With the external evidence provided by the Bodleian MS. we may now confidently exclude them from the canon.

Other poems formerly attributed to Marvell which do not appear in the Bodleian MS. and which may now also be excluded as spurious are:

'Upon his House'
'Upon his Grandchildren'
'Further Advice to a Painter'

A NOTE ON THE TEXT

'Nostradamus's Phophecy'
'A Dialogue between the Two Horses'
'An Historicall Poem'

The Bodleian MS. also augments other evidence, both internal and external, for attributing to Marvell two important verse satires which have not heretofore been included in any edition of his poems, 'The Second Advice to a Painter' and 'The Third Advice to a Painter'.

The same hand which identified the authentic poems in the manuscript portions of the Bodleian volume also checked as spurious 122 lines of 'The Loyall Scott', including most of the lines which Margoliouth has challenged on other grounds. Without these lines the poem gains immeasurably in coherence and consistency.

The authenticity of three other poems printed in the Folio is also questioned by their exclusion from the Bodleian volume. These poems are 'A Dialogue between Thyrsis and Dorinda', 'Tom May's Death', and 'On the Victory obtained by Blake'. I have not, however, felt justified in omitting pieces printed in the Folio from the present edition.

The Folio portion of the Bodleian MS. contains about 100 manuscript emendations of the text. These are in a hand which is not that of the scribe, nor of the person who crossed out the last four lines of 'A Dialogue between the Soul and Body' and wrote 'Desunt multa' (much is missing) beneath, nor, probably, that of Capt. Thompson, who explains in his preface that the Popple MS. came too late for him to make much use of it. A large proportion of the emendations are attempts through elision to reduce Marvell's lines to a somewhat cut-and-dried idea of metrical regularity by eliminating anapests and dactyls. Many more are corrections to the Latin poems, which contain many errors in the Folio. Others are more substantive, such as 'the iron *grates* of life' in 'To his Coy Mistress', an interesting reading which I do not adopt, since the Folio's *gates* presents no difficulties, or '*mads* the dog' (for *made*) in line 21 of 'Damon the Mower', which I do adopt, because the Folio reading does not make sense. I have recorded these variants when they are substantive and when they do not (as is usually the case in corrections in Latin and French) simply set right what is obviously wrong.

I have abandoned the somewhat random arrangement of poems in the Folio for one which I hope is less confusing. The lyrics are printed together in the order in which they appear in the Folio except that I have inserted after 'Clorinda and Damon' 'Two Songs at the Marriage of the Lord Fauconberg and the Lady Mary Cromwell'. At the end of the section I have placed the lines on rural solitude translated from Seneca.

In the second section I have arranged chronologically poems on political themes from the Cromwell period. The third section includes in chronological order the satires of the Restoration period. I have grouped together in the fourth section, again chronologically, poems mainly epistolary or elegiac on various individuals. The last section includes the Latin poems and Marvell's one extant poem in Greek. Most of the translations supplied are by A. B. Grosart (*The Complete Works of Andrew Marvell* [1872–75]), Marvell's nineteenth-century editor, but I am indebted to William A. McQueen and Kiffin A. Rockwell and to the University of North Carolina Press for permission to reprint their translations of '*Ros*', '*Hortus*', and '*Inscribenda Luparae*'.

I have retained the spelling, capitalization, and italics of the Folio except for the long *s*. In editing the manuscript additions I have tried to apply the principles of styling followed in the Folio. To avoid confusion I have changed the old spelling of the conjunctive particle *then* to *than*. I have lengthened the second person singular pronoun from *the* to *thee* and changed *wast* to *waste* and *chast* to *chaste*. The punctuation of the Folio is retained except in a very small number of cases where it seems to introduce serious difficulties for the modern reader.

In my notes I have tried to record specific debts to other scholars, but my indebtedness to the edition of the late H. M. Margoliouth is so extensive that it should be mentioned here.

I am indebted to Mr Richard W. Hunt, Keeper of Western Manuscripts, Bodleian Library, for permission to use the manuscript on which the present edition is largely based, Bod. MS. Eng. poet. d. 49. Warm thanks are also due to Mrs Sydney Lea, Jr., for assistance in preparing this edition.

A NOTE ON THE TEXT

I have indicated my indebtedness in particular notes by (Margoliouth) and (Cooke). The abbreviations of Bod. MS. and Folio stand for Bod. MS. Eng. poet. d. 49 (the corrected edition of the Folio with manuscript additions) and *Miscellaneous Poems* of 1681, respectively.

George deF. Lord

SELECT BIBLIOGRAPHY

EDITIONS

H. M. Margoliouth, *The Poems and Letters of Andrew Marvell*, two vols., Oxford University Press, 1971 (third edition) offers the complete poems together with a useful collection of letters and helpful annotations. In particular, Margoliouth discusses Marvell's disputed authorship of the later satires.

Andrew Marvell: Complete Poems, edited by Elizabeth Story Donno, Penguin, 1971, prints the Latin poems and provides extensive notes, though the preface is restricted to expounding the editor's textual choices.

A. B. Grosart, *The Complete Works of Andrew Marvell*, four vols., privately printed, 1872–5, includes the only complete edition of the prose.

There is also an excellent *Selected Poetry* with notes, edited by Frank Kermode, New American Library, 1967.

BACKGROUND

John M. Wallace, *Destiny His Choice: The Loyalism of Andrew Marvell*, Cambridge University Press, 1968, provides a useful guide to the historical and political context in which Marvell worked, while Hilton Kelliher, *Andrew Marvell: Poet and Politician*, British Museum Publications Ltd., 1978, originally published as an exhibition catalogue, offers a concise summary of the biographical facts.

The standard biography is still Pierre Legouis, *Andrew Marvell: Poet, Puritan, Patriot*, Clarendon Press, 1965.

A narrower consideration of the literary and cultural context can be found in Maren-Sofie Rostvig, *The Happy Man; Studies in the Metamorphosis of a Classical Ideal, 1600–1700*, Oxford University Press, 1954.

There is a huge literature on the English Civil War which has recently been the subject of renewed controversy concerning its causes, origins and effects. The most brilliant recent study is Conrad Russell, *Fall of the British Monarchies, 1637–1642*, Oxford University Press, 1991. The best disscussion of the topic à propos Marvell is still to be found in Christopher Hill, *Puritanism and Revolution*, Secker and Warburg, 1958.

CRITICAL STUDIES

Andrew Marvell by M. C. Bradbrook and M. G. Lloyd Thomas, Cambridge University Press, 1961, and J. B. Leishman's *The Art of Marvell's Poetry*, Hutchinson 1966, are probably still the most helpful extended discussions of the verse for the general reader, though anyone interested in this poet should also read the superb relevant pages in *Elizabethan and Metaphysical Imagery*, Chicago University Press, 1947, by Rosamond Tuve. J. E. Duncan, *The Revival of Metaphysical Poetry*, Oxford University Press and University of Minnesota Press, 1959, is also useful.

Duncan's book documents the rediscovery of Donne, Marvell and their contemporaries in the early years of this century. Among classic commentaries by leading figures involved in that process of rediscovery are the pieces on Marvell and metaphysical poetry by T. S. Eliot, included in *Selected Essays*, Faber and Faber, 1932, and the lengthy introduction to H. J. C. Grierson's pioneering anthology *Metaphysical Poetry: Donne to Butler*, reprinted by Oxford University Press in 1962.

Among more recent critics, Warren Chernaik in *The Poet's Time*, Cambridge University Press, 1983, focuses on the political and religious background of the verse while Margarita Stocker's *Apocalyptic Marvell: The Second Coming in Seventeenth Century Poetry*, Harvester, 1986, considers Marvell in the narrower millenarian context.

Readers will also find useful collections of essays in *Andrew Marvell: The Critical Heritage*, ed. Elizabeth S. Donno, Routledge, 1978; *Andrew Marvell: Twentieth Century Views*, ed. George de F. Lord, Prentice Hall, Englewood Cliffs, N. J.; *Andrew Marvell*, ed. John Carey, Penguin, 1969; and *Marvell: Modern Judgments*, ed. Michael Wilding, Macmillan, 1969.

CHRONOLOGY

DATE	AUTHOR'S LIFE	LITERARY CONTEXT
1621	Born at Winestead-in-Holderness, Yorkshire on Easter Eve (31 March), fourth child of the Rev. Andrew Marvell, originally from Cambridgeshire, and his wife, Anne Pease. He is	Donne writes most of his *Holy Sonnets* and many *Divine Poems* (to 1631). Burton: *The Anatomy of Melancholy*.
1622	preceded by three elder sisters; a younger brother, born 1623, dies the following year.	Drayton: *Poly-Olbion* (part I, 1612). First performance of *The Changeling* by Middleton and Rowley.
1623		Shakespeare First Folio. Marino: *Adone*. Théophile de Viau: *Elégies et sonnets*.
1624	The Rev. Andrew Marvell appointed simultaneously Master of the Charterhouse Hospital, and Lecturer in Holy Trinity Church, Hull. The	King: *The Exequy*. Lord Herbert of Cherbury: *De Veritate* (advocating religious toleration). Lope de Vega: *Circe*.
1625	former was a well endowed charitable institution maintaining thirteen poor men and thirteen poor women. The Marvells live in the Master's House. Marvell's father, later described by Thomas Fuller as	Grotius: *De jure belli ac pacis* (treatise on international law). Third, expanded, edition of Bacon's *Essays*.
1627	'an excellent preacher' and by Anthony à Wood as 'facetious and yet Calvinistic', was, according to Marvell himself 'a Conformist to the established rites of the Church of England, though I confess none of the most over-running or eager in them'.	Bacon: *New Atlantis*. May's translation of Lucan's *Pharsalia*. Fletcher's anti-Catholic *The Locusts, or The Apollyonists*. Gongara: *Sonnets*. Grotius: *De Veritate religionis christinae*.
1628		Earle: *Microcosmographie*, (character sketches). Harvey publishes his theories on the circulation of the blood: *De Motu Cordis et Sanguinis*. Saint-Amant: *Visions*.

England in depth of economic slump, blamed on James I for his interference in the wool trade and use of monopolies. Bacon and Mompesson impeached by Commons. Spread of Arminianism within Church of England. First English news-sheets published (in Holland). Death of Philip III and accession of Philip IV of Spain; ascendancy of Olivarez begins.

James I's *Direction to Preachers* aims to suppress contentious (Calvinist) preaching; arouses fears of crypto-Catholicism, exacerbated by Arminian adherence to High Church ritual, emphasis on the authority of bishops and off the sermon. Invention of sliderule by William Oughtred.
To relief of Presbyterians, James's Spanish Marriage project collapses: abortive expedition of Prince Charles and Buckingham to Spain to win hand of Infanta. Statute of Monopolies forbids royal granting of monopoly rights; allows 14-year exclusive rights for new inventions, the beginning of patent laws.
Cardinal Richelieu becomes chief minister in France. Henry Wotton's *Elements of Architecture*. Bernini's sculpture of *Apollo and Daphne*. Poussin: *Echo and Narcissus*. Rubens: *Massacre of the Innocents*.

Outbreak of plague in England. Death of James I; accession of Charles I. Marriage of Charles and Henrietta Maria. Buckingham's naval raid on Cadiz, an expensive fiasco. Nicholas Ferrar establishes Anglican community at Little Gidding (broken up by Puritans in 1647). 1625–1630: Wallenstein, new general-in-chief of Imperial forces, defeats Protestant armies under Mansfeld, and, with Tilly, overwhelms Denmark which had intervened in the Thirty Years War as champion of the Protestant cause.
England at war with France (to 1630). Buckingham leads unsuccessful naval expedition for the relief of French Huguenots besieged at La Rochelle. Charles I raises money by forced loans. Case of the Five Knights who unsuccessfully test the legality of confinement for those who refuse to contribute. Charles buys great art collection of the Gonzaga Dukes of Mantua. Inigo Jones completes Queen's Chapel at St James's Palace. Kepler compiles *Rudolphine Tables* for calculating astronomical positions.

Laud is made Bishop of London; Arminianism and support of the prerogative become inextricably linked in the minds of Presbyterians. New Parliament passes Petition of Right, masterminded by Sir Edward Coke and John Eliot, in protest against arbitrary taxation and church reform. King counters with Declaration to promote religious conformity. Assassination of Buckingham.

DATE	AUTHOR'S LIFE	LITERARY CONTEXT
1629	Marvell attends Hull Grammar School (to 1633), under two graduates of Trinity College, Cambridge, James Burney and Anthony Stevenson. Here he would have received	Milton: *On the Morning of Christ's Nativity.* Andrewes: *Ninety-Six Sermons.* Hobbes: *The Peloponnesian War of Thucydides* (trans.).
1631	a good grounding in the classical authors, and towards the end of his life recalled that	Chapman: *Caesar and Pompey.* Death of John Donne.
1632	'this *scanning* was a liberal Art that we learn'd at Grammar School; and to *scan* verses ... before we did, or were oblidged to understand them'.	Milton: *On Shakespeare.* Ford: *'Tis Pity She's a Whore*; *Love's Sacrifice.* Prynne: *Historio-Mastix* (a Puritan attack on stage plays, allegedly containing aspersions on Charles I and Henrietta Maria).
1633	Matriculates at Cambridge as a sizar of Trinity College (14 December), somewhat precociously, at the age of 13. Sizars paid for their board and education in part by the performance of menial tasks for their wealthier contemporaries, receiving an allowance of 8s 8d every year, plus a further fourpence a week for food.	Milton: *L'Allegro* and *Il Penseroso.* Death of George Herbert. Poems of Donne and Herbert (*The Temple*) published. Cowley: *Poetical Blossomes.* D'Avenant: *The Wits* first performed. Fletcher: *The Purple Island.*
1634	Poetry enjoyed a considerable vogue in the University and verses circulated widely in manuscript. Crashaw, Beaumont, Cleveland, Kynaston and Cowley were all at Cambridge with Marvell. Milton had left only a year previously.	Milton: *A Masque [Comus]* (music by Henry Lawes). *Coelum Britannicum*, masque by Carew and Inigo Jones. Shirley: *The Triumph of Peace*, a masque with music by William Lawes.
1635	The University reflected the religious divides of the country though Marvell's later Platonist and Latitudinarian tendencies have been attributed to the influence of Whichcote (lecturer in Trinity Church) and Sherman, who preached in the Chapel at Trinity College (to 1640).	Milton: *Lycidas.* Selden: *Mare Clausum.* Shirley: *The Lady of Pleasure.* Quarles: *Emblemes.* Calderón de la Barca: *La vida es Sueño.* Death of Lope de Vega.

CHRONOLOGY

HISTORICAL EVENTS

Opposition, led by Eliot and Holles, forcibly delay dissolution of
Parliament to pass three further resolutions attacking Court policy.
Ringleaders imprisoned. Charles rules for 11 years without Parliament.
Great 'Puritan migration' to New England begins. Massachusetts charter
granted. Rubens presents *Peace and War* to Charles I. Vermuyden
contracted to drain Great Fens (to 1652).
Magdeberg sacked with hideous savagery by Imperial troops under Tilly.
Gustavus Adolphus of Sweden embarks on brief but brilliant career of
victory, overthrowing Tilly at Breitenfeld.
Increasing isolation of the court, which under Henrietta Maria also begins
to take on a Roman Catholic aura. Laud, effectively chief minister, relies
on courts of the Star Chamber and High Commission to enforce policy.
Van Dyck becomes court painter to Charles I. Death of Tilly and victory of
Gustavus Adolphus at Lech. Wallenstein called out of retirement. Swedes
win battle of Lützen, but Gustavus Adolphus is killed. Accession of Queen
Christina, with Oxenstierna as regent. Thomas Wentworth (later Earl of
Strafford) Lord Deputy in Ireland.
Laud becomes Archbishop of Canterbury. Wentworth's policy of
'Thorough' in Ireland brings in revenue for the Crown but also antagonizes
Presbyterian settlers and opposition at home. Condemnation of Galileo by
Inquisition for upholding the Copernican system. In France, the Abbé de
St Cyran appointed director of Port-Royal which becomes a centre of
Jansenism. 1630s: Lord Falkland's Great Tew home becomes centre for
liberal thinkers – poets (Jonson, Carew, Waller); philosophers and
theologians (Earle, Chillingworth, Hales, Hyde) – whose Christian
humanism wholly out of sympathy with recent bitter denominational
controversy.

King follows a mercantilist, interventionist economic policy, winning the
support of merchants and financiers. Cycle of good harvests during the
1630s contributes to enhanced prosperity. First writs for ship money on
coastal counties, for naval defence of country. Settlement in Maryland
(established by Roman Catholic George Calvert). Laud's religious policy
further antagonizes Puritans: conventicles are suppressed and King James's
Declaration of Sports revised and read in churches, implying condemnation
of the Puritan sabbath. Assassination of Wallenstein.

Ship money extended to inland counties – in fact a highly efficient tax, in
spite of its unpopularity. Rubens' Banqueting House ceiling depicts
blessings of monarchical rule and apotheosis of James I. War between
France and Spain. French settlement of Martinique and Guadeloupe.
Claude Lorraine: *Rest on the Flight to Egypt*. Richelieu founds *L'Académie
française*.

DATE	AUTHOR'S LIFE	LITERARY CONTEXT
1637	Publication of his first poems (in Latin and Greek) in a congratulatory volume on the birth of Princess Anne, the fifth child of King Charles I and Queen Henrietta Maria.	Death of Ben Jonson. Corneille: *Le Cid*. Descartes: *Discourse on Method*. Calderón: *El mágico prodigioso*.
1638	Death of his mother (April); remarriage of his father (November) to the widow Lucy Harris (*née* Aldred). Marvell elected to a scholarship at Trinity (13 April).	Cowley: *Loves Riddle* and *Naufragium Joculaire*. Suckling: *Aglaura*. Filmer's *Patriarcha, or the Natural Power of Kings*, defends Divine Right.
1639	Receives his BA during the Lent Term. Begins studying for MA.	Fuller: *The History of the Holy War*. Suckling: *Brennoralt, or The Discontented Colonel*.
1640	Letter to Marvell's father from the Rev. John Norton refers to Andrew Marvell's seduction by Jesuits. This short-lived conversion to Roman Catholicism may have taken place in 1639 but might well have been earlier; tempted by Jesuits to London, he was allegedly found after some months by his father in a bookseller's shop and sent back to Cambridge.	Milton: *Epitaphium Damonis*. First volume of Donne's Sermons, prefaced by Walton's *Life of Donne*. Carew: *Poems*. Suckling: *Ballad upon a Wedding*. Jonson's *The Underwood*, and translation of Horace's *Ars Poetica*. *Wit's Recreations* (collection of epigrams and epitaphs).
1641	His father is drowned while crossing the Humber (23 January). Inheritance of some family property in Meldreth, Cambridgeshire, enables him to pursue a career outside the University. There is some speculation that he may have briefly held a clerkship in the Hull trading house of his brother-in-law, Edmund Popple, a shipwright and merchant, but he may have gone straight to London.	Milton's first three anti-episcopal pamphlets. Evelyn begins his *Diary*. Denham: *Sophy*. Overton: *Lambeth Fayre* (a Leveller attack on bishops). First publication of *Diurnal Occurrences in Parliament*. Descartes: *Meditationes de prima philosophia*. Corneille: *Polyeucte*.

CHRONOLOGY

Prynne and Puritan pamphleteers Bastwick, Burton and Lilburne are mutilated, branded and imprisoned for seditious libel. Laud attempts to impose Book of Common Prayer on the Presbyterian Kirk, leading to riots in St Giles' Cathedral. Van Dyck paints triple portrait of Charles I to help Bernini execute a bust. Bernini said to remark that he had never seen a 'countenance so unfortunate'.

D'Avenant succeeds Jonson as official poet laureate. Rex v. Hampden case; John Hampden fined for refusing to pay ship money. Growing fear that ship money might be used to finance a standing army. General Assembly of Church of Scotland assumes leadership of national revolt, organizing Covenant against episcopacy, popular subscription to which being almost unanimous. Charles I mobilizes army.

First Bishops' War. Ill-equipped English army repelled by Scots under Alexander Leslie. Truce (Treaty of Berwick) in June. General Assembly sweeps away episcopacy in Scotland. Strafford advises the king to call a new Parliament to vote the necessary supply to continue the war.

Short Parliament (April–May), refuses to vote supply until grievances settled. Dissolved when opposition (led by Pym) found to be negotiating with Scots. Scots defeat English at Newburn and take Newcastle (29 August). Subsidy of £25,000 a month imposed by Scots shackles Charles to Long Parliament (meets 3 November). King supported by only a third of MPs in 1640, even moderates opposing him. Initially reform, not revolution is their aim, though Pym's 'keynote speech' (7 November) demonstrates that a core of members existed convinced of a conspiracy to introduce despotism and papacy into the country – a fear fuelled by apocalyptic preaching of Puritan divines. Root and Branch petition (11 December) signed by 15,000 Londoners, calls for abolition of episcopacy. Laud imprisoned.

Riots in London (January). Triennial Act (February). Impeachment of Strafford, whose execution (May) Charles is obliged to sanction. Protestation (3 May) of Commons to the country. Betrothal of Princess Mary to William, son of Frederick Henry, Dutch Stadholder. Henrietta Maria found to be soliciting aid from Louis XIII. Abolition of prerogative courts. Root and Branch bill. Pym's Ten Propositions (24 June). Charles leaves for Scotland (August). Rebellion of Irish Catholics in Ulster (October) which Parliament cannot trust Charles with an army to suppress. Commons pass Grand Remonstrance (22 November) – by majority of only 159 to 148, the radical restructuring of the Church being repellant to moderate Anglicans led by Falkland, Hyde and Culpepper. Riots against bishops; 12 bishops sent to the Tower. Monteverdi: *The Return of Ulysses*.

DATE	AUTHOR'S LIFE	LITERARY CONTEXT
1642	By February 1642 Marvell lodging in Clerkenwell, where he subscribes to the Protestation 'to maintain and defend ... the true, reformed Protestant Religion ...' as compelled by the Commons. Possibly he was a student at one of the nearby Inns of Court, for his name appears as witness on some mortgage deeds at Gray's Inn. Writes (before 1645) *A Dialogue between Thyrsis and Dorinda* (set to music by William Lawes).	Denham's *Cooper's Hill* pays tribute to Charles I. Death of Cavalier poets Cartwright and Godolphin. Lovelace: 'To Althea'. Fuller: *The Holy State and the Profane State.* More: *Psychodia Platonica.* Cowley: *The Guardian.* Coke: *Second Institutes.* Milton publishes two further anti-episcopal pamphlets. Corneille: *Cinna.*
1642–7	Travels in Holland, France, Italy and Spain, 'to very good purpose, as I beleeve, & the gaining of those 4 languages', writes John Milton, and is possibly absent from England for the entire period of the first Civil War. It is generally assumed that he travelled as tutor-companion to a young man of rank or wealth, though it is possible that he was able to travel on his own small patrimony.	
1643	Marvell wrote after the Restoration when challenged for opting out of the War, that 'I think the cause was too good to have been fought for. Men ought to have trusted God; they ought to have trusted the King with that whole matter ...' Marvell experienced the dilemma of many moderates, whose loyalty to the Crown and moral support for Charles I conflicted with their hostility to the Anglican establishment and sympathy with the aims of the less extreme Puritan revolutionaries.	Prynne: *The Sovereign Power of Parliament.* Browne: *Religio Medici.* Digby: *Observations* (on the above); *Of Bodies.* Cowley: *The Puritan and the Papist; The Civil War.* Walwyn: *Power of Love*, a Leveller's arguments for religious toleration. Nedham's *Mercurius Britannicus*, a Parliamentary newsbook, established as a rival to Berkenhead's Royalist *Mercurius Aulicus.* Milton: *The Doctrine and Discipline of Divorce.*

CHRONOLOGY

Charles takes unprecedented step of entering Commons to arrest the Five Members – Pym, Hampden, Holles, Haslerigg, Strode – who have already fled. Parliament pass Militia Bill and bill excluding bishops from House of Lords. Social order breaking down. Parliament sends Charles, in the north, Nineteen Propositions, terms of unconditional surrender so harsh that Charles begins to look quite moderate in comparison. Edward Hyde (later Earl of Clarendon) becomes king's chief adviser and instrumental in building up a Royalist party. Parliament mobilizes army under Earl of Essex. King raises standard at Nottingham (21 August). Royalists win battle of Edgehill (October) but are prevented from taking London. Parliament closes all theatres. Death of Richelieu. Conspiracy of Cinq-Mars. Abel Tasman discovers Tasmania and South Island of New Zealand. Monteverdi: *The Coronation of Poppaea*. Rembrandt: *The Night Watch*.

Growing agitation for peace. King rejects 'Propositions of Oxford'. Royalist military successes. Siege of Gloucester. Pym gains support of Scots whose terms involve import of Solemn League and Covenant into England church – far too extreme for most English Presbyterians. Westminster Assembly of Divines (to 1648) set up to oversee this. Parliament proves more efficient at raising money than Royalists, with Pym's county tax assessment, excise on popular commodities and Sequestration Ordinance. King relies on voluntary contributions. Death of Pym (December).

Fall of Olivarez (Spain). Death of Louis XIII and regency of Anne of Austria. Mazarin chief minister in France. Condé's defeat of Spanish at Rocroi; Condé and Turenne win series of victories throughout remainder of the Thirty Years War, ensuring France's supremacy. Invention of the barometer by Torricelli.

DATE	AUTHOR'S LIFE	LITERARY CONTEXT
1644		Milton: *On Education*; *Areopagitica*. Cleveland: *The Rebel Scot*. Overton: *Man's Mortality*. Hammond: *Practical Catechism*. Arnauld: *Apologie pour Jansénius*.
1645		Waller: *Poems*. Fuller: *Good Thoughts in Bad Times*. Digby: *Of the Immortality of Man's Soul*. Ussher: *A Body of Divinitie*.
1646	Visits Richard Flecknoe in Rome; writes the satirical *Flecknoe, an English Priest at Rome*. This year has also been suggested for the composition of *To his Coy Mistress*, because of the reference to 'ten years before the Flood', the biblical event that was computed to have taken place *anno mundi* 1656.	Milton: *Poems*; *The Tenure of Kings and Magistrates*. Vaughan: *Poems*. Crashaw: *Steps to the Temple* and *The Delights of the Muses*. Browne: *Pseudodoxia Epidemica*. Suckling: *Fragmenta Aurea*; *The Goblins*. Clarendon begins his *History of the Rebellion*.
1647	Has returned from Europe by November, when he sells a second portion of the Meldreth property inherited from his grandfather. Described as 'of Kingstone super Hull Gentleman' though it is unlikely he had spent much time living in Yorkshire.	Cowley: *The Mistress*. Fuller: *Good Thoughts in Worse Times*. Cleveland: *Poems*. Taylor: *The Liberty of Prophesying* (an Anglican argument for religious toleration).
1648	Writes *To his Noble Friend Mr Richard Lovelace* for *Lucasta* and publishes (if it is by him) *An Elegy upon the Death of my Lord Francis Villiers*. Both might suggest Royalist sympathies, but since his main criticism is of the Army, he may well have supported Parliament's attempts to treat with the king.	Herrick, ejected from his living by Parliament in 1647, publishes *Hesperides* and religious poems, *Noble Numbers*. Lovelace writes *Lucasta*, *Odes* and *Sonnets*. Scarron: *Virgile travesti* (to 1652).

CHRONOLOGY

Sir Henry Vane, the younger, an Independent with Republican leanings, rises to prominence in the Commons, closely allied with Oliver Cromwell, rising star of the Army. Scots invade England, joining Parliamentary armies to defeat Royalists at Marston Moor (2 July), Prince Rupert's cavalry, for the first time, being beaten by Cromwell's Ironsides. After the battle of Newbury Cromwell accuses Manchester of not wanting to defeat the king conclusively. The Directory is substituted for the Book of Common Prayer. Ejection of Royalist or 'unsuitable' clergy from their livings begins (over a third by the end of the Interregnum).

Execution of Laud (January). Cromwell and Independents obtain Self-Denying Ordinance (April) whereby all MPs obliged to resign their military commands. New Model Army formed under Sir Thomas Fairfax, with Cromwell as second in command, though he does not resign his seat. Charles rejects Uxbridge peace proposals. New Model Army wins decisive victories at Naseby (June) and Langport (July). Rupert surrenders Bristol. Montrose defeated at Philiphaugh (September). Matthew Hopkins' crusade against witches in the eastern counties results in over 200 executions.

King surrenders to Scots at Newark (May). Oxford capitulates (June). Intensifying of Presbyterian–Independent conflict. Propositions put to the king in June still stipulate acceptance of the Solemn League and Covenant. Independents open separate negotiations with king. Levellers argue for the abolition of monarchy and the sovereignty of the people in *Remonstrance of Many Thousand Citizens*. John Lilburne, their leader, derives his theories from Sir Edward's Coke's proposition that the monarchy was a Norman device unconstitutionally imposed on the free and equal society of Anglo-Saxon England. Abolition of bishops (October).

Parliament pays Scots £40,000 to hand over Charles I (February). Cromwell dispatches Cornet Joyce to seize the king, who is taken into Army custody. Cromwell, Ireton and others debate constitutional issues with Army 'agitators' at Putney. Cromwell negotiating directly with the king, produces the Heads of Proposals, less extreme than Parliament's Newcastle Propositions. Charles flees from Hampton Court to Carisbrooke (November). Signs Engagement with Scots (December) accepting their support in subduing England in return for a three-year trial of Presbyterian Church government. Lely paints *The Children of Charles I*.

Second Civil War. Cromwell beats Scots at Preston (August). Army press for trial of king, referred to in Ireton's Remonstrance as 'that man of blood'. Parliament continues to negotiate with him. In Pride's Purge Army forcibly reduces membership of Parliament to 150, known as 'The Rump'. The Rump and the Army become centre of power in the country. Fronde of the parlement begins in France (May). Peace of Westphalia (October) ends Thirty Years War. France, Saxony and Bavaria chief territorial gainers; Habsburg power is contained. France and Spain fight on until 1659.

DATE	AUTHOR'S LIFE	LITERARY CONTEXT
1649	Writes *Upon the Death of the Lord Hastings* published in a volume of elegies by mainly Royalist poets (Dryden, Herrick and Denham amongst them). Assumed to be moving in London literary circles by this time.	Rous: *The Lawfulnes of Obeying the Present Government.* Ascham: *Of the Confusions and Revolutions of Government.* Winstanley: *The True Levellers' Standard Advanced.* Overton: *England's New Chains Discovered.* Madeleine de Scudéry: *Artamène, ou le Grand Cyrus* (10 vols. to 1653). Bossuet: *Méditations sur la brièveté de la vie.*
1650	Writes *An Horatian Ode upon Cromwell's Return from Ireland.* While lamenting the tragedy of 1649 and praising the courage of Charles I, Marvell now sees in Cromwell's success the workings of a divine purpose to which even the king had to consent. *Tom May's Death* repudiates the more democratic aspects of republicanism. At the end of the year Marvell becomes tutor to Mary Fairfax, daughter of the Parliamentary General, Sir Thomas Fairfax, at Appleton House in Yorkshire.	Hobbes: *Treatise of Human Nature; De Corpore Politico.* Vaughan: *Silex scintillans; Magia adamica.* Anne Bradstreet: *The Tenth Muse Lately Sprung up in America.*
1651	Fairfax in retirement devoted himself to improving his estates, translating and composing verse, collecting coins, medals and manuscripts, and Marvell would appear to have passed an agreeable time with the family. He writes the Appleton poems, notably *Upon Appleton House.* Also *In Legationem Domini Oliveri St John* on the occasion of Oliver St John's embassy to the United Provinces. His commendatory poems to Dr Witty published in Robert Witty's translation of *Popular Errors.*	Hobbes: *Leviathan.* Vaughan: *Olor Iscanus.* Donne's *Essays in Divinity* published. D'Avenant: *Gondibert.* Cartwright: *Comedies, Tragedies, with other poems.* Taylor: *The Rule and Exercise of Holy Living* (1650) and ... *of Holy Dying* (1651), for which he is charged with atheism. Corneille: *Andromède.*

CHRONOLOGY

Trial and execution of Charles I (January). Publication of the anonymous *Eikon Basilike* ('The Royal Image'), presents the late king as a martyr, and is an immediate bestseller, unlike Milton's reply (*Eikonoklastes* – 'The Image Breaker'). Monarchy and House of Lords abolished (February). All office holders subjected to an oath of loyalty 'to the Commonwealth of England'. Economic depression and unemployment. Winstanley and the Diggers occupy common land on St George's Hill, Surrey (April), denouncing property as a Norman invention. Proliferation of disaffected sectaries – Anabaptists, Ranters, Familists, Adamites, Brownists, Fifth Monarchists, etc. Cromwell and Fairfax crush Levellers as political force and Lilburne spends most of 1650s in prison. Fairfax, who had opposed the king's execution, retires from public life. Cromwell brutally suppresses Irish Catholics at Drogheda. Charles II proclaimed in Scotland. In France, end of Fronde of the parlement and beginning of Princes' Fronde, with Condé opposing Mazarin. Execution of Montrose. Cromwell returns from his subjugation of Ireland (May) to take part in the Scottish campaign. Cromwell defeats Scots at Dunbar. Ordinance repealing penalties for non-attendance at Church, provided one attended an alternative public place of worship, favours Independents, but also Roman Catholics. Society of Friends ('Quakers') founded by George Foxe.

Sudden death of William II; posthumous birth of William III. John de Witt (elected Grand Pensionary 1653) effectively becomes chief minister of a new Dutch Republic (the United Provinces). Velasquez paints *Pope Innocent X*; Claude Lorraine *The Flight into Egypt*. Giacomo Carissimi: *Jephtha* – one of the earliest oratorios. Von Guericke invents the air pump and initiates experiments with vacuums.

Charles II invades England from Scotland; defeated by Cromwell at Worcester – 'God's "crowning mercy" '. Leaves Scotland open to annexation; negotiations for union completed by 1654. English naval superiority over Dutch and French confirmed. First English Navigation Acts (October) to break hold of Dutch carrying trade between Europe and America. Milton, commissioned by Council to reply to Salmasius' indictment of the regicide government (*Defensio Regia*), issues *Pro Populo Anglicano Defensio*. Cape Colony founded by Dutch. Lely's portrait of Oliver Cromwell. Riccioli and Grimaldi's lunar map (Grimaldi also first to discover diffraction of light and evolve wave theory of light.)

xlv

DATE	AUTHOR'S LIFE	LITERARY CONTEXT
1652	It is commonly assumed that Marvell composes most of his pastoral poetry – lyrics such as 'The Garden', 'The Little T.C. in a Prospect of Flowers', the Mower poems, etc. during the Nun Appleton period, though some could well have been written during the 60s or 70s. Marvell leaves the Fairfax household during 1652, determined to begin active political service under Oliver Cromwell. Fairfax, on the other hand, becomes increasingly involved in Royalist intrigues.	Winstanley: *Law of Freedom.* Crashaw: *Carmen Deo Nostro.* Vaughan: *The Mount of Olives, or Solitary Devotions.* Letters of Dorothy Osborne to William Temple (to 1654). Robert Filmer: *Directions for Obedience to Governours in Dangerous and Doubtful Times.*
1653	Probably writes *The Character of Holland* after English naval victory off Portland. Possibly putting himself forward as official verse propagandist of the new state. Milton's letter to Bradshaw (21 February), recommending Marvell as Assistant Latin Secretary to the Council of State; no appointment forthcoming but Marvell becomes tutor to William Dutton, protégé and prospective son-in-law of Cromwell, whom he accompanies to Eton, lodging in the house of the Puritan John Oxenbridge. Probably writes *Bermudas* at this time. Meets John Hales and Nathaniel Ingelo. Writes *A Letter to Doctor Ingelo.*	Walton: *The Compleat Angler.* Shirley: *Cupid and Death* with music by Matthew Locke. 1650s: Cambridge Platonists – Whichcote, Smith, More, Cudworth, etc., try to combat the sort of materialism preached by Hobbes and to free religion from fanaticism and controversy.
1654	Writes two epigrams (April) on Cromwell's portrait sent to Queen Christina of Sweden and in the winter *The First Anniversary of the Government under His Highness The Lord Protector.* Events had confirmed in Marvell's eyes that Cromwell	Flecknoe's *Ariadne*, probably the first English opera. Madeleine de Scudéry: *Clélie, histoire romaine* (10 vols. to 1660). John Playford: *A Breif Introduction to the Skill of Musick.*

CHRONOLOGY

End of war in Ireland. Settlement of demobilized English troops on lands of former Catholic rebels. Commercial rivalry provokes Anglo-Dutch war (to 1654). Blake's victory off the Kentish Knock; his defeat off Dungeness. Foreign policy financed by sale of Crown and church lands, as well as higher taxation. Parliament resolve tithe system should continue until Committee of Propagation of the Gospel comes up with alternative system of providing for clergy, angering Milton and the Independents, who had hoped for disestablishment. Army radicals also pressing for law reform and dissolution of the Rump. Parliament passes Act of Pardon and Oblivion to reconcile Royalists. John Thurloe, a personal friend of Oliver Cromwell, and later Marvell's boss, becomes head of the government's intelligence service. Condé, with Spanish support, marches on France and occupies Paris. Dutch create colony at Cape of Good Hope. John Hilton's collection of catches, *Catch as Catch Can*. First coffee house in London in Cornhill.

Naval victories against Dutch by Blake and Monck. The Rump, finally on the point of introducing a Bill of Elections, forcibly dissolved by Cromwell. Republicans such as Vane, Haslerigg, Ludlow, Marten and Sidney thus removed from position of influence. The 'Barebones' Parliament, composed of 140 delegates personally recommended or handpicked from lists provided by separatist Puritan congregations is the high point of the revolution for Cromwell, who, believing his millennial hopes are to be realized, is prepared to resign power to them – 'Truly you are called by God to rule with him and for him'. Radicals produce programme of administrative reform and rationalization unacceptable to conservatives who feel that property is threatened; Cromwell himself sides with the Presbyterians on the matter of retaining some form of tithe system, and, on the request of the conservatives, allows the Barebones Parliament to surrender its powers back to him. In December he becomes Lord Protector under Lambert's 'Instrument of Government', refusing the title of king, but without agreeing any means of choosing his successor. Obliged to fall back for support on the Army, now purged of radicals. Protectorate represents the victory of conservatism and the end of the revolution.

First Parliament of the Protectorate (to 1655). Several moves to make the Protectorship hereditary. Pamphleteers raise the kingship issue, John Hall: *Of Government and Obedience* and Hunton: *His Highness the Protector Protected* arguing in its favour. Disaffection of Quakers, who never forgive Cromwell for not abolishing tithes, and of Fifth Monarchists who now ask whether the Lord would have 'Oliver Cromwell or Jesus Christ to rule over us?' New Parliament more Presbyterian and intolerant in religious matters; Triers and Ejectors instituted to review ecclesiastical appointments and

DATE	AUTHOR'S LIFE	LITERARY CONTEXT
1654 *cont*	indeed ruled by God's ordinance. Drawing upon the millennial hopes prevalent at the time he urges that 'If these be the Times, then this must be the Man', and, arguably, recommends popular endorsement of 'Heavens choice' – i.e. an offer of the Crown by	At Oxford, Bible translated into Irish, Welsh, Turkish and Malay (to 1658). Hooft: *History of the Low Countries*.
1655	Parliament to Cromwell – as the only secure means by which strong government can be maintained. Probably sent privately to its dedicatee, *The First Anniversary* is taken up by the Government and printed for propaganda purposes in 1655.	Fuller: *Church History*. Waller: *Ayres and Dialogues*, including 'Go Lovely Rose'; 'Panegyrick To My Lord Protector'. Stanley: *A History of Philosophy* (to 1662). Mme de Sévigné begins to write her *Letters*.
1656	Marvell and Dutton in France at Saumar on the Loire where there was a famous Protestant academy. Marvell is described by James Scudamore, a visiting Royalist, as 'a notable English Italo-Machiavellian'.	Harrington: *The Commonwealth of Oceana* in opposition to *Leviathan*. Cowley: *Poems*. D'Avenant's *The Siege of Rhodes*, one of the earliest English operas, evades ban on stage-plays.
1657	Writes *On the Victory obtained by Blake*, thought to express his regret that Cromwell had turned down the Crown. Joins Milton as Latin Secretary to the Council of State, under Secretary of State Thurloe with a stipend of £200 (September). Marvell's duties included translating correspondence and official papers from and into Latin, receiving on occasion envoys from foreign states, and probably acting as an interpreter. He was from time to time required to deputize for Milton at whose house in Petty France he was a frequent visitor.	Bunyan: *A Vindication* (anti-Quaker). Baxter: *Call to the Unconverted*. King: *Poems*. One-volume publication of the 18 *Provinciales* of Pascal. Cyrano de Bergerac: *Histoire comique des Etats de la lune et du Soleil*.

restrict uncontrolled lay preaching. Expedition of Penn and Venables to Hispaniola (part of Cromwell's grand 'Western Design' to secure settlements in West Indies). England makes commercial treaties with Sweden, Denmark and Portugal. Successful revolt of Brazil against Dutch dominion. End of Frondes in France. Mazarin's authority confirmed. Abdication of Queen Christina of Sweden. New interest, during Commonwealth, in Elizabethan diplomacy; publication of *The Compleat Ambassador* (7 vols.) by Sir Dudley Digges, Elizabeth I's Master of the Rolls.

Cromwell divides country into districts and appoints a major general to undertake the policing of each. Encourages Jews to return to England (expelled by Edward I). Jamaica seized. As centre of slave trade it was to become central to English imperial policy. Trade boom. Cromwell, living at Whitehall, assumes many of the external trappings of royalty. Secretary Thurloe given complete control of all printed material. Free discussion and pamphleteering ends. Nedham's *Mercurius Politicus* and *The Public Intelligencer* remain. John Wallis' *Arithmetica Infinitorum* contains the principles of differential calculus; becomes a standard work. Isaac Newton becomes professor of mathematics at Cambridge. Rembrandt: *Woman Bathing*. Murillo: *Birth of the Virgin*.
Alliance of England and France against Spain; Spain blockaded throughout winter. War against England's traditional enemy, regarded as war against anti-Christ, at first popular, but trade rather than religion influences Cromwell's foreign policy. That Mazarin is willing to ally with England demonstrates English government no longer regarded as revolutionary, but as a conservative national government.

In 'The Humble Petition and Advice' Parliament invites Cromwell to assume hereditary kingship, which, under pressure from Pride and other Army officers, he refuses. Republicans led by Lambert oppose any move towards a monarchy. However, by accepting the Petition but not the Crown, Cromwell becomes still more powerful, now able to appoint his own council and to consult it or not as he chooses. The old ruling families, supplanted by the major generals, begin to return to local government. Royalists intriguing with disaffected Levellers (eg. Edward Sexby, whose *Killing No Murder* calls for Cromwell's assassination). Thurloe, by an agreement with Royalist traitor Sir Richard Willis, gains advance news of all planned uprisings. Blake's destruction of Spanish silver fleet at Santa-Cruz. Clearing up of privateers protects English merchants. Republic confirmed as major maritime power and gains increased prestige in Europe. Whereas in 1620s and 30s England had been powerless to intervene when the fate of Europe was being decided in the Thirty Years War, her mediation now frequently sought; a network of ambassadors was in place throughout Europe, whereas in 1633 there had only been one in Constantinople. Invention of pendulum clock. Tea and drinking chocolate first sold in London.

DATE	AUTHOR'S LIFE	LITERARY CONTEXT

1657 *cont*   Writes *Two Songs at the Marriage of the Lord Fauconberg and the Lady Mary Cromwell* (November). Two months previously, Marvell's former pupil, Mary Fairfax, had married the Second Duke of Buckingham, a match of which Cromwell strongly disapproved.

1658   During summer composes Latin epitaph to Jane, first wife of John Oxenbridge. *A Poem upon the Death of His Late Highnesse the Lord Protector.* Marvell takes part in his funeral on 23 November. He maintains his secretaryship under Richard Cromwell.

Literary context for 1658:
Waller: *Of a war with Spain and a Fight at Sea.*
Browne: *Urne Burial.*
Phillips: *The New World of English Words.*
D'Avenant: *The Cruelty of the Spaniards in Peru* (opera).
Saint-Amant: *Oeuvres complètes.*

1659   Elected MP for Hull (January), a position he holds until 1678, though temporarily loses his seat to the Republican Sir Henry Vane on restoration of the Rump in May 1659. Marvell continues in his post after the dismissal of Thurloe, serving under Thomas Scott, an enemy of the Cromwells. He is granted lodgings in Whitehall until at least October 1659 when the Council of State is dissolved. During the winter attends meetings of 'The Rota', a club formed by the Republican James Harrington for discussion of political theories, where other members or auditors included Cyriak Skinner, Henry Neville and John Aubrey.

Literary context for 1659:
Three Poems Upon the Death of his Late Highness Oliver Lord Protector of England, Scotland, and Ireland (by Waller, Dryden and Sprat).
Stillingfleet: *Irenicum.*
Hales: *Golden Remains.*
Vane: *A Needful Corrective or Ballance in Popular Government.*
Evelyn: *Apology for the Royal Party.*
Molière: *Les Précieuses ridicules.*
Boileau: *Satire I.*

1660   Marvell resumes his seat in the Parliament that recalled Charles II and, ironically, is entrusted to answer in Latin a letter of congratulation received on that occasion. Like other loyalists, Marvell accepts the accomplished fact of the

Literary context for 1660:
Milton: *The Readie and Easie Way to Establish a Free Commonwealth* and *Brief Notes Upon a Late Sermon* for which he is arrested and imprisoned.
Pepys begins his *Diary.*
Harrington: *Political Discourses*

1

HISTORICAL EVENTS

Anglo-French siege of Dunkirk; Battle of the Dunes. Death of Cromwell at Whitehall on 3 September, the anniversary of his two great victories at Dunbar and Worcester. Protectorate passes to his son, Richard, a tool of Army chiefs Fleetwood and Disbrowe. Birth of Purcell. First bank note (in Sweden). Velasquez: *The Rokeby Venus*; Rembrandt: *Self-Portrait with a Stick*.

Parliament convened 27 January. Thurloe, as official head of Richard's supporters, introduces a bill for full recognition of the Protectorate which passes by 223 votes to 134. It is opposed by, amongst others, Thomas Scott, the regicide, who becomes Marvell's head of department shortly afterwards (and is executed at the Restoration). Fairfax returns to Parliament as member for York, voting with Haslerigg and the opposition. Under Richard Cromwell Thurloe's power increasing, but in April he unsuccessfully advises Richard against dissolving Parliament. Richard deposed by Army coup; Thurloe out of office. Rump of 1653 recalled. Derby Petition. Lambert's rising. Second forcible dissolution of the Rump. Lambert rules through the Committee of Safety. Fairfax opens negotiations with Monck. Rump reconvenes in December on news that Monck had mobilized army of occupation in Scotland. John Rushworth's first great collection of State Papers (for years 1618–29). Treaty of the Pyrenees between France and Spain.

Monck marches south, raising another regiment en route (named after border town of Coldstream), invading England 1 January. Fairfax, rallying in support, takes York. Lambert's army offers no opposition. Monck reaches London 3 February, pragmatically not having announced any intention other than to establish a free and full Parliament to replace the discredited Rump. Members of Long Parliament expelled by Pride are allowed to return and Parliament thereupon votes for its own dissolution. New Parliament (Convention Parliament), including restored House of

DATE	AUTHOR'S LIFE	LITERARY CONTEXT
1660 *cont*	Restoration. Intervenes on behalf of Milton, following his arrest and, after his release, complains about his excessive gaol fees of £150. Involved in two measures designed to create a *modus vivendi* between Presbyterians and Episcopalians, reporting favourably on a bill 'for erecting and endowing vicarages out of impropriate rectories' and acting as a teller for the ayes in the division voting on the Indulgence to Protestant Nonconformists embodied in the Declaration of Breda. Neither measure becomes law.	*tending to the introduction of a free Commonwealth in England.* Bunyan arrested for preaching without a licence and spends next 12 years in Bedford gaol. Falkland: *Discourses of Infallibility* and *a Reply.* Fuller: *Mixed Contemplations in Better Times.* Dryden: *Astraea Redux.* Cowley: *Ode, upon the Blessed Restoration.* Rochester: 'To His Sacred Majesty'. Tatham: *The Rump, or The Mirror of the Late Times.* Spinoza: *Short Treatise on God, Man and his Faith.* Brébeuf: *Entretiens solitaires.*
1661	In November 1660 Marvell begins a series of over a thousand letters to the Hull Corporation, reporting on the progress of their particular interests. In 1661 begins a parallel series of letter to Hull Trinity House (Hull Seamen's Guild) on whose behalf Marvell exerted himself throughout his political career. Marvell, having served under Cromwell, probably still less comfortable in the new Cavalier Parliament. He is called to task by the Speaker for coming to blows with Thomas Clifford (later a minister) in the Commons precincts.	Glanvill: *The Vanity of Dogmatizing.* Dryden: *To His Sacred Majesty.* Molière: *L'Ecole des maris.* La Calprenède: *Pharamond.* Scarron: *Nouvelles tragicomiques.*
1662–3	Marvell remains friends with many supporters of the Protectorate: Milton (at whose house in Jewin Street he meets Samuel Parker, formerly a fanatical Puritan, about to turn equally intransigent Anglican and to become one of Marvell's	Butler: *Hudibras.* Fuller: *History of the Worthies of England.* Howard: *The Committee.* Stillingfleet: *Origines Sacrae.* Dryden: *To My Lord Chancellor.* Molière: *L'Ecole des femmes.*

CHRONOLOGY

Lords, meets (25 April) and is presented with letter from Charles II and conciliatory Declaration of Breda, in which, subject to Parliament's approval, he promises a free pardon for his former enemies, payment of arrears to army and navy, confirmation of titles to land and limited religious toleration. Terms accepted with enthusiasm. Charles returns to England, reaching London 29 May. Montagu, Fairfax and others sent by Parliament to greet Charles at The Hague (Fairfax retires again to Nun Appleton after the accession). Thurloe offers his services to the new King but is refused and is imprisoned for a time for high treason. Secret marriage of James, Duke of York to Clarendon's daughter, Anne Hyde. Act of Indemnity and Oblivion. Of the 59 who signed Charles I's death warrant, 29 are sentenced to death, of which 10 are executed. Theatres re-open. D'Avenant and Killigrew granted monopoly of acting in London. Marriage of Louis XIV and Maria Teresa of Spain. Robert Boyle: *New Experiments Physio-mechanical, Touching the Spring of the Air and Its Effects.*

Execution of Earl of Argyll. On anniversary of king's execution, bodies of Cromwell, Ireton, and Bradshaw are dug up from Westminster Abbey and reburied at Tyburn. Convention Parliament's failure to secure accommodation for their predominantly Presbyterian views signals beginning of collapse of Puritanism as a political force. Fifth Monarchist revolt does not help cause of toleration. New 'Cavalier' Parliament with Anglican majority obliterates most of the constitutional reforms of the previous twenty years, orders burning of the Solemn League and Covenant and repeals 1642 statute excluding bishops from the House of Lords. Militia Act places armed forces under command of King. Corporation Act: all local government officers obliged to take an oath of non-resistance, abjure the Covenant and take Anglican communion. Death of Mazarin. Louis XIV assumes full powers in France; Colbert put in control of finance and economy.

Charles marries the Roman Catholic Catherine of Braganza. Parliament now defines parameters of national religion, enforcing the Clarendon Code in defiance of the King's Declaration of Indulgence. Act of Uniformity imposes oaths of non-resistance on clergy, who are obliged to accept Book of Common Prayer and the 39 Articles in their entirety. Clarendon himself, while opposed to the Declaration, was not in favour of the Act of Uniformity; though anxious to restore episcopacy he had in mind a limited episcopacy, with revision of the Prayer Book and concessions in ritual, but

DATE	AUTHOR'S LIFE	LITERARY CONTEXT
1662–3 cont	most bitter political enemies); James Harrington, Lord Wharton, a prominent Presbyterian who had fought for Parliament; Sir Edward Harley, who also had Presbyterian sympathies and later became a Whig. Spends eleven months in Holland – a political mission, at the instance of the Earl of Carlisle (also a former Cromwellian).	Mme de La Fayette: *La Princesse de Montpensier*. La Rouchefoucauld: *Mémoires*. Bossuet: *Sermons*.
1663	Accompanies the Earl of Carlisle as Secretary on embassy to Russia (where Carlisle's brief was to secure the restoration of privileges to English merchants at Archangel) and to Sweden and Denmark (to set up an alliance against the United Provinces.)	Shakespeare Third Folio. Cowley: *Verses on Several Occasions*. Herbert of Cherbury: *De religione Gentilium*. Stanley's edition of Aeschylus.
1664	Travelling by sledge, reach Moscow where they finally gain admittance 6 February, Marvell having officially complained to the Tsar about the delay. Marvell causes offence by addressing Tsar Alexis in an oration as 'Illustrissimus' instead of 'Serenissimus' but makes an eloquent reply to the objections raised. In the end the mission proves fruitless and they leave (24 June). The embassies to Sweden and Denmark are equally unsuccessful.	Etherege: *The Comical Revenge, or Love in a Tub*. Lucy Hutchinson begins her Memoirs of the Life of Colonel John Hutchison. Birth of Vanbrugh. Stillingfleet: *A Rational Account of the Grounds of the Protestant Religion*. Flecknoe: *Love's Kingdom*. Molière: *Tartuffe*.
1665	In an incident outside Hamburg Marvell is found 'clapping a pistol' to the head of a recalcitrant waggoner and has to be rescued 'out of the hands of a barbarous rout of peasants and Mechanicks'. Returns to England (January). *The Character of Holland* published.	Bunyan: *The Holy City, or the New Jerusalem*. Dryden: *The Indian Emperor* (stars Nell Gwyn). Orrery: *Mustapha*. La Rochefoucauld: *Maximes*. La Fontaine: *Contes et nouvelles en vers*.

this rejected by solidly Anglican House of Commons. Nearly 2000 (out of 9000) Presbyterian clergy give up their livings in the greatest purge since the Reformation. Lambert is imprisoned for life. Unpopular sale of Dunkirk, Cromwell's greatest foreign acquisition, to Louis XIV. Wren's Sheldonian Theatre at Oxford. Robert Boyle: *The Sceptical Chymist*, sweeps away alchemical theories and insists on the importance of experiment and sound deduction. Death of naturalist John Tradescant. Licensing Act drastically reduces number of printers and printing presses.

Attempt to impeach Clarendon. The Royal Society gains its charter. Founders and early members include Boyle, Hooke, Petty, Ray, Wilkins, Wren, Ashmole, Aubrey, Cowley, Dryden, Evelyn and Waller. Staple Act confirms 1651 Navigation Acts, closing off colonial trade to foreign shipping. America and West Indian colonies rapidly emerge as staple suppliers of tobacco, raw cotton and rice to Europe – all transhipped through England. Drury Lane Theatre opens. First Turnpike Act. John Webb begins the King Charles Building at Greenwich Palace, in Baroque style. Palladio's *First Book of Architecture*.
English capture Niew Amsterdam from Dutch and rename it New York after James Duke of York. Triennial Act made non-compulsory.
Conventicle Act to suppress Dissenting congregations; sporadically enforced but religious nonconformity too widespread now to be stamped out. Work starts on Versailles under Le Vaux and Le Nôtre. Evelyn's *Sylva*, an influential book on practical arboriculture, followed up by *Kalendarium Hortense, or the Gardener's Almanack*. Hals: *Men ... and Women Governors of the Haarlem Almshouse*.

Outbreak of bubonic plague kills 70,000 Londoners and paralyses port for three months. Five Mile Act further restricts activities of Dissenting ministers, though half-heartedly enforced. Second Dutch War (to 1667) appeases public clamour though does not resolve trade issue. James defeats Dutch off Lowestoft (June). English defeat at Bergen (August). Death of Philip IV of Spain. Newton's theory of the use of fluxions. *Philosophical Transactions*, published by the Royal Society, the first permanent scientific journal. Robert Hooke's *Micrographia* (studies crystal structure of snowflakes). Hooke's studies of microscopic fossils lead him to become one of the first proponents of a theory of evolution.

DATE	AUTHOR'S LIFE	LITERARY CONTEXT
1666	Marvell's career as a satirical poet begins. His satires reflect his disillusionment with the Government and a hatred of authoritarianism, both political and religious. *The Second* and *The third Advice to a Painter* parody Waller's *Instructions to a Painter*, and expose the conduct of the naval war against the Dutch as far from exemplary. Writes *Clarindon's House-warming*. Marvell's closest political sympathies at this time with the Duke of Buckingham who led the opposition to Clarendon.	Bunyan: *Grace Abounding*. Waller: *Instructions to a Painter* (applauds war against the Dutch). Glanvill: *Philosophical Considerations Concerning Witches and Witchcraft*. Tillotson: *The Rule of Faith*. A. Brome, *et al*, trans., *The Poems of Horace*. Parliament censures works of Hobbes. Molière: *Le Misanthrope*; *Le Médicin malgré lui*.
1667	In *The Last Instructions to a Painter* (August–September) he criticizes Clarendon, blames the Government for the humiliating victory of De Ruyter on the Medway, warns against the danger of French foreign policy, and urges the king to choose his ministers from the Country party. As with Cromwell in 1655, he defends the ruler against his worst enemies and supports the principle of a strong executive. Marvell a member of the committee set up to enquire into conduct of the Second Dutch War (17 October) and which resolves (6 November) to arraign Clarendon for high treason. Marvell speaks very strongly against Clarendon on that day.	Milton: *Paradise Lost*. Dryden: *Annus mirabilis*; *The State of Innocence and the Fall of Man* (adaptation of *Paradise Lost*). Dryden and D'Avenant: *The Tempest*. Dryden and Duke of Newcastle: *Sir Martin Mar-all*. Duchess of Newcastle: *Life* of her husband. Orrery: *The Black Prince*. More: *Enchiridion Ethicum*. Flecknoe: *Les Damoiselles a La Mode*. Birth of Jonathan Swift. Racine: *Andromaque*.
1668	On 6 February Marvell attacks – 'somewhat transportedly' – Arlington, Buckingham's principal rival, for his pitiful intelligence operation during the Dutch War. Redeems himself with the Government shortly afterwards by urging	Dryden: *Of Dramatick Poesy*. Traherne: *Centuries of Meditations*. Etherege: *She Would if she Could*. Shadwell: *The Sullen Lovers*. Cowley: *Essays in Verse and Prose*.

HISTORICAL EVENTS

French join Dutch in war against England. The Four Days' Battle at sea (1–4 June). English naval victory off North Foreland (25 July). Great Fire of London (2–6 September). *London Gazette* founded as organ of Government. Scottish Covenanters defeated at the battle of Pentland Hills. Newton's theory of gravitation. Wenceslaus Hollar, draughtsman to the king since 1660 makes the last of his famous engravings of London pre-Fire. Leibniz: *De Arte Combinatoria* in which he argues that all reasoning is reducible to an ordered combination of elements such as words, sounds and colours. Vermeer: *Allegory on the Art of Painting*.

While peace negotiations being held at Breda (treaty signed 21 July), Dutch raiding force sails up the Medway, sinks three ships and tows away the flagship, *The Royal Charles*. During summer recess, king resolves to remove Clarendon from Lord Chancellorship due to unpopularity of Court party; Great seal demanded and given up (30 August). Dismissal and exile of Clarendon, unfairly charged with embezzlement and blamed for lack of tangible war successes. Replaced by no less unpopular 'Cabal' (formed from the initials of their names – Clifford, Arlington, Buckingham, Ashley Cooper and Lauderdale). Reforms of Treasury; exchequer certificates circulate as embryonic paper currency. Lauderdale begins to impose autocratic rule on Scotland. Newton's optical discoveries begin. Naturalist John Ray, founder of modern biological science, begins his classification of species.

Peace of Aix-la-Chapelle (May). Triple Alliance of England, Holland and Sweden to protect the Netherlands against France, organized by Temple and Arlington, a rather too advanced diplomatic coup for Parliament who still regard the Dutch as England's principal enemy. Increasing distrust of the Cabal. Sir William Coventry resigns from Government and becomes focus of what for the first time is a regular Opposition or 'Country' Party, convinced of corruption in high places, suspicious of Charles' foreign policy and beginning to suspect his loyalty to Protestantism. Claude Lorraine: *Landscape with the Angel Appearing to Hagar*. Dryden becomes poet laureate.

DATE	AUTHOR'S LIFE	LITERARY CONTEXT
1668 *cont*	consideration of the King's Speech. Marvell's hopes for a change of ministers and a change of direction at first encouraged by the Triple Alliance but thereafter doomed to frustration.	Bethel: *The World's Mistake in Oliver Cromwell.* Denham: *Poems and Translations.* Boileau: *Satires VIII–IX.*
1669	*The Loyall Scott* (1669–70) inspired by Marvell's support of the king's policy of a Parliamentary union between the two countries which he blames the Anglican church for preventing. Marvell by now lodging at the Crown by Charing Cross.	Dryden: *Tyrannic Love.* Penn (from the Tower of London): *No Cross, No Crown.* Molière: *L'Avare.* Racine: *Britannicus.*
1670	Marvell expresses his suspicions about the possible duplicity of Court policy in a letter to his nephew. But his dislike of French-style absolutism does not prevent him from writing six Latin epigrams in praise of Louis XIV for submission to a competition for an inscription on the Louvre. Opposes Conventicle Act and disapproves of the rider re-affirming the king's supreme authority in matters ecclesiastical.	Parker: *A Discourse of Ecclesiastical Polity.* Dryden: *The Conquest of Granada.* Aphra Behn's first play, *The Forced Marriage.* Birth of Congreve. Walton: *Life of George Herbert.* Pascal: *Pensées.* Racine: *Bérénice.* Molière: *Le Bourgeois gentilhomme.* Spinoza: *Tractatus Theologico-Politicus.*
1671	English and Latin epigram, 'On Blood's Stealing the Crown' (of dubious attribution). Marvell's and Buckingham's names even linked with Blood's in an informer's report (September).	Milton: *Paradise Regained* and *Samson Agonistes.* Traherne: majority of *Thanksgivings* and probably collected and arranged 'Dobell' sequence of poems. Buckingham: *The Rehearsal* (attrib.).
1672	*The Rehearsal Transpros'd,* published anonymously, attacks bishops, and particularly Samuel Parker, Archdeacon of Canterbury, for refusing to slacken requirements for conformity. Also attacks Dryden, a former colleague of	Bunyan: *A Confession of my Faith and a Reason of my Practice.* Freed by the Declaration of Indulgence; resumes preaching and is again briefly imprisoned. Dryden: *Marriage à-la-Mode; Of Heroik Plays.*

James, Duke of York, acknowledges his conversion to Roman Catholicism the previous year; Charles insists his daughters are brought up as Anglicans. Death of Henrietta Maria. Sir Christopher Wren becomes Surveyor of Works and responsible for the rebuilding of London following the Great Fire. His work includes St Paul's Cathedral and 51 other London churches.

Rumours that the king was considering divorce, his wife having failed to produce an heir. Treaty of Dover, whereby Charles agrees to support Louis' annexation of the Netherlands with naval help, for which he receives a subsidy of 3 million *livres* p.a. By a secret clause Charles agrees to declare his Catholicism at an appropriate time (which never occurs), whereupon the subsidy would be increased, together with military aid if necessary. The king's public and private policies now in direct conflict. Second Conventicle Act renews persecution of Protestant Dissenters. Death of Charles' favourite sister, Henriette, Duchess of Orleans. Hudson's Bay Trading Company established.

English buccaneers destroy Panama. French Senegal Company founded. Colonel Blood attempts to steal the Crown Jewels and is pardoned. Grinling Gibbons' carving of Tintoretto's *Crucifixion* leads to Wren's patronage and his employment at St Paul's, Blenheim, Chatsworth, etc.

Charles II's Declaration of Indulgence suspends penal laws against Protestant Nonconformists and Catholics alike. Viewed by some as part of a pro-French, Roman Catholic conspiracy. Third Dutch War. Louis invades Holland (June); halted by William of Orange who is elected Stadtholder after popular uprising overthrows republic and De Witt is murdered. Indecisive battle of Southwold Bay; Earl of Sandwich lost in action. Ashley Cooper made Earl of Shaftesbury and Lord Chancellor. The Stop of the Exchequer – repayment of Government debts suspended with the promise

DATE	AUTHOR'S LIFE	LITERARY CONTEXT
1672 *cont*	Marvell's in Cromwell's civil service. When copies are confiscated by Roger L'Estrange, Surveyor of the Press, word reaches him via the Earl of Angelsey that the king wanted the book to be allowed 'for Parker has done him wrong and this man has done him Right'. According to Burnet, the king much enjoyed Marvell's amusing burlesque.	Wycherley: *Love in a Wood, or St James's Park*. Temple: *Observations upon the . . . Netherlands*. Births of Addison and Steele. Molière: *Les Femmes savantes*. Racine: *Bajazet*.
1673	Repeal of Declaration of Indulgence gives Parker the upper hand, as he advertises in his 'Reproof'. *The Rehearsal Transpros'd, The Second Part* published under Marvell's name. Parker accused Marvell of voting against the Declaration and it is not impossible that he did so, in the hope that the same end might be met by legislation, rather than by exercise of the prerogative. However, the fall of the Cabal removed any further hopes of toleration, and Marvell's complete disillusionment with Charles II has been dated from this time. Seems to have spent some time in Highgate where he retired 'to injoy the spring and my privacy'.	Wycherley: *The Gentleman Dancing-Master*. Shadwell: *Epsom Wells*. Behn: *The Dutch Lover*. Ravenscroft: *The Careless Lovers*. D'Avenant: *Works*. Temple: *Essay on the Origin and Nature of Government*. Racine: *Mithredate*. Molière: *Le Malade imaginaire*.
1674	Government spy reports Marvell's involvement (as 'Mr Thomas') in Dutch-based anti-French, anti-Catholic fifth column, even before peace with Holland concluded in February. Fear of Popery had thus driven him to adopt a position directly opposite to the one he had taken up earlier in *The Character of Holland*. Writes commendatory poem for the second, revised edition of *Paradise Lost*.	Death of Milton, Herrick and Traherne. Shadwell's opera *The Enchanted Island* (adaptation of *The Tempest*). Hobbes' translation of Homer's *Odyssey*. J. Josselyn: *Two Voyages to New England*. Lee: *Nero* (first play). Anthony à Wood: *Historia et Antiquitates Universitatis Oxoniensis*. Racine: *Iphigénie*. Boileau: *L'Art poétique*.

HISTORICAL EVENTS

of an extra 6% interest to creditors as compensation – a radical step but the only one Charles can find to finance war. Pepys appointed Secretary to the Admiralty. The two Willem van de Velde, maritime painters, enter royal service.

Parliament makes supply dependent upon withdrawal of Declaration of Indulgence; Charles humiliatingly concedes. Parliamentary opinion begins to swing in favour of William of Orange, encouraged by Dutch propaganda and bribery. Test Act passed whereby office holders are obliged to make declaration denying transubstantiation and produce a certificate that they have recently taken Anglican communion. Clifford and the Duke of York resign, confirming public's worst fears. Outrage at news of James's impending marriage to the Catholic Mary of Modena; Shaftesbury dismissed for his opposition. Sir Thomas Osborne becomes Lord Treasurer (June). Lully's *Tragédies-lyriques*. First public concerts held in London. Christian Huygen's *Horlogium Oscillatorum* contains earliest attempt to apply dynamics to bodies of finite size.

Fall of Buckingham and Arlington completes collapse of the Cabal (except Lauderdale). Treaty of Westminster; Charles pulls out of the war. Sir Thomas Osborne, later Earl of Danby, emerges as new chief minister. Anti-French, and a strong supporter of the Anglican establishment, his policies designed to restore the credit of the Court party. By good financial management he proposed that Charles should be able to rule without Parliament if necessary; in the meantime, liberal bribing of MPs would ensure that they were amenable to any requests for supply. Shaftesbury, espousing cause of popular Protestantism, leads opposition party in the Lords, supported by Buckingham and George Savile, Viscount Halifax; in the Commons, leading spokesmen are Sacheverell, Cavendish, Russell and Coventry. Death of Clarendon. Organist and composer John Blow becomes Master of the Children of the Chapel Royal.

DATE	AUTHOR'S LIFE	LITERARY CONTEXT
1675	Marvell appointed a commissioner for recusancy in Yorkshire (March). In April writes a mock 'king's speech' for the opening of the new session. Hull Corporation's cash book records Marvell paid 6s 8d a day for the 59 days he represented the town in the current session. He was one of the few members still receiving such a payment, a fact with which his enemies rather unfairly taunted him, since he appeared to have no other means of support.	Wycherley: *The Country Wife*. Shadwell: *Psyche* (opera with Matthew Locke). Otway: *Alcibiades* (first play). Lee: *Sophonisba, or Hannibal's Overthrow*. Rochester: *A Satyr Against Mankind*. Shaftesbury: *A Letter from a Person of Quality to his Friend in the Country*. Traherne: *Christian Ethics*.
1676	Publishes *Mr. Smirke: or the Divine in Mode*, with *A Short Historical Essay Concerning General Councils, Creeds, and Imposition in Religion*.	Etherege: *The Man of Mode*. Wycherley: *The Plain-Dealer*. Settle: *Ibrahim*. Otway: *Don Carlos*. Behn: *The Town-Fop*.
1677	Marvell's longest surviving speech in the House against 'An Act for securing the Protestant Religion' which would have increased the powers of the bishops. An altercation with Speaker Seymour leads one Member to demand Marvell be 'sent to the Tower'. Lodges two bankrupt relatives in a house taken in the name of his housekeeper Mary Palmer. Anonymous publication of *An Account of the Growth of Popery and Arbitrary Government*, in which Marvell calls for renewal of war with France and a new Parliament, and now interprets the Declaration of Indulgence as part of a Roman Catholic conspiracy. Shaftesbury is hailed as a martyr for English liberties and the Protestant religion, but Marvell advocates reform, not revolution.	L'Estrange: *The Parallel, or, An Account of the Growth of Knavery* (answer to Marvell). Sedley: *Antony and Cleopatra*. Tate: *Poems*. Burnet: *Memoirs of the Dukes of Hamilton*. Behn: *The Rover*. Durfey: *A Fond Husband*. Racine: *Phèdre*.

CHRONOLOGY

Opening of 13th session of the Cavalier Parliament (April). A great deal of money changing hands: Danby bribing MPs to support the Court (and offering them a Royal proclamation for enforcing laws against Nonconformists to make them more compliant): the Dutch and Spanish bribing them to press for war with France; the French bribing them *not* to enter such a war. Supply granted for naval expenses only. For the first time Charles is solvent (June). Test Act passed by Lords (opposed by Shaftesbury) which would effectively have made an opposition party unconstitutional. Moves to impeach Danby, which even Marvell opposes so that 'more usefull and publick businesse may be resumed'. In his letters he deplores the riotous behaviour in the Commons this session – on one occasion members even draw swords and tear off periwigs. Dispute over privileges between the two Houses (Shirley v. Fagg case) provokes prorogation and prevents Act from becoming law. Order for the suppression of coffee houses (for political reasons), which is almost immediately withdrawn. Work begins on St Paul's Cathedral; foundation of the Royal Observatory at Greenwich.

Artist Godfrey Kneller arrives in England and becomes attached to the Court. King makes another secret treaty with Louis XIV and becomes his pensioner (£100,000 p. a.). This enables him to manage without Parliament, which suits the French king, as English parliaments were inclined to press for war against him. Shaftesbury's Green Ribbon Club active during prorogation. Bacon's rebellion in Virginia.

Negotiations begin between French and Dutch. Louis continues to pay Charles to remain neutral. Danby recommends Parliament be summoned as he feels he will be able to obtain supply; Louis thereupon bribes the opposition to oppose Danby's anti-French policies, and ensure a stalemate. Both Shaftesbury and Buckingham in receipt of such bribes – Louis promising in return not to interefere with their liberties or their religion. Buckingham, Shaftesbury, Salisbury and Wharton committed to Tower for refusing to admit the legality of Parliament, meeting after a 15 month prorogation. Supply voted for ships. Danby's Act for securing the Protestant Religion fails to pass. Louis scores more military successes against the Dutch. Commons renew their request that England support the Dutch against France. In atmosphere of increasing suspicion of Roman Catholic conspiracy, Sacheverell demands that the king make public his alliances. Amidst rowdy scenes, Parliament is adjourned. Anglo-Dutch treaty (December) appears to detach England from France. Marriage of William III and Duke of York's daughter Mary a triumph for Danby in his efforts to forge a resplendently Protestant foreign policy.

DATE	AUTHOR'S LIFE	LITERARY CONTEXT
1678	Marvell elected younger warden of Trinity House, London. The *London-Gazette* offers a reward for information regarding the author or printer of *An Account of the Growth of Popery*. Publishes *Remarks upon a Late Disingenuous Discourse Writ by One T.D. . . . By a Protestant*. After a visit to Hull, dies of a tertian ague on 16 August at his house in Bloomsbury. Buried at St Giles-in-the-Field. Mary Palmer, acting in conjunction with the two city friends Marvell had been sheltering, gains administration of the estate, having convinced a court that she had been his wife since 1667.	Bunyan: *The Pilgrim's Progress*. Dryden: *All For Love*. Mme de La Fayette: *La Princesse de Clèves*. Vaughan: *Thalia Rediviva*. Butler: *Hudibras* (part 2). L'Estrange's digest of Seneca's *Morals*, one of the most widely read books of the period, and translation of *Lettres Portugaises* as *Five Love-Letters from a Nun to a Cavalier*.
1681	*Miscellaneous* poems published in a collection by 'Mary Marvell', 'according to the exact Copies of my late dear Husband, under his own Hand-Writing, being found among his other papers . . .'	Dryden: *The Spanish Fryar; Absalom and Achitopel; His Majesty's Declaration Defended*. Oldham: *Satyrs upon the Jesuits*. Ravenscroft: *The London Cuckolds*. Shadwell: *The Lancashire Witches*.

CHRONOLOGY

In recognition of the new treaty with the Dutch, Parliament prevailed upon to vote money for 90 ships and 30,000 troops. Charles continues to follow double foreign policy, publicly trying to set up a series of alliances against France; privately attempting to secure French money for maintaining English neutrality – to which end another secret treaty is signed, though rendered superfluous when France and Holland make peace at Nijmegen (July). Just when other European powers were in the last throes of resistance to French might, England had raised an army and conjecture as to the use to which it might be put proves explosive. Titus Oates and Israel Tonge first give evidence on oath to Sir Edmund Berry Godfrey (28 September) of a Popish plot. Mysterious death of Sir Edmund Berry Godfrey in October. Five Roman Catholic lords sent to the Tower. Execution of Edward Coleman, the Duke of York's secretary. Discovery of incriminating letter from Danby to Montagu – English ambassador in France – endorsed by Charles, and referring to French subsidies. The Commons convinced that the Court had been intriguing with the French for years to introduce Roman Catholicism and arbitrary government, and for this purpose alone had wished to raise an army. Danby impeached. Charles dissolves Parliament (January 1679).

Exclusion Crisis. Two bills to exclude James from the succession had been defeated in 1679 and 1680. Politics for the first time takes on distinctive party lines. First use of 'Whigs' (pro-Exclusion) and 'Tories' (anti-Exclusion). Whigs divided between supporters of William of Orange, the king's nephew, and the Duke of Monmouth, his illegitimate son. Even those not in favour of barring James, as a Catholic, from the throne, prepared to discuss limitations on the prerogative should he succeed. At Oxford Parliament (March) Shaftesbury proposes that Monmouth be named as Charles II's heir. New Exclusion Bill. Charles dissolves Parliament and is enabled by French subsidy to rule without Parliament until his death in 1685. Reaction in the country against the Whigs. Shaftesbury committed to Tower on treason charge.

Lyric Poems

A Dialogue, between
The Resolved Soul, and Created Pleasure

Courage my Soul, now learn to wield
The weight of thine immortal Shield.
Close on thy Head thy Helmet bright.
Ballance thy Sword against the Fight.
See where an Army, strong as fair,
With silken Banners spreads the air.
Now, if thou bee'st that thing Divine,
In this day's Combat let it shine:
And shew that Nature wants an Art
To conquer one resolved Heart.   10

Pleasure
Welcome the Creations Guest,
Lord of Earth, and Heavens Heir.
Lay aside that Warlike Crest,
And of Nature's banquet share:
Where the Souls of fruits and flow'rs
Stand prepar'd to heighten yours.

Soul
I sup above, and cannot stay
To bait so long upon the way.

Pleasure
On these downy Pillows lye,
Whose soft Plumes will thither fly: 20
On these Roses strow'd so plain
Lest one Leaf thy Side should strain.

Soul
My gentler Rest is on a Thought,
Conscious of doing what I ought.

Pleasure
If thou bee'st with Perfumes pleas'd,
Such as oft the Gods appeas'd,
Thou in fragrant Clouds shalt show
Like another God below.

Soul
A Soul that knowes not to presume
Is Heaven's and its own perfume.   30

Pleasure
Every thing does seem to vie
Which should first attract thine Eye:
But since none deserves that grace,
In this Crystal view *thy* face.

Soul
When the Creator's skill is priz'd,
The rest is all but Earth disguis'd.

Pleasure
Hark how Musick then prepares
For thy Stay these charming Aires;
Which the posting Winds recall,
And suspend the Rivers Fall.   40

Soul
Had I but any time to lose,
On this I would it all dispose.
Cease Tempter. None can chain a mind
Whom this sweet Chordage cannot bind.

Chorus
Earth cannot shew so brave a Sight
As when a single Soul does fence
The Batteries of alluring Sense,
And Heaven views it with delight.

44. *Chordage:* Note the pun.

Then preserve: for still new Charges sound:
And if thou overcom'st thou shalt be crown'd.   50

Pleasure
All this fair, and soft, and sweet,
    Which scatteringly doth shine,
Shall within one Beauty meet,
    And she be only thine.

Soul
If things of Sight such Heavens be,
What Heavens are those we cannot see?

Pleasure
Where so e're thy Foot shall go
    The minted Gold shall lie,
Till thou purchase all below,
    And want new Worlds to buy.   60

Soul
Wer't not a price who'ld value Gold?
And that's worth nought that can be sold.

Pleasure
Wilt thou all the Glory have
    That War or Peace commend?
Half the World shall be thy Slave
    The other half thy Friend.

Soul
What Friends, if to my self untrue?
What Slaves, unless I captive you?

Pleasure
Thou shalt know each hidden Cause:
    And see the future Time: 70
Try what depth the Centre draws;
    And then to Heaven climb.

51. *soft:* As in the Bod. MS.; *cost* in the Folio.
71. *Centre:* Center of the earth.

Soul
None thither mounts by the degree
Of Knowledge, but Humility.

Chorus
Triumph, triumph, victorious Soul;
The World has not one Pleasure more:
The rest does lie beyond the Pole,
And is thine everlasting Store.

On a Drop of Dew

See how the Orient Dew,
 Shed from the Bosom of the Morn
 Into the blowing Roses,
Yet careless of its Mansion new
For the clear Region where 'twas born,
 Round in its self incloses:
 And in its little Globes Extent,
Frames as it can its native Element.
 How it the purple flow'r does slight,
  Scarce touching where it lyes,   10
 But gazing back upon the Skies,
  Shines with a mournful Light;
   Like its own Tear,
Because so long divided from the Sphear.
 Restless it roules and unsecure,
  Trembling lest it grow impure:
 Till the warm Sun pitty it's Pain,
And to the Skies exhale it back again.
  So the Soul, that Drop, that Ray
Of the clear Fountain of Eternal Day,   20
Could it within the humane flow'r be seen,
  Remembering still its former height,
  Shuns the sweet leaves and blossoms green;
  And, recollecting its own Light,

---

5. *For:* Because of. 6. *incloses:* Closes in on itself all round.
8. *native Element:* Heaven. 24. *recollecting:* Collecting again.

Does, in its pure and circling thoughts, express
The greater Heaven in an Heaven less.
    In how coy a Figure wound,
    Every way it turns away:
    So the World excluding round,
    Yet receiving in the Day.   30
    Dark beneath, but bright above:
    Here disdaining, there in Love.
  How loose and easie hence to go:
  How girt and ready to ascend.
  Moving but on a point below,
  It all about does upwards bend.
Such did the Manna's sacred Dew destil;
White, and intire, though congeal'd and chill.
Congeal'd on Earth: but does, dissolving, run
Into the Glories of th' Almighty Sun.   40

The Coronet

  When for the Thorns with which I long, too long,
    With many a piercing wound,
    My Saviours head have crown'd,
I seek with Garlands to redress that Wrong;
    Through every Garden, every Mead,
I gather flow'rs (my fruits are only flow'rs)
    Dismantling all the fragrant Towers
That once adorn'd my Shepherdesses head.
And now when I have summ'd up all my store,
    Thinking (so I my self deceive)   10
    So rich a Chaplet thence to weave
As never yet the king of Glory wore:
    Alas I find the Serpent old
    That, twining in his speckled breast,
    About the flow'rs disguis'd does fold,

25. *circling:* The circle was an emblem of perfection.
27. *coy:* Modest.   37. *Such:* So.
37–40: Compare Exodus 16:21: "and they gathered it [manna] morning by morning ... and when the sun waxed hot, it melted."
7. *Towers:* Very high head-dress worn by women.
14. *twining in:* Entwining.

    With wreaths of Fame and Interest.
Ah, foolish Man, that would'st debase with them,
And mortal Glory, Heavens Diadem!
But thou who only could'st the Serpent tame,
Either his slipp'ry knots at once untie,   20
And disintangle all his winding Snare:
Or shatter too with him my curious frame:
And let these wither, so that he may die,
Though set with Skill and chosen out with Care.
That they, while Thou on both their Spoils dost tread,
May crown thy Feet, that could not crown thy Head.

Eyes and Tears

    i

How wisely Nature did decree,
With the same Eyes to weep and see!
That, having view'd the object vain,
They might be ready to complain.

    ii

And, since the Self-deluding Sight
In a false Angle takes each hight;
These Tears which better measure all,
Like wat'ry Lines and Plummets fall.

    iii

Two Tears, which Sorrow long did weigh
Within the Scales of either Eye,   10
And then paid out in equal Poise,
Are the true price of all my Joyes.

    iv

What in the World most fair appears,
Yea even Laughter, turns to Tears:

16. *wreaths:* Coils. *Interest:* Self-interest.   19. *thou:* Christ.
22: Compare John Donne, "Batter My Heart, Three-Personed God." *curious:*
Elaborately wrought.

And all the Jewels which we prize,
Melt in these Pendants of the Eyes.

    v

I have through every Garden been,
Amongst the Red, the White, the Green;
And yet, from all the flow'rs I saw,
No Hony, but these Tears could draw.   20

    vi

So the all-seeing Sun each day
Distills the World with Chymick Ray;
But finds the Essence only Show'rs,
Which straight in pity back he poures.

    vii

Yet happy they whom Grief doth bless,
That weep the more, and see the less:
And, to preserve their Sight more true,
Bath still their Eyes in their own Dew.

    viii

So *Magdalen*, in Tears more wise
Dissolv'd those captivating Eyes,   30
Whose liquid Chaines could flowing meet
To fetter her Redeemers feet.*

    ix

Not full sailes hasting loaden home,
Nor the chast Ladies pregnant Womb,
Nor *Cynthia* Teeming show's so fair,
As two Eyes swoln with weeping are.

    x

The sparkling Glance that shoots Desire,
Drench'd in these Waves, does lose its fire.
Yea oft the Thund'rer pitty takes
And here the hissing Lightning slakes.   40

* The Latin version of this stanza appears on p. 231.

xi

The Incense was to Heaven dear,
Not as a Perfume, but a Tear.
And Stars shew lovely in the Night,
But as they seem the Tears of Light.

xii

Ope then mine Eyes your double Sluice,
And practise so your noblest Use.
For others too can see, or sleep;
But only humane Eyes can weep.

xiii

Now like two Clouds dissolving, drop,
And at each Tear in Distance stop: 50
Now like two Fountains trickle down:
Now like two floods o'return and drown.

xiii

Thus let your Streams o'reflow your Springs,
Till Eyes and Tears be the same things:
And each the other's difference bears;
These weeping Eyes, those seeing Tears.

Bermudas

Where the remote *Bermudas* ride
In th' Oceans bosome unespy'd,
From a small Boat, that row'd along,
The listning Winds receiv'd this Song.
   What should we do but sing his Praise
That led us through the watry Maze,
Unto an Isle so long unknown,
And yet far kinder than our own?
Where he the huge Sea-Monsters wracks,
That lift the Deep upon their Backs.   10
He lands us on a grassy Stage;
Safe from the Storms, and Prelat's rage.

12. *Prelat's rage:* The Anglican Bishop's persecution of Nonconformists.

He gave us this eternal Spring,
Which here enamells every thing;
And sends the Fowl's to us in care,
On daily Visits through the Air.
He hangs in shades the Orange bright,
Like golden Lamps in a green Night.
And does in the Pomgranates close
Jewels more rich than *Ormus* shows.   20
He makes the Figs our mouths to meet;
And throws the Melons at our feet.
But Apples plants of such a price,
No Tree could ever bear them twice.
With Cedars, chosen by his hand,
From *Lebanon*, he stores the Land.
And makes the hollow Seas, that roar,
Proclaime the Ambergris on shoar.
He cast (of which we rather boast)
The Gospels Pearl upon our Coast.   30
And in these Rocks for us did frame
A Temple, where to sound his Name.
Oh let our Voice his Praise exalt,
Till it arrive at Heavens Vault:
Which thence (perhaps) rebounding, may
Eccho beyond the *Mexique Bay*.
Thus sung they, in the *English* boat,
An holy and a chearful Note,
And all the way, to guide their Chime,
With falling Oars they kept the time.   40

Clorinda *and* Damon

C.   *Damon* come drive thy flocks this way.
D.   No: 'tis too late they went astray.
C.   I have a grassy Scutcheon spy'd,
     Where *Flora* blazons all her pride.
     The Grass I aim to feast thy Sheep:
     The Flow'rs I for thy Temples keep.
D.   Grass withers; and the Flow'rs too fade.

20. *Ormus:* Hormuz, on the Persian Gulf.

C.   Seize the short Joyes then, ere they vade.
      Seest thou that unfrequented Cave?
D.   That den?   *C.*   Loves Shrine.   *D.*   But
          Virtue's Grave.   10
C.   In whose cool bosome we may lye
      Safe from the sun.   *D.*   Not Heaven's Eye.
C.   Near this, a Fountaines liquid Bell
      Tinkles within the concave Shell.
D.   Might a Soul bath there and be clean,
      Or slake its Drought?   *C.*   What is't you mean?
D.   These once had been enticing things,
      Clorinda, Pastures, Caves, and Springs.
C.   And what late change?   *D.*   The other day
      Pan met me.   *C.*   What did great *Pan* say?   20
D.   Words that transcend poor Shepherds skill;
      But He e'er since my Songs does fill:
      And his Name swells my slender Oate.
C.   Sweet must *Pan* sound in *Damons* Note.
D.   *Clorinda's* voice might make it sweet.
C.   Who would not in *Pan's* Praises meet?

Chorus
Of Pan *the flowry Pastures sing,*
Caves eccho, and the Fountains ring.
Sing then while he doth us inspire;
For all the World is our Pan's *Quire.*   30

Two Songs at the Marriage of the Lord Fauconberg *and the Lady* Mary Cromwell

First Song

Chorus. Endymion. Luna.

Chorus
Th' *Astrologers* own Eyes are set,
And even Wolves the Sheep forget;
Only *this Shepheard*, late and soon,
Upon this Hill outwakes the *Moon*.
Heark how he sings, with sad delight,
Thorough the clear and silent Night.

Endymion
Cynthia, O Cynthia, turn thine Ear,
Nor scorn *Endymions* plaints to hear.
As we our Flocks, so you command
The fleecy Clouds with silver wand.   10

Cynthia
If thou a *Mortal*, rather sleep;
Or if a *Shepheard*, watch thy Sheep.

Endymion
The *Shepheard*, since he saw thine Eyes,
And *Sheep* are both thy *Sacrifice*.
Nor merits he a *Mortal's* name,
That burns with an *immortal Flame*.

Two Songs at the Marriage of the Lord Fauconberg and the Lady Mary Cromwell: Thomas Belasye (1627–1700), second Viscount Fauconberg, a kinsman of Lord Fairfax, married Mary, the Protector's third daughter, on November 19, 1657.
   The two dialogues come at the very end of the Folio, following a number of poems dealing with the Cromwell era, but I have put them among the other pastoral dialogues since the only thing topical about them is their title.

Cynthia
I have enough for me to do,
Ruling the Waves that Ebb and flow.

Endymion
Since thou disdain'st not then to share
On Sublunary things thy care;   20
Rather restrain these double Seas,
Mine Eyes uncessant deluges.

Cynthia
My wakeful Lamp all night must move,
Securing their Repose above.

Endymion
If therefore thy resplendent Ray
Can make a Night more bright than Day;
Shine thorough this obscurer Brest,
With shades of deep Despair opprest.

Chorus
Courage, *Endymion*, boldly Woo,
Anchises was a *Shepheard* too;   30
Yet is *her younger Sister* laid
Sporting with him in *Ida's Shade:*
    And *Cynthia*, though the strongest,
Seeks but the honour to have held out longest.

Endymion
Here unto *Latmos Top* I climbe:
How far below thine *Orbe* sublime?
O why, as well as Eyes to see,
Have I not Armes that reach to thee?

Cynthia
'Tis needless then that I refuse,
Would you but your own Reason use.   40

30–32. *Anchises:* Robert Rich, who married Cromwell's fourth daughter Frances
a week earlier.

Endymion
Though I so high may not pretend,
It is the same so you descend.

Cynthia
These Stars would say I do them wrong,
Rivals each one for thee too strong.

Endymion
The Stars are fix'd unto their *Sphere*,
And cannot, though they would, come near.
Less Loves set off each others praise,
While *Stars* Eclipse by mixing Rayes.

Cynthia
That Cave is dark.

Endymion
       Then none can spy: 50
Or shine Thou there and 'tis the Sky.

Chorus
    Joy to *Endymion*,
  For he has *Cynthia's* favour won.
    And *Jove* himself approves
With his serenest influence their Loves.
  For he did never love to pair
  His Progeny above the Air;
  But to be honest, valiant, wise,
Makes *Mortals* matches fit for *Deityes*.

Second Song

Hobbinol. Phillis. Tomalin.

Hobbinol
Phillis, Tomalin, away:
Never such a merry day.
For *the Northern Shepheard's Son*
Has *Menalca's daughter* won.

Phillis
Stay till I some flow'rs ha' ty'd
In a Garland for the Bride.

Tomalin
If thou would'st a Garland bring,
Phillis you may wait the Spring:
They ha' chosen such an hour
When *She* is the only flow'r.   10

Phillis
Let's not then at least be seen
Without each a Sprig of Green.

Hobbinol
Fear not; at *Menalca's Hall*
There is Bayes enough for all.
He when Young as we did graze,
But when Old he planted Bayes.

Tomalin
Here *She* comes; but with a Look
Far more catching than my Hook.
'Twas those Eyes, I now dare swear,
Led our Lambs we knew not where.   20

Hobbinol
Not our Lambs own Fleeces are
Curl'd so lovely as her Hair:
Nor our Sheep new Wash'd can be
Half so white or sweet as *She*.

Phillis
He so looks as fit to keep
Somewhat else then silly *Sheep*.

Hobbinol
Come, lets in some Carol new
Pay to Love and Them their due.

All
    Joy to that *happy Pair*,
Whose Hopes united banish our Despair.   30
    What *Shepheard* could for Love pretend,
Whil'st all the *Nymphs* on *Damon's* choice attend?
    What *Shepherdess* could hope to wed
    Before *Marina's* turn were sped?
    Now lesser Beauties may take place,
    And meaner Virtues come in play;
           While they,
           Looking from high,
           Shall grace
Our Flocks and us with a propitious Eye.   40
    But what is most, the gentle Swain
    No more shall need of Love complain;
    But Virtue shall be Beauties hire,
And those be equal that have equal Fire.
    Marina yields. Who dares be coy?
Or who despair, now *Damon* does enjoy?
        Joy to that happy Pair,
Whose Hopes united banish our Despair.

A Dialogue between the Soul and Body

Soul
    O Who shall, from this Dungeon, raise
A Soul enslav'd so many wayes?
With bolts of Bones, that fetter'd stands
In Feet; and manacled in Hands.
Here blinded with an Eye; and there
Deaf with the drumming of an Ear.
A Soul hung up, as 'twere, in Chains
Of Nerves, and Arteries, and Veins.
Tortur'd, besides each other part,
In a vain Head, and double Heart.   10

Body
    O who shall me deliver whole,
From bonds of this Tyrannic Soul?

Which, stretcht upright, impales me so,
That mine own Precipice I go;
And warms and moves this needless Frame:
(A Fever could but do the same.)
And, wanting where its spight to try,
Has made me live to let me dye.
A Body that could never rest,
Since this ill Spirit it possest.   20

Soul
    What Magick could me thus confine
Within anothers Grief to pine?
Where whatsoever it complain,
I feel, that cannot feel, the pain.
And all my Care its self employes,
That to preserve, which me destroys:
Constrain'd not only to indure
Diseases, but, whats worse, the Cure:
And ready oft the Port to gain,
Am Shipwrackt into Health again.   30

Body
    But Physick yet could never reach
The Maladies Thou me dost teach;
Whom first the Cramp of Hope does Tear:
And then the Palsie Shakes of Fear.
The Pestilence of Love does heat:
Or Hatred's hidden Ulcer eat.
Joy's chearful Madness does perplex:
Or Sorrow's other Madness vex.
Which Knowledge forces me to know;
And Memory will not foregoe.   40
What but a Soul could have the wit
To build me up for Sin so fit?
So Architects do square and hew
Green Trees that in the Forest grew.

13-14: "After he was stretch'd to such an height in his own fancy, that he could not look down from top to toe but his Eyes dazled at the Precipice of his Stature" (Marvell, *Rehearsal Transpros'd*, in *Complete Works*, 4 vols., ed. A. B. Grosart, London, 1872-1875, Vol. I, p. 64. Also see "On a Drop of Dew," l. 13, p. 6.
15. *needless:* Having no want.

The Nymph complaining for the death of her Faun

The wanton Troopers riding by
Have shot my Faun and it will dye.
Ungentle men! They cannot thrive
To kill thee. Thou neer didst alive
Them any harm: alas nor cou'd
Thy death yet do them any good.
I'me sure I never wisht them ill;
Nor do I for all this; nor will:
But, if my simple Pray'rs may yet
Prevail with Heaven to forget   10
Thy murder, I will Joyn my Tears
Rather than fail. But, O my fears!
It cannot dye so. Heavens King
Keeps register of every thing:
And nothing may we use in vain.
Ev'n Beasts must be with justice slain;
Else Men are made their *Deodands.*
Though they should wash their guilty hands
In this warm life-blood, which doth part
From thine, and wound me to the Heart,   20
Yet could they not be clean: their Stain
Is dy'd in such a Purple Grain.
There is not such another in
The World, to offer for their Sin.
Unconstant *Sylvio,* when yet
I had not found him counterfeit,
One morning (I remember well)
Ty'd in this silver Chain and Bell,
Gave it to me: nay and I know
What he said then; I'me sure I do.   30
Said He, look how your Huntsman here
Hath taught a Faun to hunt his *Dear.*

3-4: That is, they who have killed thee cannot thrive.
17. *Deodand:* In English law a personal chattel which, having been the immediate
occasion of the death of a human being, was given to God as an expiatory offering.

But *Sylvio* soon had me beguil'd.
This waxed tame, while he grew wild,
And quite regardless of my Smart,
Left me his Faun, but took his Heart.
 Thenceforth I set my self to play
My solitary time away,
With this: and very well content,
Could so mine idle Life have spent.   40
For it was full of sport; and light
Of foot, and heart; and did invite,
Me to its game: it seem'd to bless
Its self in me. How could I less
Than love it? O I cannot be
Unkind, t' a Beast that loveth me.
 Had it liv'd long, I do not know
Whether it too might have done so
As *Sylvio* did: his Gifts might be
Perhaps as false or more than he.   50
But I am sure, for ought that I
Could in so short a time espie,
Thy Love was far more better then
The love of false and cruel men.
 With sweetest milk, and sugar, first
I it at mine own fingers nurst.
And as it grew, so every day
It wax'd more white and sweet than they.
It had so sweet a Breath! And oft
I blush to se its foot more soft,   60
And white, (shall I say then my hand?)
NAY any Ladies of the Land.
 It is a wond'rous thing, how fleet
'Twas on those little silver feet.
With what a pretty skipping grace,
It oft would challenge me the Race:
And when 't had left me far away,
'Twould stay, and run again, and stay.
For it was nimbler much than Hindes;
And trod, as on the four Winds.   70
 I have a Garden of my own,
But so with Roses over grown,
And Lillies, that you would it guess

To be a little Wilderness.
And all the Spring time of the year
It onely loved to be there.
Among the beds of Lillyes, I
Have sought it oft, where it should lye;
Yet could not, till it self would rise,
Find it, although before mine Eyes.   80
For, in the flaxen Lillies shade,
It like a bank of Lillies laid.
Upon the Roses it would feed,
Until its Lips ev'n seem'd to bleed:
And then to me 'twould boldly trip,
And print those Roses on my Lip.
But all its chief delight was still
On Roses thus its self to fill:
And its pure virgin Limbs to fold
In whitest sheets of Lillies cold.   90
Had it liv'd long, it would have been
Lillies without, Roses within.
     O help! O help! I see it faint:
And dye as calmely as a Saint.
See how it weeps. The Tears do come
Sad, slowly dropping like a Gumme.
So weeps the wounded Balsome: so
The holy Frankincense doth flow.
The brotherless *Heliades*
Melt in such Amber Tears as these.   100
     I in a golden Vial will
Keep these two crystal Tears; and fill
It till it do o'reflow with mine;
Then place it in *Diana's* Shrine.
     Now my sweet Faun is vanish'd to
Whither the Swans and Turtles go:
In fair *Elizium* to endure,
With milk-white Lambs, and Ermins pure.
O do not run too fast: for I
Will but bespeak thy Grave, and dye.   110
     First my unhappy Statue shall
But cut in Marble; and withal,
Let it be weeping too: but there
Th'Engraver sure his Art may spare;

For I so truly thee bemoane,
That I shall weep though I be Stone:
Until my Tears, still dropping, wear
My breast, themselves engraving there.
There at my feet shalt thou be laid,
Of purest Alabaster made: 120
For I would have thine Image be
White as I can, though not as Thee.

Young Love

i

Come little Infant, Love me now,
    While thine unsuspected years
Clear thine aged Fathers brow
    From cold Jealousie and Fears.

ii

Pretty surely 'twere to see
    By young Love old Time beguil'd:
While our Sportings are as free
    As the Nurses and the Child.

iii

Common Beauties stay fifteen;
    Such as yours should swifter move;   10
Whose fair Blossoms are too green
    Yet for Lust, but not for Love.

iv

Love as much the snowy Lamb
    Or the wanton kid does prize,
As the lusty Bull or Ram,
    For his morning Sacrifice.

v

Now then love me: time may take
    Thee before thy time away:
Of this Need wee'l Virtue make,
    And learn Love before we may.   20

vi

So we win of doubtful Fate;
    And, if good she to us meant,
We that Good shall antedate,
    Or, if ill, that Ill prevent.

vii

Thus as Kingdomes, frustrating
    Other Titles to their Crown,
In the craddle crown their King,
    So all Forraign Claims to drown,

viii

So, to make all Rivals vain,
    Now I crown thee with my Love: 30
Crown me with thy Love again,
    And we both shall Monarchs prove.

To his Coy Mistress

    Had we but World enough, and Time,
This coyness Lady were no crime.
We would sit down, and think which way
To walk, and pass our long Loves Day.
Thou by the *Indian Ganges* side
Should'st Rubies find: I by the Tide
Of *Humber* would complain. I would
Love you ten years before the Flood:
And you should, if you please, refuse
Till the Conversion of the *Jews*.   10
My vegetable Love should grow
Vaster than Empires, and more slow.
An hundred years should go to praise

13-18: Compare Abraham Cowley, *The Mistress* (1647), "My Dyet":
    O'n a *Sigh* of Pity I a year can live,
        One *Tear* will keep me twenty at least,
        Fifty a gentle *Look* will give;
    An hundred years on one *kind word* I'll feast:
        A thousand more will added be,
    If you an *Inclination* have for me;
    And all beyond is vast *Eternity*.
(Margoliouth)

Thine Eyes, and on thy Forehead Gaze.
Two hundred to adore each Breast:
But thirty thousand to the rest.
An Age at least to every part,
And the last Age should show your Heart.
For Lady you deserve this State;
Nor would I love at lower rate.   20
  But at my back I alwaies hear
Times winged Charriot hurrying near:
And yonder all before us lye
Deserts of vast Eternity.
Thy Beauty shall no more be found;
Nor, in thy marble Vault, shall sound
My ecchoing Song; then Worms shall try
That long preserv'd Virginity:
And your quaint Honour turn to dust;
And into ashes all my Lust.   30
The Grave's a fine and private place,
But none I think do there embrace.
  Now therefore, while the youthful hew
Sits on thy skin like morning glew,
And while thy willing Soul transpires
At every pore with instant Fires,
Now let us sport us while we may;
And now, like am'rous birds of prey,
Rather at once our Time devour,
Than languish in his slow-chapt pow'r.   40
Let us roll all our Strength, and all
Our sweetness, up into one Ball:
And tear our Pleasures with rough strife,

29. *dust:* As in Cooke; *durst* in the Folio.

33-34. *hew . . . glew:* These lines have long been regarded as a critical and editorial crux. Bod. MS. compounds the difficulty by emending *hew* to *glew* and *glew* to *dew*. Margoliouth emends *glew* to *dew*. Professor Louis L. Martz has long felt that no emendation was necessary and that *glew* must be a dialectal form of *glow*. Professor Cleanth Brooks has just provided me with philological evidence for retaining *glew* in the form of a note by the late Professor Helge Kökeritz, which concludes: "Doubtless . . . a vowel or diphthong, spelled *ew* and capable of rhyming with *ue* in *hue*, existed in the earlier periods of these northern dialects. Marvell's *glew* must consequently be a dialectal form of *glow*." As a Yorkshireman Marvell would have known this form. The youthful *hue* of the lady is compared with the tints of the sky at dawn.

Thorough the Iron gates of Life.
Thus, though we cannot make our Sun
Stand still, yet we will make him run.

The unfortunate Lover

i

Alas, how pleasant are their dayes
With whom the Infant Love yet playes!
Sorted by pairs, they still are seen
By Fountains cool, and Shadows green.
But soon these Flames do lose their light,
Like Meteors of a Summers night:
Nor can they to that Region climb,
To make impression upon Time.

ii

'Twas in a Shipwrack, when the Seas
Rul'd, and the Winds did what they please,   10
That my poor Lover floting lay,
And, e're brought forth, was cast away:
Till at the last the master-Wave
Upon the Rock his Mother drave;
And there she split against the Stone,
In a *Cesarian Section*.

iii

The Sea him lent these bitter Tears
Which at his Eyes he alwaies bears:
And from the Winds the Sighs he bore,
Which through his surging Breast do roar.   20
No Day he saw but that which breaks,
Through frighted Clouds in forked streaks.
While round the ratling Thunder hurl'd,
As at the Fun'ral of the World.

iv

While Nature to his Birth presents
This masque of quarrelling Elements;

44. *gates:* The Bod. MS. changes *gates* to *grates*.

A num'rous fleet of Corm'rants black,
That sail'd insulting o're the Wrack,
Receiv'd into their cruel Care,
Th' unfortunate and abject Heir: 30
Guardians most fit to entertain
The Orphan of the *Hurricane*.

v

They fed him up with Hopes and Air,
Which soon digested to Despair.
And as one Corm'rant fed him, still
Another on his Heart did bill.
Thus while they famish him, and feast,
He both consumed, and increast:
And languished with doubtful Breath,
Th' *Amphibium* of Life and Death.   40

vi

And now, when angry Heaven wou'd
Behold a spectacle of Blood,
Fortune and He are call'd to play
At sharp before it all the day:
And Tyrant Love his brest does ply
With all his wing'd Artillery.
Whilst he, betwixt the Flames and Waves,
Like *Ajax* the mad Tempest braves.

vii

See how he nak'd and fierce does stand,
Cuffing the Thunder with one hand;   50
While with the other he does lock,
And grapple, with the stubborn Rock:
From which he with each Wave rebounds,
Torn into Flames, and ragg'd with Wounds.
And all he saies, a Lover drest
In his own Blood does relish best.

---

36. *bill:* Peck.   44. *At sharp:* With sharpened weapons.
48: Ajax, son of Oïleus, boasted he had escaped from a storm against the will of the
gods. Poseidon, his rescuer, shattered the rock on which he had found refuge and
drowned him.

viii
This is the only *Banneret*
That ever Love created yet:
Who though, by the Malignant Starrs,
Forced to live in Storms and Warrs;   60
Yet dying leaves a Perfume here,
And Musick within every Ear:
And he in Story only rules,
In a Field *Sable* a Lover *Gules*.

The Gallery

i
Clora come view my Soul, and tell
Whether I have contriv'd it well.
Now all its several lodgings lye
Compos'd into one Gallery;
And the great *Arras*-hanings, made
Of various Faces, by are laid;
That, for all furniture, you'l find
Only your Picture in my Mind.

ii
Here Thou art painted in the Dress
Of an Inhumane Murtheress;   10
Examining upon our Hearts
Thy fertile Shop of cruel Arts:
Engines more keen than ever yet
Adorned Tyrants Cabinet;
Of which the most tormenting are
Black Eyes, red Lips, and curled Hair.

57. *Banneret:* A grade of knighthood first conferred by Charles I at the Battle of
Edgehill (1642). Compare Richard Lovelace, "Lucasta" (1649):
    Love nee're his Standard when his Hoste he sets,
    Creates alone fresh-bleeding Bannerets.
64. *Sable ... Gules:* Heraldic colors, black and crimson.
11. *Examining:* Testing.

iii

But, on the other side, th'art drawn
Like to *Aurora* in the Dawn;
When in the East she slumb'ring lyes,
And stretches out her milky Thighs;   20
While all the morning Quire does sing,
And *Manna* falls, and Roses spring;
And, at thy Feet, the wooing Doves
Sit perfecting their harmless Loves.

iv

Like an Enchantress here thou show'st,
Vexing thy restless Lover's Ghost;
And, by a Light obscure, dost rave
Over his Entrails, in the Cave;
Divining thence, with horrid Care,
How long thou shalt continue fair;   30
And (when inform'd) them throw'st away,
To be the greedy Vultur's prey.

v

But, against that, thou sit'st a float
Like *Venus* in her pearly Boat.
The *Halcyons*, calming all that's nigh,
Betwixt the Air and Water fly.
Or, if some rowling Wave appears,
A Mass of Ambergris it bears.
Nor blows more Wind than what may well
Convoy the Perfume to the Smell.   40

vi

These Pictures and a thousand more,
Of Thee, my Gallery do store;
In all the Forms thou can'st invent
Either to please me, or torment:
For thou alone to people me,
Art grown a num'rous Colony;
And a Collection choicer far
Than or *White-hall's*, or *Mantua's* were.

48. *Mantua:* Charles I bought the entire "cabinet" of Vincenzo Gonzaga,

vii

But, of these Pictures and the rest,
That at the Entrance likes me best: 50
Where the same Posture, and the Look
Remains, with which I first was took.
A tender Shepherdess, whose Hair
Hangs loosely playing in the Air,
Transplanting Flow'rs from the green Hill,
To crown her Head, and Bosome fill.

The Fair Singer

i

To make a final conquest of all me,
Love did compose so sweet an Enemy,
In whom both Beauties to my death agree,
Joyning themselves in fatal Harmony;
That while she with her Eyes my Heart does bind,
She with her Voice might captivate my Mind.

ii

I could have fled from One but singly fair:
My dis-intangled Soul it self might save,
Breaking the curled trammels of her hair.
But how should I avoid to be her Slave,   10
Whose subtile Art invisibly can wreath
My Fetters of the very Air I breath?

iii

It had been easie fighting in some plain,
Where Victory might hang in equal choice.
But all resistance against her is vain,
Who has th' advantage both of Eyes and Voice.
And all my Forces needs must be undone,
She having gained both the Wind and Sun.

Duke of Mantua, and added it to his great collection at Whitehall. (Margoliouth)
18: In a sea-battle having the wind and sun at one's back is a double advantage.

Mourning

i

You, that decipher out the Fate
Of humane Off-springs from the Skies,
What mean these Infants which of late
Spring from the Starrs of *Chlora's* Eyes?

ii

Her Eyes confus'd, and doubled ore,
With Tears suspended ere they flow;
Seem bending upwards, to restore
To Heaven, whence it came, their Woe:

iii

When, molding off the watry Sphears,
Slow drops unty themselves away;   10
As if she, with those precious Tears,
Would strow the ground where *Strephon* lay.

iv

Yet some affirm, pretending Art,
Her Eyes have so her Bosome drown'd,
Only to soften near her Heart
A place to fix another Wound.

v

And, while vain Pomp does her restrain
Within her solitary Bowr,
She courts her self in am'rous Rain;
Her self both *Danae* and the Showr.   20

vi

Nay others, bolder, hence esteem
Joy now so much her Master grown,
That whatsoever does but seem
Like Grief, is from her Windows thrown.

vii

Nor that she payes, while she survives,
To her dead Love this Tribute due;
But casts abroad these Donatives,
At the installing of a new.

viii

How wide they dream! The *Indian* Slaves
That sink for Pearl through Seas profound,   30
Would find her Tears yet deeper Waves
And not of one the bottom sound.

ix

I yet my silent Judgment keep,
Disputing not what they believe:
But sure as oft as Women weep,
It is to be suppos'd they grieve.

Daphnis *and* Chloe

i

Daphnis must from *Chloe* part:
Now is come the dismal Hour
That must all his Hopes devour,
All his Labour, all his Art.

ii

Nature, her own Sexes foe,
Long had taught her to be coy:
But she neither knew t'enjoy,
Nor yet let her Lover go.

iii

But, with this sad News supriz'd,
Soon she let that Niceness fall;   10
And would gladly yield to all,
So it had his stay compriz'd.

30. *sink:* Bod. MS. changes to *dive.*

iv

Nature so her self does use
To lay by her wonted State,
Lest the World should separate;
Sudden Parting closer glews.

v

He, well read in all the wayes
By which men their Siege maintain,
Knew not that the Fort to gain
Better 'twas the Siege to raise.   20

vi

But he came so full possest
With the Grief of Parting thence,
That he had not so much Sence
As to see he might be blest.

vii

Till Love in her Language breath'd
Words she never spake before;
But than Legacies no more
To a dying Man bequeath'd.

viii

For, Alas, the time was spent,
Now the latest minut's run   30
When poor *Daphnis* is undone,
Between Joy and Sorrow rent.

ix

At that *Why*, that *Stay my Dear*,
His disorder'd Locks he tare;
And with rouling Eyes did glare,
And his cruel Fate forswear.

x

As the Soul of one scarce dead,
With the shrieks of Friends aghast,

Looks distracted back in hast,
And then streight again is fled.   40

xi

So did wretched *Daphnis* look,
Frighting her he loved most.
At the last, this Lovers Ghost
Thus his Leave resolved took.

xii

Are my Hell and Heaven Joyn'd
More to torture him that dies?
Could departure not suffice,
But that you must then grow kind?

xiii

Ah my *Chloe* how have I
Such a wretched minute found,   50
When thy Favours should me wound
More than all thy Cruelty?

xiv

So to the condemned Wight
The delicious Cup we fill;
And allow him all he will,
For his last and short Delight.

xv

But I will not now begin
Such a Debt unto my Foe;
Nor to my Departure owe
What my Presence could not win.   60

xvi

Absence is too much alone:
Better 'tis to go in peace,
Than my Losses to increase
By a late Fruition.

xvii

Why should I enrich my Fate?
'Tis a Vanity to wear,
For my Executioner,
Jewels of so high a rate.

xviii

Rather I away will pine
In a manly stubborness   70
Than be fatted up express
For the *Canibal* to dine.

xix

Whilst this grief does thee disarm,
All th' Enjoyment of our Love
But the ravishment would prove
Of a Body dead while warm.

xx

And I parting should appear
Like the Gourmand *Hebrew* dead,
While with Quailes and *Manna* fed,
He does through the Desert err;   80

xxi

Or the Witch that midnight wakes
For the Fern, whose magick Weed
In one minute casts the Seed,
And invisible him makes.

xxii

Gentler times for Love are ment:
Who for parting pleasure strain

79–80: I adopt Cooke's emendations. The Folio reads:
    While he Quailes and *Manna* fed,
    And does through the Desert err.
81–84: Fern-seed was thought to be invisible and with appropriate rituals to
render the bearer invisible. Compare *I Henry IV*, II.ii.96: "We have the receit of
fern-seed, we walk invisible." (Margoliouth)
84. *him*: There were male as well as female witches.

Gather Roses in the rain,
Wet themselves and spoil their Scent.

xxiii
Farewel therefore all the fruit
Which I could from Love receive: 90
Joy will not with Sorrow weave,
Nor will I this Grief pollute.

xxiv
Fate I come, as dark, as sad,
As thy Malice could desire;
Yet bring with me all the Fire
That Love in his Torches had.

xxv
At these words away he broke;
As who long has praying ly'n,
To his Heads-man makes the Sign,
And receives the parting stroke.   100

xxvi
But hence Virgins all beware.
Last night he with *Phlogis* slept;
This night for *Dorinda* kept;
And but rid to take the Air.

xxvii
Yet he does himself excuse,
Nor indeed without a Cause.
For, according to the Lawes,
Why did *Chloe* once refuse?

The Definition of Love

i
My Love is of a birth as rare
As 'tis for object strange and high:
It was begotten by despair
Upon Impossibility.

ii

Magnanimous Despair alone
Could show me so divine a thing,
Where feeble Hope could ne'r have flown
But vainly flapt its Tinsel Wing.

iii

And yet I quickly might arrive
Where my extended Soul is fixt,　　　　　　　　　　　10
But Fate does Iron wedges drive,
And alwaies crouds it self betwixt.

iv

For Fate with jealous Eye does see
Two perfect Loves; nor lets them close;
Their union would her ruine be,
And her Tyrannick pow'r depose.

v

And therefore her Decrees of Steel
Us as the distant Poles have plac'd,
(Though Loves whole World on us doth wheel)
Not by themselves to be embrac'd.　　　　　　　　　20

vi

Unless the giddy Heaven fall,
And Earth some new Convulsion tear;
And, us to joyn, the World should all
Be cramp'd into a *Planisphere*.

vii

As Lines so Loves *oblique* may well
Themselves in every Angle greet:
But ours so truly *Paralel*,
Though infinite can never meet.

24. *Planisphere:* A map or chart formed by the projection of a sphere on a plane.

viii
Therefore the Love which us doth bind,
But Fate so enviously debarrs,   30
Is the Conjunction of the Mind,
And Opposition of the Stars.

The Picture of little T. C.
in a Prospect of Flowers

i
See with what simplicity
This Nimph begins her golden daies!
In the green Grass she loves to lie,
And there with her fair Aspect tames
The Wilder flow'rs, and gives them names:
But only with the Roses playes;
            And them does tell
What Colour best becomes them, and what Smell.

ii
Who can foretel for what high cause
This Darling of the Gods was born!   10
Yet this is She whose chaster Laws
The wanton Love shall one day fear,
And, under her command severe,
See his Bow broke and Ensigns torn.
            Happy, who can
Appease this virtuous Enemy of Man!

iii
O then let me in time compound,
And parly with those conquering Eyes;
Ere they have try'd their force to wound,
Ere, with their glancing wheels, they drive   20
In Triumph over Hearts that strive,
And them that yield but more despise.
            Let me be laid,
Where I may see thy Glories from some Shade.

iv

Mean time, whilst every verdant thing
It self does at thy Beauty charm,
Reform the errours of the Spring;
Make that the Tulips may have share
Of sweetness, seeing they are fair;
And Roses of their thorns disarm: 30
        But most procure
That Violets may a longer Age endure.

v

But O young beauty of the Woods,
Whom Nature courts with fruits and flow'rs,
Gather the Flow'rs, but spare the Buds;
Lest *Flora* angry at thy crime,
To kill her Infants in their prime,
Do quickly make th' Example Yours;
        And, ere we see,
Nip in the blossome all our hopes and Thee.   40

The Match

i

Nature had long a Treasure made
  Of all her choisest store;
Fearing, when She should be decay'd,
  To beg in vain for more.

ii

Her *Orientest* Colours there,
  And Essences most pure,
With sweetest Perfumes hoarded were,
  All as she thought secure.

iii

She seldom them unlock'd, or us'd,
  But with the nicest care;   10

5. *Orientest:* Most precious, most brilliant.

For, with one grain of them diffus'd,
   She could the World repair.

   iv

But likeness soon together drew
   What she did sep'rate lay;
Of which one perfect Beauty grew,
   And that was *Celia*.

   v

Love wisely had of long fore-seen
   That he must once grow old;
And therefore stor'd a Magazine,
   To save him from the cold.   20

   vi

He kept the several Cells repleat
   With Nitre thrice refin'd;
The Naphta's and the Sulphur's heat,
   And all that burns the Mind.

   vii

He fortifi'd the double Gate,
   And rarely thither came;
For, with one Spark of these, he streight
   All Nature could inflame.

   viii

Till, by vicinity so long,
   A nearer Way they sought;   30
And, grown magnetically strong,
   Into each other wrought.

   ix

Thus all his fewel did unite
   To make one fire high:
None ever burn'd so hot, so bright:
   And *Celia* that am I.

x
So we alone the happy rest,
 Whilst all the World is poor,
And have within our Selves possest
 All Love's and Nature's store.   40

The Mower against Gardens

Luxurious Man, to bring his Vice in use,
 Did after him the World seduce:
And from the fields the Flow'rs and Plants allure,
 Where Nature was most plain and pure.
He first enclos'd within the Gardens square
 A dead and standing pool of Air:
And a more luscious Earth for them did knead,
 Which stupifi'd them while it fed.
The Pink grew then as double as his Mind;
 The nutriment did change the kind.   10
With strange perfumes he did the Roses taint,
 And Flow'rs themselves were taught to paint.
The Tulip, white, did for complexion seek;
 And learn'd to interline its cheek:
Its Onion root they then so high did hold,
 That one was for a Meadow sold.
Another World was search'd, through Oceans new,
 To find the *Marvel of Peru.*
And yet these Rarities might be allow'd,
 To Man, that sov'raign thing and proud; 20
Had he not dealt between the Bark and Tree,
 Forbidden mixtures there to see.
No Plant now knew the Stock from which it came;
 He grafts upon the Wild the Tame:
That the uncertain and adult'rate fruit

1. *Luxurious:* Voluptuous.
9: Compare "vain Head and double Heart" of "A Dialogue between the Soul and Body," 1. 10, p. 17.
16: During the tulip mania of the 1630s a single bulb sold for 5,500 florins or 550 times the value of a sheep. (Margoliouth)
18. *The Marvel of Peru, Mirabilis Jalapa,* grew in the West Indies. (Margoliouth)

Might put the Palate in dispute.
His green *Seraglio* has its Eunuchs too;
    Lest any Tyrant him out-doe.
And in the Cherry he does Nature vex,
    To procreate without a Sex.   30
'Tis all enforc'd; the Fountain and the Grot;
    While the sweet Fields do lye forgot:
Where willing Nature does to all dispence
    A wild and fragrant Innocence:
And *Fauns* and *Faryes* do the Meadows till,
    More by their presence than their skill.
Their Statues polish'd by some ancient hand,
    May to adorn the Gardens stand:
But howso'ere the Figures do excel,
    The *Gods* themselves with us do dwell.   40

Damon *the Mower*

i

Heark how the Mower *Damon* Sung.
With love of *Juliana* stung!
While ev'ry thing did seem to paint
The Scene more fit for his complaint.
Like her fair Eyes the day was fair;
But scorching like his am'rous Care.
Sharp like his Sythe his Sorrow was,
And wither'd like his Hopes the Grass.

ii

Oh what unusual Hearts are here,
Which thus our Sun-burn'd Meadows fear!   10
The Grass-hopper its pipe gives ore;
And hamstring'd Frogs can dance no more.
But in the brook the green Frog wades;
And Grass-hoppers seek out the shades.
Only the Snake, that kept within,
Now glitters in its second skin.

12. *hamstring'd:* Rendered inert by the heat.

iii

This heat the Sun could never raise,
Nor Dog-star so inflame's the dayes.
It from an higher Beauty grow'th,
Which burns the Fields and Mower both: 20
Which mads the Dog, and makes the Sun
Hotter than his own *Phaeton*.
Not *July* causeth these Extremes,
But *Juliana's* scorching beams.

iv

Tell me where I may pass the Fires
Of the hot day, or hot desires.
To what cool Cave shall I descend,
Or to what gelid Fountain bend?
Alas! I look for Ease in vain,
When Remedies themselves complain.   30
No moisture but my Tears do rest,
Nor Cold but in her Icy Breast.

v

How long wilt Thou, fair Shepheardess,
Esteem me, and my Presents less?
To Thee the harmless Snake I bring,
Disarmed of its teeth and sting.
To Thee *Chameleons* changing-hue,
And Oak leaves tipt with hony-dew.
Yet Thou ungrateful hast not sought
Nor what they are, nor who them brought.   40

vi

I am the Mower *Damon*, known
Through all the Medows I have mown.
On me the Morn her dew distills
Before her darling Daffadils.
And, if at Noon my toil me heat,
The Sun himself licks off my Sweat.

21. *mads:* As in the Bod. MS.; *made* in the Folio.

While, going home, the Ev'ning sweet
In cowslip-water bathes my feet.

vii

What, though the piping Shepherd stock
The plains with an unnumber'd Flock,   50
This Sithe of mine discovers wide
More ground than all his Sheep do hide.
With this the golden fleece I shear
Of all these Closes ev'ry Year.
And though in Wooll more poor than they,
Yet am I richer far in Hay.

viii

Nor am I so deform'd to sight,
If in my Sithe I looked right;
In which I see my Picture done,
As in a crescent Moon the Sun.   60
The deathless Fairyes take me oft
To lead them in their Danses soft:
And, when I tune my self to sing,
About me they contract their Ring.

ix

How happy might I still have mow'd,
Had not Love here his Thistles sow'd!
But now I all the day complain,
Joyning my Labour to my Pain;
And with my Sythe cut down the Grass,
Yet still my Grief is where it was: 70
But, when the Iron blunter grows,
Sighing I whet my Sythe and Woes.

x

While thus he threw his Elbow round,
Depopulating all the Ground,
And, with his whistling Sythe, does cut
Each stroke between the Earth and Root,
The edged Stele by careless chance

48. *cowslip-water:* Used by fashionable ladies to preserve the complexion.

Did into his own Ankle glance:
And there among the Grass fell down,
By his own Sythe, the Mower mown.   80

xi

Alas! said He, these hurts are slight
To those that dye by Loves despight.
With Shepherds-purse, and Clowns-all-heal,
The Blood I stanch, and Wound I seal.
Only for him no Cure is found,
Whom *Julianas* Eyes do wound.
'Tis death alone that this must do:
For Death thou art a Mower too.

The Mower to the Glo-Worms

i

Ye living Lamps, by whose dear light
The Nightingale does sit so late,
And studying all the Summer-night,
Her matchless Songs does meditate;

ii

Ye Country Comets, that portend
No War, nor Princes funeral,
Shining unto no higher end
Than to presage the Grasses fall;

iii

Ye Glo-worms, whose officious Flame
To wandring Mowers shows the way.   10
That in the Night have lost their aim,
And after foolish Fires do stray;

iv

Your courteous Lights in vain you waste,
Since *Juliana* here is come,

---

83. *Shepherds-purse:* Used to stop bleeding. *Clowns-all-heal:* Used to cure wounds.
9. *officious:* Zealous, attentive.

For She my Mind hath so displac'd
That I shall never find my home.

The Mower's Song

i

My Mind was once the true survey
Of all these Medows fresh and gay;
And in the greeness of the Grass
Did see its Hopes as in a Glass;
When *Juliana* came, and She
What I do to the Grass, does to my Thoughts and Me.

ii

But these, while I with Sorrow pine,
Grew more luxuriant still and fine;
That not one Blade of Grass you spy'd,
But had a Flower on either side;   10
When *Juliana* came, and She
What I do to the Grass, does to my Thoughts and Me.

iii

Unthankful Medows, could you so
A fellowship so true forego.
And in your gawdy May-games meet,
While I lay trodden under feet?
When *Juliana* came, and She
What I do to the Grass, does to my Thoughts and Me.

iv

But what you in Compassion ought
Shall now by my Revenge be wrought: 20
And Flow'rs, and Grass, and I and all,
Will in one common Ruine fall.
For Juliana comes, and She
What I do to the Grass, does to my Thoughts and Me.

1. *survey:* Inventory.   4. *its:* My mind's.

v
And thus, ye Meadows, which have been
Companions of my thoughts more green,
Shall now the Heraldry become
With which I shall adorn my Tomb;
For *Juliana* comes, and She
What I do to the Grass, does to my Thoughts and Me.   30

Ametas *and* Thestylis *making Hay-Ropes*

i

Ametas
Think'st Thou that this Love can stand,
Whilst Thou still dost say me nay?
Love unpaid does soon disband:
Love binds Love as Hay binds Hay.

ii

Thestylis
Think'st Thou that this Rope would twine
If we both should turn one way?
Where both parties so combine,
Neither Love will twist nor Hay.

iii

Ametas
Thus you vain Excuses find,
Which your selves and us delay: 10
And Love tyes a Womans Mind
Looser than with Ropes of Hay.

iv

Thestylis
What you cannot constant hope
Must be taken as you may.

v

Ametas
Then let's both lay by our Rope,
And go kiss within the Hay.

Musicks Empire

i

First was the World as one great Cymbal made,
Where Jarring Windes to infant Nature plaid.
All Musick was a solitary sound,
To hollow Rocks and murm'ring Fountains bound.

ii

Jubal first made the wilder Notes agree;
and *Jubal* tun'd Musick's first *Jubilee:*
He call'd the *Ecchoes* from their sullen Cell,
And built the Organs City where they dwell.

iii

Each sought a consort in that lovely place;
And Virgin Trebles wed the manly Base.   10
From whence the Progeny of numbers new
Into harmonious Colonies withdrew.

iv

Some to the Lute, some to the Viol went,
And others chose the Cornet eloquent.
These practising the Wind, and those the Wire,
To sing Mens Triumphs, or in Heavens quire.

v

Then Musick, the Mosaique of the Air,
Did of all these a solemn noise prepare:
With which She gain'd the Empire of the Ear,
Including all between the Earth and Sphear.   20

---

5. *Jubal:* The "father of all such as handle the harp and organ" (Genesis, 4:21).
6. *first:* The Bod. MS. and Cooke both insert *first.*

vi

Victorious sounds! yet here your Homage do
Unto a gentler Conqueror than you;
Who though He flies the Musick of his praise,
Would with you Heavens Hallelujahs raise.

The Garden

i

How vainly men themselves amaze
To win the Palm, the Oke, or Bayes;
And their uncessant Labours see
Crown'd from some single Herb or Tree,
Whose short and narrow verged Shade
Does prudently their Toyles upbraid;
While all Flow'rs and all Trees do close
To weave the Garlands of repose.

ii

Fair quiet, have I found thee here,
And Innocence thy Sister dear!   10
Mistaken long, I sought you then
In busie Companies of Men.
Your sacred Plants, if here below,
Only among the Plants will grow.
Society is all but rude,
To this delicious Solitude.

iii

No white nor red was ever seen
So am'rous as this lovely green.
Fond Lovers, cruel as their Flame,
Cut in these Trees their Mistress name.   20

22. *Conqueror:* Perhaps the Lord General Fairfax, of Appleton House. See "Upon the Hill and Grove at Bill-borow," ll. 75–76, p. 61.
2. *Palm, the Oke, or Bayes:* For, respectively, military, civic or literary distinction.

Little, Alas, they know, or heed,
How far these Beauties Hers exceed!
Fair Trees! where s'ere your barkes I wound,
No Name shall but your own be found.

    iv

When we have run our Passions heat,
Love hither makes his best retreat.
The *Gods*, that mortal Beauty chase,
Still in a Tree did end their race.
Apollo hunted *Daphne* so,
Only that She might Laurel grow.   30
And *Pan* did after *Syrinx* speed,
Not as a Nymph, but for a Reed.

    v

What wond'rous Life in this I lead!
Ripe Apples drop about my head;
The Luscious Clusters of the Vine
Upon my Mouth do crush their Wine;
The Nectaren, and curious Peach,
Into my hands themselves do reach;
Stumbling on Melons, as I pass,
Insnar'd with Flow'rs, I fall on Grass.   40

    vi

Mean while the Mind, from pleasures less,
Withdraws into its happiness:
The Mind, that Ocean where each kind
Does streight its own resemblance find;
Yet it creates, transcending these,
Far other Worlds, and other Seas;

23. *your:* As in Cooke; *you* in Folio.
41–42: The emendation in the Bod. MS. of *pleasure* (in Folio) to *pleasures* points up the primary meaning of these lines: that soul, mind, and body have their appropriate pleasures, ranked accordingly.
43–44: Sir Thomas Browne in *Vulgar Errors*, 3.24, discusses the popular misconception "that all animals of the Land are in their kind in the Sea." (Margoliouth)

Annihilating all that's made
To a green Thought in a green Shade.

   vii
Here at the Fountains sliding foot,
Or at some Fruit-tree's mossy root,   50
Casting the Bodies Vest aside,
My Soul into the boughs does glide:
There like a Bird it sits, and sings,
Then whets, and combs its silver Wings;
And, till prepar'd for longer flight,
Waves in its Plumes the various Light.

   viii
Such was that happy Garden-state,
While Man there walk'd without a Mate:
After a Place so pure, and sweet,
What other Help could yet be meet!   60
But 'twas beyond a Mortal's share
To wander solitary there:
Two Paradises 'twere in one
To live in Paradise alone.

   ix
How well the skilful Gardner drew
Of flow'rs and herbes this Dial new;
Where from above the milder Sun
Does through a fragrant Zodiack run;
And, as it works, th' industrious Bee
Computes its time as well as we.   70
How could such sweet and wholsome Hours
Be reckon'd but with herbs and flow'rs!

47–48. *Annihilating ... Thought:* Either reducing the whole material world to nothing material or considering the whole material world as of no value compared to a green thought. In the second sense, to = compared to. (Margoliouth)
54. *whets:* Preens.

The Second Chorus from Seneca's *Tragedy,* Thyestes

Stet quicunque volet potens
Aulae culmine lubrico etc.

TRANSLATION

Climb at *Court* for me that will
Tottering Favour's slipp'ry hill.
All I seek is to lye still.
Settled in some secret Nest
In calm Leisure let me rest;
And far off the publick Stage
Pass away my silent Age.
Thus when without noise, unknown,
I have liv'd out all my span,
I shall dye, without a groan,   10
An old honest Country man.
Who expos'd to others Eyes,
Into his own Heart ne'r pry's,
Death to him's a Strange surprise.

2. *Tottering . . . hill;* Bod. MS. reads: *Giddy Favour's slipp'ry hill.*

The Cromwell Era

An Horatian *Ode upon* Cromwel's *Return from* Ireland

The forward Youth that would appear
Must now forsake his *Muses* dear,
    Nor in the Shadows sing
    His Numbers languishing.
'Tis time to leave the Books in dust,
And oyl th' unused Armours rust:
    Removing from the Wall
    The Corslet of the Hall.
So restless *Cromwel* could not cease
In the inglorious Arts of Peace,   10
    But through adventrous War
    Urged his active Star:
And, like the three-fork'd Lightning, first
Breaking the Clouds where it was nurst,
    Did thorough his own Side
    His fiery way divide.
For 'tis all one to Courage high
The Emulous or Enemy;
    And with such to inclose
    Is more then to oppose.   20
Then burning through the Air he went,
And Pallaces and Temples rent:
    And *Cæsars* head at last

An Horatian Ode: Cromwell returned from his devastating war in Ireland late in May 1650 to take part in the Scottish campaign as Lieutenant-General to Fairfax, then Commander-in-Chief. Fairfax resigned his appointment, refusing to participate in an attack on Scotland, and retired to his Yorkshire estate. Cromwell was made head of the Parliamentary forces and invaded Scotland on July 22, 1650.
13-20: The dynamic and ambitious Cromwell finds the emulous members of his own party ("side") as intolerable as the enemy. Cromwell became pre-eminent among Parliamentary leaders after the battle of Marston Moor in 1644.
23. *Cæsar's head:* Note that the title of Caesar, here applied to Charles I, is transferred to Cromwell in l. 101.

Did through his Laurels blast.
'Tis Madness to resist or blame
The force of angry Heavens flame;
    And, if we would speak true,
    Much to the Man is due:
Who, from his private Gardens, where
He liv'd reserved and austere,   30
    As if his highest plot
    To plant the Bergamot,
Could by industrious Valour climbe
To ruine the great Work of Time,
    And cast the Kingdoms old
    Into another Mold.
Though Justice against Fate complain,
And plead the antient Rights in vain:
    But those do hold or break
    As Men are strong or weak.   40
Nature that hateth emptiness,
Allows of penetration less:
    And therefore must make room
    Where greater Spirits come.
What Field of all the Civil Wars
Where his were not the deepest Scars?
    And *Hampton* shows what part
    He had of wiser Art:
Where, twining subtile fears with hope,
He wove a Net of such a scope,   50
    That *Charles* himself might chase
    To *Caresbrooks* narrow case:
That thence the *Royal Actor* born
The *Tragick Scaffold* might adorn,
    While round the armed Bands
    Did clap their bloody hands.
He nothing common did, or mean,

---

24. *Laurels:* Supposed to be immune to lightning.

32. *Bergamot:* A pear associated with royalty.

42. *penetration:* The supposed occupation of the same space by two bodies at the same time.

47–52: Charles I fled from Hampton Court to Carisbrooke Castle on the Isle of Wight in November 1647. In March 1648 he was apprehended in a vain attempt to escape through a barred casement window ("Caresbrooks narrow case").

Upon the memorable Scene:
  But with his keener Eye
    The Axes edge did try: 60
Nor call'd the *Gods* with vulgar spight
To vindicate his helpless Right,
  But bow'd his comely Head
    Down, as upon a Bed.
This was that memorable Hour
Which first assur'd the forced Pow'r.
  So when they did design
    The *Capitols* first Line,
A bleeding Head where they begun,
Did fright the Architects to run;   70
  And yet in that the *State*
    Foresaw its happy Fate.
And now the *Irish* are asham'd
To see themselves in one Year tam'd:
  So much one Man can do,
    That does both act and know.
They can affirm his Praises best,
And have, though overcome, confest
  How good he is, how just,
    And fit for highest Trust: 80
Nor yet grown stiffer with Command,
But still in the *Republick's* hand:
  How fit he is to sway
    That can so well obey.
He to the *Commons Feet* presents
A *Kingdome*, for his first years rents:
  And, what he may, forbears
    His Fame to make it theirs:
And has his Sword and Spoyls ungirt,
To lay them at the *Publick's* skirt.   90
  So when the Falcon high
    Falls heavy from the Sky,
She, having kill'd, no more does search,
But on the next green Bow to pearch;

67–72: Pliny (*Natural History*, 28, 2) relates how a human head was found in laying the foundations of the Capitol and how the most celebrated priest of Etruria, Olenus Calenus, interpreted the head as a favorable omen. (Margoliouth)

Where, when he first does lure,
The Falckner has her sure.
What may not then our *Isle* presume
While Victory his Crest does plume;
What may not others fear,
If thus he crown each Year!   100
A *Cæsar* he ere long to *Gaul*,
To *Italy* an *Hannibal*,
And to all States not free
Shall *Clymacterick* be.
The *Pict* no shelter now shall find
Within his party-colour'd Mind;
But from this Valour sad
Shrink underneath the Plad:
Happy if in the tufted brake
The *English Hunter* him mistake,   110
Nor lay his Hounds in near
The *Caledonian* Deer.
But thou the Wars and Fortunes Son
March indefatigably on,
And for the last effect
Still keep thy Sword erect:
Besides the force it has to fright
The Spirits of the shady Night;
The same *Arts* that did *gain*
A *Pow'r* must it *maintain*.   120

Upon the Hill and Grove at Bill-borow
To the Lord Fairfax

i

See how the arched Earth does here
Rise in a perfect Hemisphere!

104. *Clymacterick:* Critical, epoch-making.
105–106: *party-colour'd* is a pun on the assumed derivation of Pict (here alluding to the Scots) from *pingere*, the Latin verb to *paint*.   107. *sad:* Steadfast.
117–118: Mrs E. E. Duncan-Jones rightly interprets these lines as alluding to Odysseus' and Aeneas' warding off the spirits of the dead with swords.
Upon the Hill and Grove at Bill-borow: Bilborough manor, bought in 1546 by Sir William Fairfax, was five miles northwest of the Fairfax property at Nun Appleton.

The stiffest Compass could not strike
A Line more circular and like;
Nor softest Pensel draw a Brow
So equal as this Hill does bow.
It seems as for a Model laid,
And that the World by it was made.

ii

Here learn ye Mountains more unjust,
Which to abrupter greatness thrust,   10
That do with your hook-shoulder'd height
The Earth deform and Heaven fright.
For whose excrescence ill design'd,
Nature must a new Center find,
Learn here those humble steps to tread,
Which to securer Glory lead.

iii

See what a soft access and wide
Lyes open to its grassy side;
Nor with the rugged path deterrs
The feet of breathless Travellers.   20
See then how courteous it ascends,
And all the way it rises bends;
Nor for it self the height does gain,
But only strives to raise the Plain.

iv

Yet thus it all the field commands,
And in unenvy'd Greatness stands,
Discerning further than the Cliff
Of Heaven-daring *Teneriff*.
How glad the weary Seamen hast
When they salute it from the Mast!   30
By Night the Northern Star their way
Directs, and this no less by Day.

4. *like:* Even.   5. *Pensel:* Paintbrush.
14. *Center:* That is, of the earth.

v

Upon its crest this Mountain grave
A Plump of aged Trees does wave.
No hostile hand durst ere invade
With impious Steel the sacred Shade.
For something alwaies did appear
Of the *great Master's* terrour there:
And Men could hear his Armour still
Ratling through all the Grove and Hill.   40

vi

Fear of the *Master*, and respect
Of the great *Nymph* did it protect;
Vera the *Nymph* that him inspir'd,
To whom he often here retir'd,
And on these Okes ingrav'd her Name;
Such Wounds alone these Woods became:
But ere he well the Barks could part
'Twas writ already in their Heart.

vii

For they ('tis credible) have sense,
As We, of Love and Reverence,   50
And underneath the Courser Rind
The *Genius* of the house do bind.
Hence they successes seem to know,
And in their *Lord's* advancement grow;
But in no Memory were seen
As under this so streight and green.

viii

Yet now no further strive to shoot,
Contented if they fix their Root.
Nor to the wind's uncertain gust,
Their prudent Heads too far intrust.   60
Onely sometimes a flutt'ring Breez
Discourses with the breathing Trees;

34. *Plump:* Clump. Margoliouth's conjectural emendation. The Folio reads *Plum.*   38. *great Master:* Lord Fairfax.
43. *Vera:* Anne, daughter of Sir Horace Vere and wife of Lord Fairfax.

Which in their modest Whispers name
Those Acts that swell'd the Cheek of Fame.

   ix

Much other Groves, say they, than these
And other Hills him once did please.
Through Groves of Pikes he thunder'd then,
And Mountains rais'd of dying Men.
For all the *Civick Garlands* due
To him our Branches are but few.   70
Nor are our Trunks enow to bear
The *Trophees* of one fertile Year.

   x

'Tis true, yee Trees, nor ever spoke
More certain *Oracles* in Oak.
But Peace (if you his favour prize),
That Courage its own Praises flies.
Therefore to your obscurer Seats
From his own Brightness he retreats:
Nor he the Hills without the Groves,
Nor Height but with Retirement loves.   80

Upon Appleton *House*
to my Lord Fairfax

   i

Within this sober Frame expect
Work of no Forrain *Architect*;
That unto Caves the Quarries drew,
And Forrests did to Pastures hew;
Who of his great Design in pain
Did for a Model vault his Brain,
Whose Columnes should so high be rais'd
To arch the Brows that on them gaz'd.

73. *yee:* Bod. MS.; Folio reads *the.*   74. *Oak:* That is, at Dodona.
75–76: Compare "Musicks Empire", ll. 21–22, p. 48.

ii

Why should of all things Man unrul'd
Such unproportion'd dwellings build?   10
The Beasts are by their Denns exprest:
And Birds contrive an equal Nest;
The low roof'd Tortoises do dwell
In cases fit of Tortoise-shell:
No Creature loves an empty space;
Their Bodies measure out their Place.

iii

But He, superfluously spread,
Demands more room alive than dead.
And in his hollow Palace goes
Where Winds (as he) themselves may lose.   20
What need of all this Marble Crust
T'impark the wanton Mote of Dust,
That thinks by Breadth the World t'unite
Though the first Builders fail'd in Height?

iv

But all things are composed here
Like Nature, orderly and near:
In which we the Dimensions find
Of that more sober Age and Mind,
When larger sized Men did stoop
To enter at a narrow loop;   30
As practising, in doors so strait,
To strain themselves through *Heavens Gate*.

v

And surely when the after Age
Shall hither come in *Pilgrimage*,
These sacred Places to adore,
By *Vere* and *Fairfax* trod before,
Men will dispute how their Extent
Within such dwarfish Confines went:

12. *equal:* Adequate, fit.   22. *Mote:* As in the Bod. MS.; *Mose* in the Folio.
30. *loop*: Loop-hole.   36. *Vere:* Fairfax married Anne Vere in 1637.

And some will smile at this, as well
As *Romulus* his Bee-like Cell.   40

    vi
Humility alone designs
Those short but admirable Lines,
By which, ungirt and unconstrain'd,
Things greater are in less contain'd.
Let others vainly strive t'immure
The *Circle* in the *Quadrature!*
These *holy Mathematicks* can
In ev'ry Figure equal Man.

    vii
Yet thus the laden house does sweat,
And scarce indures the *Master* great: 50
But where he comes the swelling Hall
Stirs, and the *Square* grows *Spherical*;
More by his *Magnitude* distrest,
Than he is by its straitness prest:
And too officiously it slights
That in it self which him delights.

    viii
So Honour better Lowness bears,
Than That unwonted Greatness wears.
Height with a certain Grace does bend,
But low Things clownishly ascend.   60
And yet what needs there here Excuse,
Where ev'ry Thing does answer Use?
Where neatness nothing can condemn,
Nor Pride invent what to contemn?

    ix
A Stately *Frontispice of Poor*
Adorns without the open Door:
Nor less the Rooms within commends

40. *Cell:* A thatched hut traditionally held to be Romulus' was in antiquity
preserved on the Palatine. (Margoliouth)
52: The hall had a domed cupola.   65. *Frontispice:* Decorated entrance.

Daily new *Furniture of Friends*.
The House was built upon the Place
Only as for a *Mark of Grace*;   70
And for an *Inn* to entertain
Its *Lord* a while, but not remain.

x

Him *Bishops-Hill*, or *Denton* may,
Or *Bilbrough*, better hold than they:
But Nature here hath been so free
As if she said leave this to me.
Art would more neatly have defac'd
What she had laid so sweetly waste;
In fragrant Gardens, shady Woods,
Deep Meadows, and transparent Floods.   80

xi

While with slow Eyes we these survey,
And on each pleasant footstep stay,
We opportunly may relate
The Progress of this Houses Fate.
A *Nunnery* first gave it birth.
For *Virgin-Buildings* oft brought forth.
And all that Neighbour-Ruine shows
The Quarries whence this dwelling rose.

71. *Inn:* Fairfax wrote the following lines, of which his own MS. is in the Bodleian
Library (MS. Fairfax 40), "Upon the New-built House att Apleton";
    Thinke not O man that dwells herein
    This House's a stay but as an Inne
    Which for Convenience fittly stands
    In way to one nott made with hands
    But if a time here thou take Rest
    Yett thinke Eternity's the Best.
(Margoliouth)
73. *Bishops-Hill:* A house on the River Ouse in York where Mary Fairfax was born.
Denton: Another Fairfax estate, lies about thirty miles up the Wharfe River from
Nun Appleton.
74. *Bilbrough:* Another Fairfax manor near Nun Appleton.
84: The heiress Isabel Thwaites, being wooed by William Fairfax of Steeton, was
shut up by her guardian, the Lady Anna Langton, Prioress of Nun Appleton; but
an appeal was made to higher authority, she was released by force, and Fairfax
married her in 1518. It was to their sons that the house was surrendered, it is said
by the same Prioress, at its dissolution in 1542. (Margoliouth)

xii

Near to this gloomy Cloysters Gates
There dwelt the blooming Virgin *Thwates*,   90
Fair beyond Measure, and an Heir
Which might Deformity make fair.
And oft She spent the Summer Suns
Discoursing with the *Suttle Nunns*.
Whence in these Words one to her weav'd,
(As 'twere by Chance) Thoughts long conceiv'd.

xiii

"Within this holy leisure we
Live innocently as you see.
These Walls restrain the World without,
But hedge our Liberty about.   100
These Bars inclose that wider Den
Of those wild Creatures, called Men.
The Cloyster outward shuts its Gates,
And, from us, locks on them the Grates.

xiv

"Here we, in shining Armour white,
Like *Virgin-Amazons* do fight.
And our chaste *Lamps* we hourly trim,
Lest the great *Bridegroom* find them dim.
Our *Orient* Breaths perfumed are
With incense of incessant Pray'r.   110
And Holy-water of our Tears
Most strangely our Complexion clears.

xv

"Not Tears of Grief; but such as those
With which calm Pleasure overflows;
Or Pity, when we look on you
That live without this happy Vow.
How should we grieve that must be seen
Each one a *Spouse*, and each a *Queen*;
And can in *Heaven* hence behold
Our brighter Robes and Crowns of Gold?   120

xvi
"When we have prayed all our Beads,
Some One the holy *Legend* reads;
While all the rest with Needles paint
The Face and Graces of the *Saint*.
But what the Linnen can't receive
They in their Lives do interweave.
This Work the *Saints* best represents;
That serves for *Altar's Ornaments*.

xvii
"But much it to our work would add
If here your hand, your Face we had: 130
By it we would *our Lady* touch;
Yet thus She you resembles much.
Some of your Features, as we sow'd,
Through ev'ry *Shrine* should be bestow'd.
And in one Beauty we would take
Enough a thousand *Saints* to make.

xviii
"And (for I dare not quench the Fire
That me does for your good inspire)
'Twere Sacriledge a Man t'admit
To holy things, for *Heaven* fit.   140
I see the *Angels* in a Crown
On you the Lillies show'ring down:
And round about your Glory breaks,
That something more than humane speaks.

xix
"All Beauty, when at such a height,
Is so already consecrate.
Fairfax I know; and long ere this
Have mark'd the Youth, and what he is.
But can he such a *Rival* seem
For whom you Heav'n should disesteem?   150
Ah, no! and 'twould more Honour prove
He your *Devoto* were, than *Love*.

xx

"Here live beloved, and obey'd:
Each one your Sister, each your Maid.
And, if our Rule seem strictly pend,
The Rule it self to you shall bend.
Our *Abbess* too, now far in Age,
Doth your succession near presage.
How soft the yoke on us would lye,
Might such fair Hands as yours it tye!   160

xxi

"Your voice, the sweetest of the Quire,
Shall draw *Heav'n* nearer, raise us higher.
And your Example, if our Head,
Will soon us to perfection lead.
Those Virtues to us all so dear,
Will straight grow Sanctity when here:
And that, once sprung, increase so fast
Till Miracles it work at last.

xxii

"Nor is our *Order* yet so nice,
Delight to banish as a Vice.   170
Here Pleasure Piety doth meet;
One perfecting the other Sweet.
So through the mortal fruit we boyl
The Sugars uncorrupting Oyl:
And that which perisht while we pull,
Is thus preserved clear and full.

xxiii

"For such indeed are all our Arts;
Still handling Natures finest Parts.
Flow'rs dress the Altars; for the Clothes,
The Sea-Born Amber we compose;   180
Balms for the griev'd we draw; and Pastes
We mold, as Baits for curious tastes.
What need is here of Man? unless
These as sweet Sins we should confess.

181. *griev'd:* Hurt in body.

xxiv

"Each Night among us to your side
Appoint a fresh and Virgin Bride;
Whom if *our Lord* at midnight find,
Yet Neither should be left behind.
Where you may lye as chaste in Bed,
As Pearls together billeted.   190
All Night embracing Arm in Arm,
Like Chrystal pure with Cotton warm.

xxv

"But what is this to all the store
Of Joys you see, and may make more!
Try but a while, if you be wise:
The Tryal neither Costs, nor Tyes."
Now *Fairfax* seek her promis'd faith:
Religion that dispensed hath,
Which She hence forward does begin;
The *Nuns* smooth Tongue has suckt her in.   200

xxvi

Oft, though he knew it was in vain,
Yet would he valiantly complain.
"Is this that *Sanctity* so great,
An Art by which you finly'r cheat?
Hypocrite Witches, hence *avant*,
Who though in prison yet inchant!
Death only can such Theeves make fast,
As rob though in the Dungeon cast.

xxvii

"Were there but, when this House was made,
One Stone that a just Hand had laid,   210
It must have fall'n upon her Head
Who first Thee from thy Faith misled.
And yet, how well soever ment,
With them 'twould soon grow fraudulent,
For like themselves they alter all,
And vice infects the very Wall.

197-199: Now claim her plighted word, from which religion (*which She hence forward does begin*) has released her.

xxviii

"But sure those Buildings last not long,
Founded by Folly, kept by Wrong.
I know what Fruit their Gardens yield,
When they it think by Night conceal'd.   220
Fly from their Vices. 'Tis thy 'state,
Not Thee, that they would consecrate.
Fly from their Ruine. How I fear
Though guiltless lest thou perish there."

xxix

What should he do? He would respect
Religion, but not Right neglect:
For first Religion taught him Right,
And dazled not but clear'd his sight.
Sometimes resolv'd his Sword he draws,
But reverenceth then the Laws: 230
For Justice still that Courage led;
First from a Judge, then Souldier bred.

xxx

Small Honour would be in the Storm.
The *Court* him grants the lawful Form;
Which licens'd either Peace or Force,
To hinder the unjust Divorce.
Yet still the *Nuns* his Right debar'd,
Standing upon their holy Guard.
Ill-counsell'd Women, do you know
Whom you resist, or what you do?   240

xxxi

Is not this he whose Offspring fierce
Shall fight through all the *Universe*;
And with successive Valour try
France, Poland, either *Germany;*

---

221. *'state:* Property.   232. *Judge ... Souldier:* His father was judge of Common
Pleas and his mother daughter of George Manners, twelfth Lord Roos, a
distinguished soldier who died at the siege of Tournay in 1513. (Margoliouth)
241-244: Sir Thomas Fairfax (son of William Fairfax and Isabel Thwaites) fought
in Italy and Germany; his son Thomas, first Lord Fairfax, was knighted for

Till one, as long since prophecy'd,
His Horse through conquer'd *Britain* ride?
Yet, against Fate, his Spouse they kept;
And the great Race would intercept.

xxxii

Some to the Breach against their Foes
Their *Wooden Saints* in vain oppose.   250
Another bolder stands at push
With their old *Holy-Water Brush*.
While the disjointed *Abbess* threads
The gingling Chain-shot of her *Beads*.
But their lowd'st Cannon were their Lungs;
And sharpest Weapons were their Tongues.

xxxiii

But, waving these aside like Flyes,
Young *Fairfax* through the Wall does rise.
Then th' unfrequented Vault appear'd,
And superstitions vainly fear'd.   260
The *Relicks false* were set to view;
Only the Jewels there were true:
But truly bright and holy *Thwaites*
That weeping at the *Altar* waites.

xxxiv

But the glad Youth away her bears,
And to the *Nuns* bequeaths her Tears:
Who guiltily their Prize bemoan,
Like Gipsies that a child had stoln.
Thenceforth (as when th' Inchantment ends
The Castle vanishes or rends)   270
The wasting Cloister with the rest
Was in one instant dispossest.

---

gallantry before Rouen. Two sons of the first Lord Fairfax fell at Frankenthal in
Germany, one died at Scanderoon in Turkey, and one after an affray with French
soldiers in Paris. The great Lord himself fought at Bois-le-Duc; he applied for leave
to join the forces of Gustavus Adolphus (see his letter of February 22, 1631/2 in
Fairfax Correspondence, i.163), but does not appear to have done so. (Margoliouth)
268. *had:* Bod. MS.; Folio reads *hath.*

xxxv

At the demolishing, this Seat
To *Fairfax* fell as by Escheat.
And what both *Nuns* and *Founders* will'd
'Tis likely better thus fulfill'd.
For if the *Virgin* prov'd not theirs,
The *Cloyster* yet remained hers.
Though many a *Nun* there made her Vow,
'Twas no *Religious House* till now.   280

xxxvi

From that blest Bed the *Heroe* came,
Whom *France* and *Poland* yet does fame:
Who, when retired here to Peace,
His warlike Studies could not cease;
But laid these Gardens out in sport
In the just Figure of a Fort;
And with five Bastions it did fence,
As aiming one for ev'ry Sense.

xxxvii

When in the *East* the Morning Ray
Hangs out the Colours of the Day,   290
The Bee through these known Allies hums,
Beating the *Dian* with its *Drumms*.
Then Flow'rs their drowsie Eylids raise,
Their Silken Ensigns each displays,
And dries its Pan yet dank with Dew,
And fills its Flask with Odours new.

xxxviii

These, as their *Governour* goes by,
In fragrant Vollyes they let fly;

---

274. *Escheat:* The lapsing of land to the lord of the manor when an owner dies
intestate and without heirs.
281–288: These lines refer to Sir Thomas Fairfax, son of Sir William Fairfax and
Isabel Thwaites.   292. *Dian*: Reveille.
295–296: The military metaphor is elaborated by allusions to the *pan* which holds
the priming in a musket and the powder *flask*.

And to salute their *Governess*
Again as great a charge they press: 300
None for the *Virgin Nymph;* for She
Seems with the Flow'rs a Flow'r to be.
And think so still! though not compare
With Breath so sweet, or Cheek so faire.

　xxxix
Well shot ye Firemen! Oh how sweet,
And round your equal Fires do meet;
Whose shrill report no Ear can tell,
But Ecchoes to the Eye and smell.
See how the Flow'rs, as at *Parade*,
Under their *Colours* stand displaid: 310
Each *Regiment* in order grows,
That of the Tulip, Pinke, and Rose.

　xl
But when the vigilant *Patroul*
Of Stars walks round about the *Pole*,
Their Leaves, that to the stalks are curl'd,
Seem to their Staves the *Ensigns* furl'd.
Then in some Flow'rs beloved Hut
Each Bee as Sentinel is shut;
And sleeps so too: but, if once stir'd,
She runs you through, nor askes *the Word*.   320

　xli
Oh Thou, that dear and happy Isle
The Garden of the World ere while,
Thou *Paradise* of four Seas,
Which *Heaven* planted us to please,
But, to exclude the World, did guard
With watry if not flaming Sword;
What luckless Apple did we taste,
To make us Mortal, and Thee Waste?

301. *the Virgin Nymph:* Mary Fairfax, whom Marvell tutored.
303. *think . . . compare:* Imperatives addressed to the flowers. *Compare* here means to
challenge comparison with.

xlii

Unhappy! shall we never more
That sweet *Militia* restore,   330
When Gardens only had their Towrs,
And all the Garrisons were Flowrs,
When Roses only Arms might bear,
And Men did rosie Garlands wear?
Tulips, in several Colours barr'd,
Were then the *Switzers* of our *Guard*.

xliii

The *Gardiner* had the *Souldiers* place,
And his more gentle Forts did trace.
The Nursery of all things green
Was then the only *Magazeen*.   340
The *Winter Quarters* were the Stoves,
Where he the tender Plants removes.
But War all this doth overgrow:
We Ord'nance Plant and Powder sow.

xliv

And yet there walks one on the Sod
Who, had it pleased him and *God*,
Might once have made our Gardens spring
Fresh as his own and flourishing.
But he preferr'd to the *Cinque Ports*
These five imaginary Forts: 350
And, in those half-dry Trenches, spann'd
Pow'r which the Ocean might command.

xlv

For he did, with his utmost Skill,
Ambition weed, but *Conscience* till.

336. *Switzers:* The Swiss Guards at the Vatican still (1967) wear uniforms with
black, yellow, and red stripes.
349. *Cinque Ports:* A group of five seaports having jurisdiction along the southern
coast of England; here an image of the public responsibilities Fairfax has
relinquished in favor of the "five Bastions" (l. 288) of the spirit.
351. *spann'd:* Limited.

Conscience, that Heaven-nursed Plant,
Which most our Earthly Gardens want.
A prickling leaf it bears, and such
As that which shrinks at ev'ry touch;
But Flowrs eternal, and divine,
That in the Crowns of Saints do shine.   360

   xlvi

The sight does from these *Bastions* ply,
Th' invisible *Artilery;*
And at proud *Cawood-Castle* seems
To point the *Battery* of its Beams.
As if it quarrell'd in the Seat
Th' Ambition of its *Prelate* great.
But ore the Meads below it plays,
Or innocently seems to gaze.

   xlvii

And now to the Abbyss I pass
Of that unfathomable Grass,   370
Where Men like Grashoppers appear,
But Grashoppers are Gyants there:
They, in there squeaking Laugh, contemn
Us as we walk more low than them:
And, from the Precipices tall
Of the green spires, to us do call.

   xlviii

To see Men through this Meadow Dive,
We wonder how they rise alive.
As, under Water, none does know

355–360: Compare the plant Hæmony "Of sov'ran use/ 'Gainst all inchantments,
mildew blast, or damp/ Or gastly fumes apparition" in Milton's *Comus* (*A Mask
Presented at Ludlow-Castle*, 1634), which has similar characteristics:
    The leaf was darkish, and had prickles on it,
    But in another Countrey, as he said,
    Bore a bright golden flowre, but not in this soyl.
                              (ll. 630–632)
363. *Cawood:* Two miles southeast of Nun Appleton, a seat of the Archbishop of
York, who fled from it in 1642.
365. *quarrell'd:* Transitive, *found fault with.*
368. *gaze:* Bod. MS. reads *graze.*

Whether he fall through it or go.   380
But, as the Marriners that sound,
And show upon their Lead the Ground,
They bring up Flow'rs so to be seen,
And prove they've at the Bottom been.

   xlix
No Scene that turns with Engines strange
Does oftner than these Meadows change.
For when the Sun the Grass hath vext,
The tawny Mowers enter next;
Who seem like *Israelites* to be,
Walking on foot through a green Sea.   390
To them the Grassy Deeps divide,
And crowd a Lane to either Side.

   l
With whistling Sithe, and Elbow strong,
These Massacre the Grass along:
While one, unknowing, carves the *Rail*,
Whose yet unfeather'd Quils her fail.
The Edge all bloody from its Breast
He draws, and does his stroke detest;
Fearing the Flesh untimely mow'd
To him a Fate as black forebode.   400

   li
But bloody *Thestylis*, that waites
To bring the mowing Camp their Cates,
Greedy as Kites has trust it up,
And forthwith means on it to sup:
When on another quick She lights,
And cryes, "He call'd us *Israelites*;
But now, to make his saying true,
Rails rain for Quails, for Manna Dew."

380: That is, whether he is going downwards or forwards.
385. *Scene:* Stage. Elaborate machinery (*Engines strange*) was used for scenic effects in masques produced at the Court of Charles I.
392: That is, crowd to either side to form a lane.

lii

Unhappy Birds! what does it boot
To build below the Grasses Root;   410
When Lowness is unsafe as Hight,
And Chance o'retakes what scapeth spight?
And now your Orphan Parents Call
Sounds your untimely Funeral.
Death Trumpets creak in such a Note,
And 'tis the *Sourdine* in their Throat.

liii

Or sooner hatch or higher build:
The Mower now commands the Field;
In whose new Traverse seemeth wrought
A Camp of Battail newly fought: 420
Where, as the Meads with Hay, the Plain
Lyes quilted ore with Bodies slain:
The Women that with forks it fling,
Do represent the Pillaging.

liv

And now the careless Victors play,
Dancing the Triumphs of the Hay;
Where every Mowers wholesome Heat
Smells like an *Alexanders sweat*.
Their Females fragrant as the Mead
Which they in *Fairy Circles* tread: 430
When at their Dances End they kiss,
Their new-made Hay not sweeter is.

lv

When after this 'tis pil'd in Cocks,
Like a calm Sea it shews the Rocks:
We wondring in the River near
How Boats among them safely steer.
Or, like the *Desert Memphis Sand*,

416. *Sourdine:* A muted trumpet.
426. *Hay:* Also the name of a country dance.
428: Alexander's body "had so sweet a smell of it selfe, that all the apparrell he
wore next unto his body took thereof a passing delightful savour, as it had been
perfumed" (North's Plutarch, *Alexander*). (Margoliouth)

Short *Pyramids* of Hay do stand.
And such the *Roman Camps* do rise
In Hills for Soldiers Obsequies.   440

lvi

This *Scene* again withdrawing brings
A new and empty Face of things;
A levell'd space, as smooth and plain,
As Clothes for *Lilly* strecht to stain.
The World when first created sure
Was such a Table rase and pure.
Or rather such is the *Toril*
Ere the Bulls enter at Madril.

lvii

For to this naked equal Flat,
Which *Levellers* take Pattern at,   450
The Villagers in common chase
Their Cattle, which it closer rase;
And what below the Scythe increast
Is pincht yet nearer by the Beast.
Such, in the painted World, appear'd
Davenant with th' Universal Heard.

lviii

They seem within the polisht Grass
A Landskip drawen in Looking-Glass.
And shrunk in the huge Pasture show
As Spots, so shap'd, on Faces do,   460
Such Fleas, ere they approach the Eye,
In Multiplying Glasses lye.
They feed so wide, so slowly move,
As *Constellations* do above.

439. *rise:* Erect.
444. *Lilly:* Sir Peter Lely, the famous painter, who came to England from Holland
in 1641. The *Clothes* are his canvasses.
446. *Table rase: Tabula rasa.*   447. *Toril:* Bullring.
448. *Madril:* Madrid.   454. *Beast:* As in Bod. MS.; Folio reads *Breast*.
455–456: Davenant describes a painting of the six days of Creation. On the sixth
day "... strait an universal Herd appears" (*Gondibert*, II.vi). (Margoliouth)
461–462. *Such:* Here, as often in Marvell, means *so*. *Multiplying Glasses:*
Microscopes.

lix

Then, to conclude these pleasant Acts,
Denton sets ope its *Cataracts*;
And makes the Meadow truly be
(What it but seem'd before) a Sea.
For, jealous of its *Lords* long stay,
It try's t'invite him thus away.   470
The River in it self is drown'd,
And Isles th' astonisht Cattle round.

lx

Let others tell the *Paradox*,
How Eels now bellow in the Ox;
How Horses at their Tails do kick,
Turn'd as they hang to Leeches quick;
How Boats can over Bridges sail;
And Fishes do the Stables scale.
How *Salmons* trespassing are found;
And Pikes are taken in the Pound.   480

lxi

But I, retiring from the Flood,
Take Sanctuary in the Wood;
And, while it lasts, my self imbark
In this yet green, yet growing Ark;
Where the first Carpenter might best
Fit Timber for his Keel have Prest.
And where all Creatures might have shares,
Although in Armies, not in Paires.

lxii

The double Wood of ancient Stocks
Link'd in so thick, an Union locks,   490
It like two *Pedigrees* appears,
On one hand *Fairfax*, th' other *Veres*:

484: In contrast to the "yet green, yet growing" timbers of this Ark, compare the
Body's final complaint against the Soul:
    So Architects do square and hew
    Green Trees that in the Forest grew.
        ("A Dialogue between the Soul and the Body")
486. *Prest:* Taken for public use.   491. *Pedigrees:* Genealogical trees.

Of whom though many fell in War,
Yet more to Heaven shooting are:
And, as they Natures Cradle deckt,
Will in green Age her Hearse expect.

lxiii

When first the Eye this Forrest sees
It seems indeed as *Wood* not *Trees*:
As if their Neighbourhood so old
To one great Trunk them all did mold.   500
There the huge Bulk takes place, as ment
To thrust up a *Fifth Element*;
And stretches still so closely wedg'd
As if the Night within were hedg'd.

lxiv

Dark all without it knits; within
It opens passable and thin;
And in as loose an order grows,
As the *Corinthean Porticoes*.
The arching Boughs unite between
The Columnes of the Temple green;   510
And underneath the winged Quires
Echo about their tuned Fires.

lxv

The *Nightingale* does here make choice
To sing the Tryals of her Voice.
Low Shrubs she sits in, and adorns
With Musick high the squatted Thorns.
But highest Oakes stoop down to hear,
And listning Elders prick the Ear.
The Thorn, lest it should hurt her, draws
Within the Skin its shrunken claws.   520

lxvi

But I have for my Musick found
A Sadder, yet more pleasing Sound:

499. *Neighbourhood:* Proximity.
502. *Fifth Element:* Quintessence, supposed to be the substance of which the heavenly bodies were composed.

The *Stock-doves*, whose fair necks are grac'd
With Nuptial Rings their Ensigns chast;
Yet always, for some Cause unknown,
Sad pair unto the Elms they moan.
O why should such a Couple mourn,
That in so equal Flames do burn!

 lxvii

Then as I carless on the Bed
Of gelid *Straw-berryes* do tread,   530
And through the Hazles thick espy
The hatching *Thrastle's* shining Eye,
The *Heron* from the Ashes top,
The eldest of its young lets drop,
As if it Stork-like did pretend
That *Tribune* to *its Lord* to send.

 lxviii

But most the *Hewel's* wonders are,
Who here has the *Holt-felsters* care.
He walks still upright from the Root,
Meas'ring the Timber with his Foot;   540
And all the way, to keep it clean,
Doth from the Bark the Wood-moths glean.
He, with his Beak, examines well
Which fit to stand and which to fell.

 lxix

The good he numbers up, and hacks;
As if he mark'd them with the Ax.
But where he, tinkling with his Beak,
Does find the hollow Oak to speak,
That for his building he designs,
And through the tainted Side he mines.   550
Who could have thought the *tallest Oak*
Should fall by such a *feeble Stroke*!

535-536: In Holland the stork was traditionally thought to leave one of her young
for the houseowner who had encouraged her to build her nest. (Margoliouth)
537-538. *Hewel:* The green woodpecker. *Holt-felsters:* Woodcutters.

lxx

Nor would it, had the Tree not fed
A *Traitor-Worm*, within it bred.
(As first our *Flesh* corrupt within
Tempts impotent and bashful *Sin*.)
And yet that *Worm* triumphs not long,
But serves to feed the *Hewels young*.
While the Oake seems to fall content,
Viewing the Treason's Punishment.   560

lxxi

Thus I, *easie Philosopher*,
Among the *Birds* and *Trees* confer:
And little now to make me, wants
Or of the *Fowles*, or of the *Plants*.
Give me but Wings as they, and I
Streight floting on the Air shall fly:
Or turn me but, and you shall see
I was but an inverted Tree.

lxxii

Already I begin to call
In their most learn'd Original: 570
And where I Language want, my Signs
The Bird upon the Bough divines;
And more attentive there doth sit
Than if She were with Lime-twigs knit.
No Leaf does tremble in the Wind
Which I returning cannot find.

lxxiii

Out of these scatter'd *Sibyls* Leaves
Strange *Prophecies* my Phancy weaves:
And in one History consumes,
Like *Mexique-Paintings*, all the *Plumes*.   580
What *Rome, Greece, Palestine*, ere said
I in this light *Mosaick* read.

---

580. *Mexique-Paintings:* Cortez found elaborate pictures made with colored
feathers in the palace of Montezuma. (Margoliouth). Compare with "Last
Instructions," l. 14, p. 151.

Thrice happy he who, not mistook,
Hath read in *Natures mystick Book*.

   lxxiv
And see how Chance's better Wit
Could with a Mask my studies hit!
The Oak-Leaves me embroyder all,
Between which Caterpillars crawl:
And Ivy, with familiar trails,
Me licks, and clasps, and curles, and hales.   590
Under this *antick Cope* I move
Like some great *Prelate of the Grove*,

   lxxv
Then, languishing with ease, I toss
On Pallets swoln of Velvet Moss;
While the Wind, cooling through the Boughs,
Flatters with Air my panting Brows.
Thanks for my Rest ye *Mossy Banks*,
And unto you *cool Zephyr's* Thanks,
Who, as my Hair, my Thoughts too shed,
And winnow from the Chaff my Head.   600

   lxxvi
How safe, methinks, and strong, behind
These Trees have I incamp'd my Mind;
Where Beauty, aiming at the Heart,
Bends in some Tree its useless Dart;
And where the World no certain Shot
Can make, or me it toucheth not.
But I on it securely play,
And gaul its Horsemen all the Day.

   lxxvii
Bind me ye *Woodbines* in your twines,
Curle me about ye gadding *Vines*,   610
And Oh so close your Circles lace,
That I may never leave this Place:
But, lest your Fetters prove too weak,

586: That is, could fit me with a costume suitable to my studies.
591. *antick:* (1) antique, (2) antic.   599. *shed:* Separate.

Ere I your Silken Bondage break,
Do you, *O Brambles*, chain me too,
And courteous *Briars* nail me through.

lxxviii
Here in the Morning tye my Chain,
Where the two Woods have made a Lane;
While, like a *Guard* on either side,
The Trees before their *Lord* divide: 620
This, like a long and equal Thread,
Betwixt two *Labyrinths* does lead.
But, where the Floods did lately drown,
There at the Ev'ning stake me down.

lxxix
For now the Waves are fal'n and dry'd,
And now the Meadow's fresher dy'd;
Whose Grass, with moister colour dasht,
Seems as green Silks but newly washt.
No *Serpent* new nor *Crocodile*
Remains behind our little *Nile*,   630
Unless it self you will mistake,
Among these Meads the only Snake.

lxxx
See in what wanton harmless folds
It ev'ry where the Meadow holds;
And its yet muddy back doth lick,
Till as a *Chrystal Mirrour* slick;
Where all things gaze themselves, and doubt
If they be in it or without.
And for his shade which therein shines,
Narcissus like, the *Sun* too pines.   640

lxxxi
Oh what a Pleasure 'tis to hedge
My Temples here with heavy sedge;
Abandoning my lazy Side,
Stretcht as a Bank unto the Tide;
Or to suspend my sliding Foot

636. *slick*: Sleek.   645. *sliding Foot*: Compare "The Garden," l. 49, p. 50.

On the Osiers undermined Root,
And in its Branches tough to hang,
While at my Lines the Fishes twang!

lxxxii
But now away my Hooks, my Quills,
And Angles, idle Utensils.   650
The *young Maria* walks to night:
Hide trifling Youth thy Pleasures slight.
'Twere shame that such judicious Eyes
Should with such Toyes a Man surprize;
She that already is the *Law*
Of all her *Sex*, her *Ages Aw*.

lxxxiii
See how loose Nature, in respect
To her, it self doth recollect;
And every thing so whisht and fine,
Starts forthwith to its *Bonne Mine*.   660
The *Sun* himself, of *Her* aware,
Seems to descend with greater Care;
And lest *She* see him go to Bed,
In blushing Clouds conceales his Head.

lxxxiv
So when the Shadows laid asleep
From underneath these Banks do creep,
And on the River as it flows
With *Eben Shuts* begin to close;
The modest *Halcyon* comes in sight,
Flying betwixt the Day and Night;   670
And such an horror calm and dumb,
Admiring Nature does benum.

lxxxv
The viscous Air, wheres'ere She fly,
Follows and sucks her Azure dy;

659. *whisht:* Hushed. 660. *Bonne Mine:* Good appearance. *Bonne* has two syllables.
668. *Eben Shuts:* Ebony shutters.
671. *horror:* A feeling of awe or reverent fear (without any suggestion of repugnance).

The gellying Stream compacts below,
If it might fix her shadow so;
The stupid Fishes hang, as plain
As *Flies* in *Chrystal* overt'ane;
And Men the silent *Scene* assist,
Charm'd with the *Saphir-winged Mist*.   680

    lxxxvi
Maria such, and so doth hush
The *World*, and through the *Ev'ning* rush.
No new-born *Comet* such a Train
Draws through the Skie, nor Star new-slain.
For streight those giddy Rockets fail,
Which from the putrid Earth exhale,
But by her *Flames*, in *Heaven* try'd,
Nature is wholly *vitrifi'd*.

    lxxxvii
'Tis *She* that to these Gardens gave
That wondrous Beauty which they have;   690
She streightness on the Woods bestows;
To *Her* the Meadow sweetness owes;
Nothing could make the River be
So Chrystal-pure but only *She*;
She yet more Pure, Sweet, Streight, and Fair,
Than Gardens, Woods, Meads, Rivers are.

    lxxxviii
Therefore what first *She* on them spent,
They gratefully again present.
The Meadow Carpets where to tread;
The Garden Flow'rs to Crown *Her* Head;   700
And for a Glass the limpid Brook,
Where *She* may all *her* Beautyes look;
But, since *She* would not have them seen,
The Wood about *her* draws a Skreen.

    lxxxix
For *She*, to higher Beauties rais'd,
Disdains to be for lesser prais'd.
She counts her Beauty to converse

In all the Languages as hers;
Nor yet in those *her self* imployes
But for the *Wisdome*, not the *Noyse*;   710
Nor yet that *Wisdome* would affect,
But as 'tis *Heavens Dialect*.

    lxxxx
Blest Nymph! that couldst so soon prevent
Those *Trains* by Youth against thee meant;
Tears (watry Shot that pierce the Mind;)
And *Sighs* (Loves Cannon charg'd with Wind;)
True Praise (That breaks through all defence;)
And *feign'd complying Innocence*;
But knowing where this *Ambush* lay,
She scap'd the safe, but roughest Way.   720

    lxxxxi
This 'tis to have been from the first
In a *Domestick Heaven* nurst;
Under the *Discipline* severe
Of *Fairfax*, and the starry *Vere*;
Where not one object can come nigh
But pure, and spotless as the Eye;
And *Goodness* doth it self intail
On *Females*, if there want a *Male*.

    lxxxxii
Go now fond Sex that on your Face
Do all your useless Study place,   730
Nor once at Vice your Brows dare knit
Lest the smooth Forehead wrinkled sit:
Yet your own Face shall at you grin,
Thorough the Black-bag of your Skin;
When *knowledge* only could have fill'd
And *Virtue* all of those *Furrows till'd*.

708: Compare a possible allusion to Mary Fairfax's linguistic talents in "To his worthy Friend Doctor Witty," ll. 17-26 and note, p. 216. (Margoliouth)
714. *Trains:* That is, of artillery.
734. *Black-bag:* Mask.

lxxxxiii

Hence *She* with Graces more divine
Supplies beyond her *Sex* the *Line*;
And, like a *sprig of Misleto*,
On the *Fairfacian Oak* does grow;   740
Whence, for some universal good,
The *Priest* shall cut the sacred Bud;
While her *glad Parents* most rejoice,
And make their *Destiny* their *Choice*.

lxxxxiv

Mean time ye Fields, Springs, Bushes, Flow'rs,
Where yet She leads her studious Hours,
(Till Fate her worthily translates,
And find a *Fairfax* for our *Thwaites*)
Employ the means you have by Her,
And in your kind your selves preferr;   750
That, as all *Virgins* She precedes,
So you all *Woods, Streams, Gardens, Meads*.

lxxxxv

For you *Thessalian Tempe's Seat*
Shall now be scorn'd as obsolete;
Aranjuez, as less, disdain'd;
The *Bel-Retiro* as constrain'd;
But name not the *Idalian Grove*,
For 'twas the seat of wanton Love;
Much less the Deads' *Elysian Feilds*,
Yet nor to them your Beauty yeilds.   760

lxxxxvi

'Tis not, what once it was, the *World*;
But a rude heap together hurl'd;
All negligently overthrown,
Gulfes, Deserts, Precipices, Stone.
Your lesser World contains the same.
But in more decent Order tame;

755-756. *Aranjuez:* On the Tagus thirty miles from Madrid, was known for its gardens. *Bel-Retiro* (Buen Retiro) was another royal residence near Madrid. (Margoliouth)   765. *Your lesser World:* Nun Appleton.

You Heaven's Center, Nature's Lap.
And Paradice's only Map.

 lxxxxvii
But now the *Salmon-Fishers* moist
Their *Leathern Boats* begin to hoist;   770
And, like *Antipodes* in Shoes,
Have shod theyr *Heads* in their *Canoos.*
How Tortoise like, but not so slow,
These rational *Amphibii* go?
Let's in: for the dark *Hemisphere*
Does now like one of them appear.

The Character of Holland

 Holland, that scarce deserves the name of *Land*,
As but th' Off-scouring of the *Brittish Sand*;
And so much Earth as was contributed
By *English Pilots* when they heav'd the Lead;
Or what by th' Oceans slow alluvion fell,
Of shipwrackt Cockle and the Muscle-shell;
This indigested vomit of the Sea
Fell to the *Dutch* by just Propriety.
 Glad then, as Miners that have found the Ore,
They with mad labour fish'd the *Land* to *Shoar;*   10
And div'd as desperately for each piece
Of Earth, as if't had been of *Ambergreece*;
Collecting anxiously small Loads of Clay,
Less than what building Swallows bear away;
Or than those Pills which sordid Beetles roul,
Transfusing into them their Dunghil Soul.
 How did they rivet, with Gigantick Piles,
Thorough the Center their new-catched Miles;
And to the stake a strugling Country bound,
Where barking Waves still bait the forced Ground;   20

The Character of Holland: Deane, Monck, and Blake served together as Generals at
sea from November 1652 to June 1653, and "The Character of Holland" was
probably written after their victory over the Dutch off Portland in February 1653.
5. *alluvion:* In law the formation of new land by the slow and imperceptible action
of flowing water.

Building their *watry Babel* far more high
To reach the *Sea*, than those to scale the *Sky*?
   Yet still his claim the injur'd Ocean laid,
And oft at Leap-frog ore their Steeples plaid:
As if on purpose it on Land had come
To shew them what's their *Mare Liberum.*
A daily deluge over them does boyl;
The Earth and Water play at *Level-coyl*;
The Fish oft-times the Burger dispossest,
And sat not as a Meat but as a Guest;   30
And oft the *Tritons* and the *Sea-Nymphs* saw
Whole sholes of *Dutch* serv'd up for *Cabillau;*
Or as they over the new Level rang'd
For pickled *Herring*, pickled *Heeren* chang'd.
Nature, it seem'd, asham'd of her mistake,
Would throw their Land away at *Duck* and *Drake.*
   Therefore *Necessity*, that first made *Kings*,
Something like *Government* among them brings.
For as with *Pygmees* who best kills the *Crane*,
Among the *hungry* he that treasures *Grain*,   40
Among the *blind* the one-ey'd *blinkard* reigns,
So rules among the *drowned* he that *draines.*
Not who first sees the *rising Sun* commands,
But who could first discern the *rising Lands.*
Who best could know to pump an Earth so leak
Him they their *Lord* and *Country's Father* speak.
To make a *Bank* was a great *Plot of State*;
Invent a *Shov'l* and be a *Magistrate.*
Hence some small *Dyke-grave* unperceiv'd invades
The *Pow'r*, and grows as 'twere a *King of Spades*.   50
But for less envy some *joynt States* endures,
Who look like a *Commission of the Sewers.*
For these *Half-anders*, half wet, and half dry,
Nor bear *strict service*, nor *pure Liberty.*
   'Tis probable *Religion* after this

26. *Mare Liberum:* An allusion to Grotius' doctrine of freedom of the seas, which the
Dutch tried to claim in the English Channel. (Margoliouth)
28. *Level-coyl:* A boisterous game in which each player was unseated in turn.
32. *Cabillau:* From the Dutch word for cod-fish.
36. *Duck and Drake:* A game of skipping stones.
45. *leak:* Leaky.   49. *Dyke-grave:* Officer in charge of sea-walls.
53. *Half-anders:* As opposed to Hollanders. (Margoliouth)

Came next in order; which they could not miss,
How could the *Dutch* but be converted, when
Th' *Apostles* were so many Fishermen?
Besides the Waters of themselves did rise,
And, as their Land, so them did re-baptize.   60
Though *Herring* for their *God* few voices mist,
And *Poor-John* to have been th' *Evangelist*.
Faith, that could never Twins conceive before,
Never so fertile, spawn'd upon this shore:
More pregnant then their *Marg'ret*, that laid down
For *Hans-in-Kelder* of a whole *Hans-Town*.
    Sure when *Religion* did it self imbark,
And from the *East* would *Westward* steer its Ark,
It struck, and splitting on this unknown ground,
Each one thence pillag'd the first piece he found;   70
Hence *Amsterdam*, *Turk-Christian-Pagan-Jew*,
Staple of Sects and Mint of Schisme grew;
That *Bank of Conscience*, where not one so strange
Opinion but finds Credit, and Exchange.
In vain for *Catholicks* our selves we bear;
The *universal Church* is onely there.
Nor can Civility there want for *Tillage*,
Where wisely for their *Court* they chose a *Village*.
How fit a Title clothes their *Governours*,
Themselves the *Hogs* as all their Subjects *Bores!*   80
    Let it suffice to give their Country Fame
That it had one *Civilis* call'd by Name,
Some Fifteen hundred and more years ago;
But surely never any that was so.
    See but their *Mairmaids* with their *Tails of Fish*,
Reeking at *Church* over the *Chafing-Dish*.
A vestal Turf enshrin'd in Earthen Ware
Fumes through the loop-holes of a wooden Square.

62. *Poor-John:* Dried fish.
65–66. *Marg'ret:* A Dutch woman was supposed to have born 365 children at once.
Hans-in-Kelder: Child in the womb. *Hans-Town:* Member of the Hanseatic League.
75. *Catholicks:* The "one catholic, true and apostolic Church" of the Anglicans.
80. *Hogs:* A common pun on Hoog-mogenden, the official title of the Dutch legislature. *Bores:* Boers.
82. *Civilis:* Leader of the Batavian revolt against Rome, 69 A.D.
85–92: These lines refer to portable stoves used in Dutch churches.

Each to the *Temple* with these *Altars* tend,
But still does place it at her *Western End:*   90
While the fat steam of *Female Sacrifice*
Fills the *Priests Nostrils* and puts out his *Eyes.*
    Or what a Spectacle the *Skipper gross,*
A water-Hercules *Butter-Coloss,*
Tunn'd up with all their sev'ral *Towns of Beer;*
When Stagg'ring upon some Land, *Snick and Sneer,*
They try, like Statuaries, if they can
Cut out each others *Athos* to a Man:
And carve in their large Bodies, where they please,
The Armes of the *United Provinces.*   100
    But when such Amity at home is show'd;
What then are their confederacies abroad?
Let this one court'sie witness all the rest;
When their whole Navy they together prest,
Not Christian Captives to redeem from Bands:
Or intercept the Western golden Sands:
No, but all ancient Rights and Leagues must vail,
Rather than to the *English* strike their sail;
To whom their weather beaten *Province* ows
It self, when at some greater Vessel tows   110
A Cock-boat tost with the same wind and fate,
We buoy'd so often up their *sinking State.*
    Was this *Jus Belli & Pacis*; could this be
Cause why their *Burgomaster of the Sea*
Ram'd with Gun-powder, flaming with Brand wine,
Should raging hold his Linstock to the Mine?
While, with feign'd *Treaties*, they invade by stealth

94. *Butter-Coloss:* Variant nickname for Dutchman. Compare butter-box, butter-bag.
95. *Beer* or Bier occurs frequently in the names of Dutch towns.
96. *Snick and Sneer:* Cut and thrust.
97–98: Deinocrates the sculptor proposed to carve Mt. Athos into an effigy of Alexander the Great. (Margoliouth)
107–108: Under Grotius' doctrine of *Mare Liberum* the Dutch ships refused to lower their colors in salute to British warships. (Margoliouth)
113: Another tract, *De Jure belli et pacis*, was published by Grotius in 1625. (Margoliouth)
114. *Burgomaster of the Sea:* Admiral Van Trump. He refused to salute an English ship and fired on it instead.
115: Old sea-dogs were reputed to drink brandy fortified with gunpowder.
116. *Linstock:* A match-holder for firing cannon.

Our sore new circumcised *Common wealth*.
    Yet of his vain Attempt no more he sees
Then of *Case-Butter* shot and *Bullet-Cheese*.   120
And the torn Navy stagger'd with him home,
While the Sea laught it self into a foam,
'Tis true since that (as fortune kindly sports,)
A wholesome Danger drove us to our Ports.
While half their banish'd keels the Tempest tost,
Half bound at home in Prison to the frost:
That ours mean time at leizure might careen,
In a calm Winter, under Skies Serene.
As the obsequious Air and Waters rest,
Till the dear *Halcyon* hatch out all its nest.   130
The *Common wealth* doth by its losses grow;
And, like its own Seas, only Ebbs to flow.
Besides that very Agitation laves,
And purges out the corruptible waves.
    And now again our armed *Bucentore*
Doth yearly their *Sea-Nuptials* restore.
And now the *Hydra of seaven Provinces*
Is strangled by our *Infant Hercules*.
Their Tortoise wants its vainly stretched neck;
Their Navy all our Conquest or our Wreck: 140
Or, what is left, their *Carthage* overcome
Would render fain unto our better *Rome*,
Unless our *Senate*, lest their Youth disuse
The War, (but who would) Peace if begg'd refuse.
    For now of nothing may our *State* despair,
Darling of Heaven, and of Men the Care;
Provided that they be what they have been,
Watchful abroad, and honest still within.
For while our *Neptune* doth a *Trident* shake,
Steel'd with those piercing Heads, *Dean, Monk*, and *Blake*, 150

118: Compare Genesis 34:25.
120. *Case-Butter:* Butter used for canister shot.
123. *kindly:* By nature.   127. *careen:* Heel over on shore for repairs.
135. *Bucentore:* The state-barge in which the marriage of Venice and the Adriatic was celebrated each Ascension Day.
137–140: The English victory over the Seven Provinces of Holland is compared to the infant Hercules strangling the monstrous seven-headed Hydra.
141–144: I cannot make sense out of these lines.

And while *Jove* governs in the highest Sphere,
Vainly in *Hell* let *Pluto* domineer.

The First Anniversary of the Government Under His Highness The Lord Protector

Like the vain Curlings of the Watry maze,
Which in smooth Streams a sinking Weight dos raise;
So Man, declining always, disappears
In the weak Circles of increasing Years;
And his short Tumults of themselves Compose,
While flowing Time above his Head does close.
      Cromwell alone with greater Vigour runs,
(Sun-like) the Stages of succeeding Suns:
And still the Day which he doth next restore,
Is the just Wonder of the Day before.   10
Cromwell alone doth with new Lustre spring,
And shines the Jewell of the yearly Ring.
      'Tis he the force of scatter'd Time contracts,
And in one Year the work of Ages acts:
While heavie Monarchs make a wide Return,
Longer, and more Malignant then *Saturn*:
And though they all *Platonique* years should raign,
In the same Posture would be found again.
Their earthy Projects under ground they lay,
More slow and brittle then the *China* clay: 20
Well may they strive to leave them to their Son,
For one Thing never was by one King don.
Yet some more active for a Frontier Town
Took in by Proxie, beggs a false Renown;

The First Anniversary: One of the few poems by Marvell published during his
lifetime, celebrates Cromwell's first remarkable year as Protector. It appeared
anonymously in 1655 and was reprinted in 1681 but cancelled from all known
copies of the Folio except for one in the British Museum. I have adopted the first
edition as copy text.
15–16: Monarchs are associated with the leaden and unpropitious planet Saturn,
whose orbit was the longest known before the discovery of Uranus and Neptune.
(Margoliouth)
17–18. *Platonique:* The Platonic Great Year was 26,000 to 36,000 solar years.
19–20: Clay for Chinese porcelain was thought to have been prepared by being
buried for many years.

Another triumphs at the publique Cost,
And will have Wonn, if he no more have Lost;
They fight by Others, but in Person wrong,
And only are against their Subjects strong;
Their other Wars seem but a feign'd contest,
This Common Enemy is still opprest;   30
If Conquerors, on them they turn their might;
If Conquered, on them they wreak their Spight:
They neither build the Temple in their dayes,
Nor Matter for succeeding Founders raise;
Nor sacred Prophecies consult within,
Much less themselves to perfect them begin;
No other care they bear of things above,
But with Astrologers divine, and *Jove*,
To know how long their Planet yet Reprives
From the deserved Fate their guilty lives: 40
Thus (Image-like) an useless time they tell,
And with vain Scepter strike the hourly Bell;
Nor more contribute to the state of Things,
Than wooden Heads unto the Violls strings.
    While indefatigable *Cromwell* hyes,
And cuts his way still nearer to the Skyes,
Learning a Musique in the Region clear,
To tune this lower to that higher Sphere.
    So when *Amphion* did the Lute command,
Which the God gave him, with his gentle hand,   50
The rougher Stones, unto his Measures hew'd,
Dans'd up in order from the Quarreys rude:
This took a Lower, that an Higher place,
As he the Treble alter'd, or the Base:
No Note he struck, but a new Story lay'd,
And the great Work ascended while he play'd.
    The listning Structures he with Wonder ey'd,
And still new Stopps to various Time apply'd:

33-34: I Chronicles 28.
41-42: Like the mechanical figures striking the hour on certain types of clocks.
47-48: The heavenly bodies were thought to form an octave scale which had its counterpart in the soul.
49-50. *Amphion:* The architect of Greek legend raised the walls of Thebes by playing a lute given to him by Hermes.
58. *Stopps:* A *stop* is the part of the string pressed in order to produce a required note; sometimes mechanically marked, as by the frets of a lute or guitar.

Now through the Strings a Martial rage he throws,
And joyning streight the *Theban* Tow'r arose;   60
Then as he strokes them with a touch more sweet,
The flocking Marbles in a Palace meet;
But, for he most the graver Notes did try,
Therefore the Temples rear'd their Columns high:
Thus, ere he ceas'd, his sacred Lute creates
Th' harmonious City of the seven Gates.

Such was that wondrous Order and Consent,
When *Cromwell* tun'd the ruling Instrument;
While tedious Statesmen many years did hack,
Framing a Liberty that still went back;   70
Whose num'rous Gorge could swallow in an hour
That Island, which the Sea cannot devour:
Then our *Amphion* issues out and sings,
And once he struck, and twice, the pow'rful Strings.

The Commonwealth then first together came,
And each one enter'd in the willing Frame;
All other Matter yields, and may be rul'd;
But who the Minds of stubborn Men can build?
No Quarry bears a Stone so hardly wrought,
Nor with such labour from its Center brought: 80
None to be sunk in the Foundation bends,
Each in the House the highest Place contends,
And each the Hand that lays him will direct,
And some fall back upon the Architect;
Yet all compos'd by his attractive Song,
Into the Animated City throng.

The Common-wealth does through their Centers all
Draw the Circumf'rence of the publique Wall;
The crossest Spirits here do take their part,
Fast'ning the Contignation which they thwart;   90

---

68. *Instrument:* The Instrument of Government, 1653, established Cromwell's
Protectorate.
69. *hack:* To break a note in music or to mangle words.
87–98: These lines enunciate widely-held seventeenth-century political beliefs: (1)
that the best state was a mixed monarchy composed of a sovereign, a legislature,
and a judiciary, and (2) that such a state could best harmonize discordant
interests, a doctrine known as *concordia discors*.
89–90. *Contignation:* Framework. Opposing tensions contribute to its strength just
as an arch is supported by downward pressures.

And they, whose Nature leads them to divide,
Uphold, this one, and that the other Side:
But the most Equall still sustein the Height,
And they as Pillars keep the Work upright;
While the resistance of opposed Minds,
The Fabrique as with Arches stronger binds,
Which on the Basis of a Senate free,
Knit by the Roofs Protecting weight agree.

When for his Foot he thus a place had found,
He hurles e'r since the World about him round;   100
And in his sev'rall Aspects, like a Star,
Here shines in Peace, and thither shoots a War.
While by his Beams observing Princes steer,
And wisely court the Influence they fear;
O would they rather by his Pattern wonn,
Kiss the approaching, nor yet angry Sonn;
And in their numbred Footsteps humbly tread
The path where holy Oracles do lead;
How might they under such a Captain raise
The great Designes kept for the latter Dayes!   110
But mad with Reason, so miscall'd, of State
They know them not, and what they know not hate.
Hence still they sing Hosanna to the Whore,
And her whom they should Massacre adore:
But Indians whom they should convert, subdue;
Nor teach, but traffique with, or burn the Jew.

Unhappy Princes, ignorantly bred,
By Malice some, by Errour more misled;
If gracious Heaven to my Life give length,
Leisure to Time, and to my Weakness Strength,   120
Then shall I once with graver Accents shake
Your Regall sloth, and your long Slumbers wake:
Like the shrill Huntsman that prevents the East,
Winding his Horn to Kings that chase the Beast.

---

98. *the Roofs Protecting weight:* The authority of the Protector.

105–106: "Kiss the Son, lest he be angry, and ye perish *from* the way, when his wrath is kindled but a little. Blessed are they that put their trust in him" (Psalms, 2:10).

107–108: The footsteps are numbered by the *holy Oracles.* As Margoliouth observes, the entire passage down to l. 158 is millennial orthodoxy based on the apocalytic prophecies of Daniel 7:8 and Revelation 12:20.

Till then my Muse shall hollow farr behind
Angelique *Cromwell* who outwings the wind;
And in dark Nights, and in cold Dayes alone
Pursues the Monster thorough every Throne:
Which shrinking to her *Roman* Denn impure,
Gnashes her Goary teeth; nor there secure.   130
    Hence oft I think, if in some happy Hour
High Grace should meet in one with highest Pow'r,
And then a seasonable People still
Should bend to his, as he to Heavens will,
What we might hope, what wonderfull Effect
From such a wish'd Conjuncture might reflect.
Sure, the mysterious Work, where none withstand,
Would forthwith finish under such a Hand:
Fore-shortned Time its useless Course would stay,
And soon precipitate the latest Day.   140
But a thick Cloud about that Morning lyes,
And intercepts the Beams of Mortall eyes,
That 'tis the most which we determine can,
If these the Times, then this must be the Man.
And well he therefore does, and well has guest,
Who in his Age has always forward prest:
And knowing not where Heavens choice may light,
Girds yet his Sword, and ready stands to fight;
But Men alass, as if they nothing car'd,
Look on, all unconcern'd, or unprepar'd;   150
And Stars still fall, and still the Dragons Tail
Swindges the Volumes of its horrid Flail.
For the great Justice that did first suspend
The World by Sinn, does by the same extend.
Hence that blest Day still counterpoysed wastes,
The Ill delaying, what th' Elected hastes;
Hence landing Nature to new Seas is tost,
And good Designes still with their Authors lost.
    And thou, great *Cromwell*, for whose happy birth
A Mold was chosen out of better Earth;   160

125. *hollow:* Call after in hunting.
131–144: Marvell here expreses the hope that Cromwell's power will coincide with
divine purpose (High Grace) and a responsive people to bring in the Millennium
("precipitate the latest day"), but ll. 145–158 show his doubt as to whether this
hope is to be realized.   153. *suspend:* At the Flood.

Whose Saint-like Mother we did lately see
Live out an Age, long as a Pedigree;
That shee might seem, could we the Fall dispute,
T'have smelt the Blossome, and not eat the Fruit;
Though none does of more lasting Parents grow,
But never any did them honor so;
Though thou thine Heart from Evil still unstain'd,
And always hast thy Tongue from fraud refrain'd;
Thou, who so oft through Storms of thundring Lead
Hast born securely thine undaunted Head,   170
Thy Brest though ponyarding Conspiracies,
Drawn from the Sheath of lying Prophecies;
Thee proof beyond all other Force or Skill,
Our Sinns endanger, and shall one day kill.
   How near they fail'd, and in thy sudden Fall
At once assay'd to overturn us all.
Our brutish fury strugling to be Free,
Hurry'd thy Horses while they hurry'd thee.
When thou hadst almost quit thy Mortall cares,
And soyl'd in Dust thy Crown of silver Hairs.   180
   Let this one Sorrow interweave among
The other Glories of our yearly Song.
Like skilful Looms which through the costly thred
Of purling Ore, a shining wave do shed.
So shall the Tears we on past Grief employ,
Still as they trickle, glitter in our Joy.
So with more Modesty we may be True,
And speak as of the Dead the Praises due:
While impious Men deceiv'd with pleasure short,
On their own Hopes shall find the Fall retort.   190
   But the poor Beasts wanting their noble Guide,
What could they more? shrunk guiltily aside.
First winged Fear transports them far away,
And leaden Sorrow then their flight did stay.
See how they each his towring Crest abate,
And the green Grass, and their known Mangers hate,

161–162: Elizabeth Cromwell died November 16, 1654, at the age of 94.
175. *How near*: By what a narrow margin.
177–178: Cromwell upset his coach in Hyde Park September 29, 1654, while
driving a team of six horses.   184. *purling*: Embroidering.

Nor through wide Nostrils snuffe the wanton aire,
Nor their round Hoofs, or curled Manes compare;
With wandring Eyes, and restless Ears they stood
And with shrill Neighings ask'd him of the Wood.   200
   Thou *Cromwell* falling not a stupid Tree,
Or Rock so savage, but it mourn'd for thee:
And all about was heard a Panique groan,
As if that Natures self were overthrown.
It seem'd the Earth did from the Center tear;
It seem'd the Sun was faln out of the Sphere:
Justice obstructed lay, and Reason fool'd;
Courage disheartned, and Religion cool'd.
A dismall Silence through the Palace went,
And then loud Shreeks the vaulted Marbles rent.   210
Such as the dying Chorus signs by turns,
And to deaf Seas, and ruthless Tempest mourns,
When now they sink, and now the plundring Streams
Break up each Deck, and rip the Oaken seams.
   But thee triumphant hence the firy Carr,
And firy Steeds had born out of the Warr,
From the low World, and thankless Men above,
Unto the Kingdom blest of Peace and Love:
We only mourn'd our selves, in thine Ascent,
Whom thou hadst left beneath with Mantle rent.   220
   For all delight of Life thou then didst lose,
When to Command, thou didst thy self Depose;
Resigning up thy Privacy so dear,
To turn the headstrong Peoples Charioteer;
For to be *Cromwell* was a greater thing,
Than ought below, or yet above a King:
Therefore thou rather didst thy Self depress,

---

203. *Panique:* Derived from the nature god Pan.
215–220: The passage describes the imagined death of Cromwell in terms of the
death and apotheosis of Elijah and the grief of Elisha:

> And it came to pass as they still went on, and talked, that, behold, there
> appeared a chariot of fire, and parted them both asunder; and Elijah when up
> by a whirlwind into heaven.
>
> And Elisha saw it, and he cried, My father, my father, the chariot of Israel,
> and the horsemen thereof. And he saw him no more: and he took his own
> clothes, and rent them in two pieces.   (II Kings 2:11–12)

Yielding to Rule, because it made thee Less.
  For neither didst thou from the first apply
Thy sober Spirit unto things too High,   230
But in thine own Fields exercisedst long,
An healthfull Mind within a Body strong;
Till at the Seventh time thou in the Skyes,
As a small Cloud, like a Mans hand didst rise;
Then did thick Mists and Winds the aire deform,
And down at last thou pour'dst the fertile Storm;
Which to the thirsty Land did plenty bring,
But, though forewarn'd, o'r-took and wet the King.
  What since he did, an higher Force him push'd
Still from behind, and it before him rush'd,   240
Though undiscern'd among the tumult blind,
Who think those high Decrees by Man design'd.
'Twas Heav'n would not that his Pow'r should cease,
But walk still middle betwixt Warr and Peace;
Choosing each Stone, and poysing every weight,
Trying the Measures of the Bredth and Height;
Here pulling down, and there erecting New,
Founding a firm State by Proportions true.
  When *Gideon* so did from the Warr retreat,
Yet by the Conquest of two Kings grown great,   250
He on the Peace extends a Warlike power,
And *Is'rel* silent saw him rase the Tow'r;
And how he Succoths Elders durst suppress,
With Thorns and Briars of the Wilderness.
No King might ever such a Force have don;
Yet would not he be Lord, nor yet his Son.
  Thou with the same strength, and an Heart as plain,
Didst (like thine Olive) still refuse to Reign;
Though why should others all thy Labor spoil,

249-264: Compare Gideon's punishment of the elders of Succoth in Judges 8
and 9.
258: "But the olive tree said unto them, Should I leave my fatness ... and go to be
promoted over the trees?" (Judges 9:9)
259-262: "And the bramble said unto the trees, If in truth ye anoint me king over
you, then come and put your trust in my shadow: and if not, let fire come out of the
bramble, and devour the cedars of Lebanon" (Judges 9:15).

And Brambles be anointed with thine Oil,   260
Whose climbing Flame, without a timely stop,
Had quickly Levell'd every Cedar's top.
Therefore first growing to thy self a Law,
Th' ambitious Shrubs thou in just time didst aw.
    So have I seen at Sea, when whirling Winds,
Hurry the Bark, but more the Seamens minds,
Who with mistaken Course salute the Sand,
And threat'ning Rocks misapprehend for Land;
While balefull *Tritons* to the shipwrack guide,
And Corposants along the Tacklings slide.   270
The Passengers all wearyed out before,
Giddy, and wishing for the fatall Shore;
Some lusty Mate, who with more carefull Ey
Counted the Hours, and ev'ry Star did spy,
The Helm does from the artless Steersman strain,
And doubles back unto the safer Main.
What though a while they grumble discontent,
Saving himself he does their loss prevent.
    'Tis not a Freedome, that where All command;
Nor Tyrannie, where One does them withstand: 280
But who of both the Bounders knows to lay
Him as their Father must the State obey.
    Thou, and thine House, like *Noahs* Eight did rest,
Left by the Warrs Flood on the Mountains crest:
And the large Vale lay subject to thy Will,
Which thou but as an Husbandman wouldst Till:
And only didst for others plant the Vine
Of Liberty, not drunken with its Wine.
    That sober Liberty which men may have,
That they enjoy, but more they vainly crave: 290
And such as to their Parents Tents do press,
May shew their own, not see his Nakedness.
    Yet such a *Chammish* issue still does rage,

---

262. *Levell'd:* The brambles or shrubs represent the party of Levellers, an extreme
egalitarian sect.
270. *Corposants:* Shining exhalations like St. Elmo's fire.
286-292: Compare Genesis 9:20-22.
293. *Chammish:* Like Ham (or Cham) who revealed the nakedness of the drunken
Noah to Shem and Japheth (Genesis 9:20-22). The succeeding passage attacks the
extreme religious sects which multiplied in the 1650s.

The Shame and Plague both of the Land and Age,
Who watch'd thy halting, and thy Fall deride,
Rejoycing when thy Foot had slipt aside;
That their new King might the fifth Scepter shake,
And make the World, by his Example, Quake:
Whose frantique Army should they want for Men
Might muster Heresies, so one were ten.   300
What thy Misfortune, they the Spirit call,
And their Religion only is to Fall.
Oh *Mahomet!* now couldst thou rise again,
Thy Falling sickness should have made thee Reign,
While *Feake* and *Simpson* would in many a Tome,
Have writ the Comments of thy sacred Foame:
For soon thou mightst have past among their Rant
Wer't but for thine unmoved Tulipant;
As thou must needs have own'd them of thy band
For Prophecies fit to be *Alcorand.*   310
    Accursed Locusts, whom your King does spit
Out of the Center of th' unbottom'd Pit;
Wand'rers, Adult'rers, Lyers, *Munser's* rest,
Sorcerers, Atheists, Jesuites, Possest;
You who the Scriptures and the Laws deface
With the same liberty as Points and Lace;
Oh Race most hypocritically strict!
Bent to reduce us to the ancient Pict;
Well may you act the *Adam* and the *Eve,*
Ay, and the Serpent too that did deceive.   320
    But the great Captain, now the danger's ore,
Makes you for his sake Tremble one fit more;
And, to your spight, returning yet alive
Does with himself all that is good revive.
    So when first Man did through the Morning new
See the bright Sun his shining Race pursue,
All day he follow'd with unwearied sight,
Pleas'd with that other World of moving Light;
But thought him when he miss'd his setting beams,
Sunk in the Hills, or plung'd below the Streams.   330

304. *Falling sickness:* Epilepsy.
305. *Feake and Simpson*: Preachers of sedition against Cromwell.
308. *Tulipant:* Turban.
313. *Munser's rest:* The extreme Anabaptist remnant in Münster.

While dismal blacks hung round the Universe,
And Stars (like Tapers) burn'd upon his Herse:
And Owls and Ravens with their screeching noyse
Did make the Fun'rals sadder by their Joyes.
His weeping Eys the dolefull Vigills keep,
Not knowing yet the Night was made for sleep:
Still to the West, where he him lost, he turn'd,
And with such accents, as Despairing, mourn'd:
Why did mine Eyes once see so bright a Ray;
Or why Day last no longer than a Day?   340
When streight the Sun behind him he descry'd,
Smiling serenely from the further side.

So while our Star that gives us Light and Heat,
Seem'd now a long and gloomy Night to threat,
Up from the other World his Flame he darts,
And Princes, shining through their windows, starts;
Who their suspected Counsellors refuse,
And credulous Ambassadors accuse.

"Is this," saith one, "the Nation that we read
Spent with both Wars, under a Captain dead?   350
Yet rigg a Navie while we dress us late;
And ere we Dine, rase and rebuild their State.
What Oaken Forrests, and what golden Mines!
What Mints of Men, what Union of Designes!
Unless their Ships, do, as their Fowle proceed
Of shedding Leaves, that with their Ocean breed.
Theirs are not Ships, but rather Arks of War,
And beaked Promontories sail'd from farr;
Of floting Islands a new hatched Nest;
A Fleet of Worlds, of other Worlds in quest;   360
An hideous shole of wood-Leviathans,
Arm'd with three Tire of brazen Hurricans;
That through the Center shoot their thundring side
And sink the Earth that does at Anchor ride.
What refuge to escape them can be found,
Whose watry Leaguers all the world surround?
Needs must we all their Tributaries be,
Whose Navies hold the Sluces of the Sea.

350. *both Wars:* The Civil War and the war with Holland 1652–54.
355–356: Leaves of a certain tree falling into water were believed to turn into
solan geese. (Margoliouth)   366. *Leaguers:* Besieging forces.

The Ocean is the Fountain of Command,
But that once took, we Captives are on Land.   370
And those that have the Waters for their share,
Can quickly leave us neither Earth nor Aire.
Yet if through these our Fears could find a pass;
Through double Oak, and lin'd with treble Brass;
That one Man still, although but nam'd, alarms
More than all Men, all Navies, and all Arms.
Him, all the Day, Him, in late Nights I dread,
And still his Sword seems hanging ore my head.
The Nation had been ours, but his one Soule
Moves the great Bulk, and animates the whole.   380
He Secrecy with Number hath inchas'd,
Courage with Age, Maturity with Haste:
The Valiants Terror, Riddle of the Wise;
And still his Fauchion all our Knots unties.
Where did he learn those Arts that cost us dear?
Where below Earth, or where above the Sphere?
He seems a King by long Succession born,
And yet the same to be a King does scorn.
Abroad a King he seems, and something more,
At Home a Subject on the equall Floor.   390
O could I once him with our Title see,
So should I hope yet he might Dye as wee.
But let them write his Praise that love him best,
It grieves me sore to have thus much confest."
    Pardon, great Prince, if thus their Fear or Spight
More than our Love and Duty do thee Right.
I yield, nor further will the Prize contend;
So that we both alike may miss our End:
While thou thy venerable Head dost raise
As far above their Malice as my Praise.   400
And as the *Angell* of our Commonweal,
Troubling the Waters, yearly mak'st them Heal.

.

381. *inchas'd:* Worked in together.
384. *Fauchion*: Falchion. The man who loosed the Gordian knot was to be master of
the world.

A Poem upon the Death of His late Highnesse the Lord Protector

That Providence which had so long the care
Of *Cromwell's* head, and numbred ev'ry haire,
Now in it self (the Glasse where all appears)
Had seen the period of his golden yeares:
And thenceforth only did attend to trace
What Death might least so faire a Life deface.

The people, which what most they fear esteem,
Death when more horrid, so more noble deem,
And blame the last *Act*, like Spectators vaine,
Unlesse the *Prince* whom they applaud be slaine;   10
Nor Fate indeed can well refuse that right
To those that liv'd in Warre, to dye in Fight.

But long his *Valour* none had left that could
Indanger him, or *Clemency* that would:
And he whom Nature all for Peace had made
But angry Heaven unto Warre had sway'd,
And so lesse usefull where he most desir'd,
For what he least affected was admir'd,
Deserved yet an End whose ev'ry part
Should speak the wondrous softnesse of his Heart.   20

To *Love* and *Griefe* the fatall writt was sign'd
(Those nobler weaknesses of humane Kinde,
From which those Powers that issu'd the Decree,
Although immortall, found they were not free),
That they, to whom his brest still open lyes,
In gentle Passions should his Death disguise:
And leave suceeding Ages cause to mourne,
As long as Griefe shall weep, or Love shall burne.

Streight does a slow and languishing Disease
Eliza, Natures and his darling, seize: 30

A Poem upon the Death of His late Highnesse the Lord Protector: This elegy on Cromwell,
who died September 3, 1658, together with "An Horatian Ode" and "The First
Anniversary," was cancelled from all known copies of the Folio except for one in
the British Museum which contains only lines 1–184. I have adopted the Bod. MS.
as copy text.   21: That is, Love and Grief were appointed his executioners.
30. *Eliza:* Elizabeth Claypole died August 6, 1658.

Her when an Infant, taken with her Charms,
He oft would flourish in his mighty Arms;
And, lest their force the tender burthen wrong,
Slacken the vigour of his Muscles strong;
Then to the Mother's brest her softly move,
Which, while she drain'd of Milke, she fill'd with Love:
But as with riper Years her Vertue grew,
And every minute adds a Lustre new;
When with Meridian height her Beauty shin'd,
And thorough that sparkled her fairer Mind;   40
When shee with Smiles serene in Words discreet
His hidden Soule at every turne could meet;
Then might y' ha' daily his Affection spy'd,
Doubling that knott which Destiny had ty'd;
While they by sense, not knowing, comprehend
How on each other both theyr Fates depend.
With her each day the pleasing Houres he shares,
And at her Aspect calmes his growing Cares:
Or with a Grand Sire's joy her children sees
Hanging about her neck or at his knees,   50
Hold fast, dear Infants, hold them both or none!
This will not stay when once the other's gone.
    A silent fire now wastes those Limbs of Wax
And him within his tortur'd Image racks.
So the Flow'r with'ring which the Garden crown'd,
The sad Roote pines in secret under ground.
Each Groane he doubled and each Sigh he sigh'd
Repeated over to the restlesse Night;
No trembling String compos'd to numbers new
Answers the touch in Notes more sad, more true.   60
She, lest he grieve, hides what she can her pains,
And he to lessen hers his Sorrow feigns;
Yet both perceiv'd, yet both conceal'd their Skills,
And so diminishing increas'd their ills,
That whether by each other's Griefe they fell,
Or on their own redoubled, none can tell.
    And now *Eliza's* purple Locks were shorn,

53–54: Witches tormented their enemies by melting wax images of them.
62. *feigns:* Dissimulates.
67: An allusion to the death of Nisus which occurred when his daughter Scylla cut his purple locks (Ovid, *Metamorphoses*, 8).

Where she so long her *Father's* Fate had worn,
And frequent Lightning to her Soule that flyes
Devides the Aire and opens all the Skyes: 70
And now his Life, suspended by her breath,
Ran out impetuously to hasting Death.
Like polish'd Mirrours so his steely Brest
Had every figure of her woes exprest,
And with the damp of her last Gasps obscur'd
Had drawn such staines as were not to be cur'd.
Fate could not either reach with single stroke,
But, the dear Image fled, the Mirrour broke.

     Who now shall tell us more of mournfull Swans,
Of Halcyons kinde, or bleeding Pelicans?   80
No downy brest did ere so gently beate,
Or fanne with airy plumes so soft an heat.
For he no duty by his height excus'd,
Nor, though a *Prince*, to be a *Man* refus'd;
But rather than in his *Eliza's* paine
Not love, not grieve, would neither live nor reigne;
And in himself so oft immortall try'd,
Yet in compassion of another dy'd.

     So have I seen a Vine whose lasting Age
Of many a Winter hath surviv'd the rage,   90
Under whose shady tent Men every yeare
At its rich blood's expence their Sorrows cheare,
If some deare branch where it extends its life
Chance to be prun'd by an untimely Knife
The Parent tree unto the Griefe succeeds,
And through the Wound its vital humour bleeds;
Trickling in watry drops, whose flowing shape
Weeps that it falls ere fix'd into a Grape.
So the dry Stock, no more that spreading Vine,
Frustrates the Autumne and the hopes of Wine.   100

     A secret Cause does sure those Signes ordaine
Foreboding Princes falls, and seldome vaine:
Whether some kinder Powers that wish us well,
What they above can not prevent, foretell;
Or the great World do by consent presage,
As hollow Seas with future Tempests rage:
Or rather *Heav'n* which us so long foresees,
Their fun'ralls celebrates while it decrees.

But never yet was any humane Fate
By nature solemniz'd with so much state.   110
He unconcern'd the dreadful passage crost;
But oh what Pangs that Death did Nature cost!
   First the great Thunder was shot off and sent,
The signall from the starry Battlement:
The Winds receive it and its force out do,
As practising how they could thunder too;
Out of the Binders Hand the Sheaves they tore,
And thrash'd the Harvest in the airy floore;
Or of huge Trees, whose growth with his did rise,
The deep foundations open'd to the Skyes.   120
Then heavy Showres the winged Tempests lead
And powre the deluge ore the Chaos head.
The Race of warlike Horses at his Tombe
Offer themselves in many a Hecatombe;
With pensive head towards the grounde they fall,
And helpless languish at the tainted Stall.
Numbers of men decrease with pains unknown,
And hasten not to see his Death their own.
Such Tortures all the Elements unfix'd,
Troubled to part where so exactly mixd: 130
And as through Aire his wasting Spirits flow'd,
The Universe labour'd beneath their load.
   Nature it seem'd with him would Nature vye;
He with *Eliza*, it with him would dye.
   He without noyse still travell'd to his End,
As silent Sunns to meet the Night descend.
The Starrs that for him fought had only power
Left to determine now his fatall Houre;
Which, since they might not hinder, yet they cast
To choose it worthy of his Gloryes past.   140
   No part of time but bare his marke away
Of honour, all the year was *Cromwell's* day,
But this, of all the most auspicious found,
Twice had in open feild him Victour crownd:
When up the armed Mountains of *Dunbarre*

112: Violent storms occurred at the time of Cromwell's death.
127: An allusion to a fever epidemic in 1658.
139. *Cast:* Calculate astrologically.

He march'd, and through deep *Severn* ending warre.
What day should him eternize but the same
That had before immortaliz'd his Name?
That so who ere would at his death have joyd,
In their own Griefs might find themselves imployd;   150
But those that sadly his departure griev'd,
Yet joy'd remembring what he once atchiev'd.
And the last minute his victorious Ghost
Gave chase to *Ligny* on the *Belgick* coast.
Here ended all his mortal toyles; he layd
And slept in peace under the Laurell shade.

    O *Cromwell, Heavens Favourite!* To none
Have such high honours from above been showne:
For whom the Elements we Mourners see,
And *Heav'n* it selfe would the great Herald be;   160
Which with more Care set forth his Obsequyes
Than those of *Moses* hid from humane Eyes:
As jealous onely here lest all be lesse,
That we could to his Memory expresse.

    Then let us too our course of Mourning keep:
Where *Heaven* leads, 'tis Piety to weep.
Stand back ye, Seas, and shrunck beneath the vaile
Of your Abisse, with cover'd Head bewaile
Your *Monarch:* We demand not your supplyes
To compass in our *Isle;* our Teares suffice;   170
Since him away the dismall Tempest rent,
Who once more joyn'd us to the Continent;
Who planted *England* on the *Flandrick* shore,
And stretch'd our frontire to the *Indian* Ore;
Whose greater Truths obscure the Fables old:
Whether of *British Saints* or *Worthyes* told;
And in a Valour less'ning *Arthur's* deeds,
For Holinesse the *Confessour* exceeds.

    He first put Armes into *Religion's* hand,
And tim'rous *Conscience* unto *Courage* mann'd;   180
The soldier taught that inward Maile to weare,

154: On September 3, 1658, an English contingent in Flanders helped to defeat a Spanish force under the Prince de Ligne.
162: Deuteronomy 34:6.
172–174: By the capture of Dunkirk (1658) and Jamaica (1655).

And *fearing God* how they should *nothing feare*.
Those strokes, he said, will pierce through all below
Where those that strike from *Heaven* fetch their Blow.
Astonish'd Armyes did their Flight prepare:
And Cityes strong were stormed by his Prayer.
Of that for ever *Prestons* field shall tell
The story, and impregnable *Clonmell*;
And where the sandy mountain *Fenwick* scal'd,
The Sea between, yet hence his Pray'r prevail'd.   190
What man was ever so in *Heav'n* obey'd
Since the commanded Sun ore *Gibeon* stayd?
In all his Warrs needs must he triumph, when
He conquer'd *God* still ere he fought with *Men*.
    Hence, though in Battle none so brave or fierce,
Yet him the adverse Steel could never pierce:
Pitty it seem'd to hurt him more that felt
Each Wound himself which he to others delt;
Danger it self refusing to offend
So loose an Enemy, so fast a Friend.   200
    Friendship that sacred vertue, long does claime
The first foundation of his House and Name:
But within one its narrow limitts fall;
His Tendernesse extended unto all:
And that deep Soule through every chanell flows,
Where kindly Nature loves it self to lose.
More strong affections never Reason serv'd
Yet still affected most what best deserv'd.
If he *Eliza* lov'd to that degree
(Though who more worthy to be lov'd than she?)   210
If so indulgent to his own, how deare
To him the Children of the *Highest* were?
For her he once did Natures tribute pay:
For these his Life adventur'd every day.

187: Cromwell defeated the Scots near Preston, August 17, 1648.
188: The Irish successfully resisted Cromwell's attack on Clonmell but subsequently evacuated the town in May 1650.
189: Lt. Col. Roger Fenwick died in the Battle of the Dunes which led to the capture of Dunkirk. A day of public prayer was proclaimed. (Margoliouth)
191–192: See Joshua 10:12–14.

And 'twould be found, could we his thoughts have cast,
Their Griefs struck deepest, if *Eliza's* last.
   What Prudence more than humane did he need
To keep so deare, so diff'ring mindes agreed?
The worser sort, as conscious of their ill,
Lye weak and easy to the Rulers will: 220
But to the good (too many or too few),
All Law is uselesse, all reward is due.
Oh ill advis'd if, not for love, for shame!
Spare yet your own if you neglect his Fame,
Lest others dare to think your Zeale a maske,
And you to govern only *Heavens* taske.
   Valour, Religion, Friendship, Prudence dy'd
At once with him and all that's good beside:
And we, Deaths reffuse, Natures dregs, confin'd
To loathsome life, Alas! are left behinde,   230
Where we (so once we us'd) shall now no more
To fetch day presse about his Chamber Door;
From which he issu'd with that awfull State,
It seem'd *Mars* broke through *Janus* double Gate:
Yet alwayes temper'd with an Aire so mild,
No Aprill Suns that ere so gently smil'd;
No more shall heare that powerfull Language charm,
Whose force oft spar'd the labour of his arm;
No more shall follow where he spent the dayes
In warre, in counsell, or in pray'r, and praise,   240
Whose meanest Acts he would himself advance,
As ungirt *David* to the *Arke* did dance.
All, All is gone of ours or his delight
In Horses fierce, wild Deer or Armour bright.
Francisca faire can nothing now but weep,
Nor with soft Notes shall sing his Cares asleep.
   I saw him dead, a leaden Slumber lyes,
And mortall Sleep, over those wakefull Eys:
Those gentle Rayes under the lidds were fled
Which through his lookes that piercing Sweetnesse shed;   250

215. *cast:* Calculated.   242: II Samuel 6:14–22.
245. *Francisca:* Cromwell's youngest daughter, Frances.

That Port which so Majestique was and strong,
Loose, and depriv'd of Vigour, stretch'd along:
All wither'd, all discolour'd, pale and wan,
How much another thing, no more than Man?
Oh humane Glory vaine, Oh Death, Oh Wings,
Oh worthless World, oh transitory Things!
   Yet dwelt that Greatnesse in his shape decay'd
That still, though dead, greater than death he layd.
And in his alter'd face you something faigne
That threatens Death he yet will live againe: 260
Not much unlike the sacred Oake which shoots
To heav'n its branches and through earth its roots,
Whose spacious boughs are hung with Trophees round,
And honour'd wreaths have oft the Victour crown'd.
When angry *Jove* darts Lightning through the Aire
At mortalls sins, nor his own Plant will spare
(It groanes and bruses all below that stood
So many yeares the shelter of the wood),
The tree, ere while foreshorten'd to our view,
When faln shews taller yet than as it grew.   270
   So shall his Praise to after times increase,
When Truth shall be allow'd and Faction cease,
And his own shadows with him fall. The Eye
Detracts from objects than it selfe more high:
But when Death takes them from that envy'd seate,
Seeing how little, we confesse how greate.
   Thee many ages hence in martiall Verse
Shall *th' English* Souldier, 'ere he charge, rehearse:
Singing of thee, inflame themselves to fight,
And with the name of *Cromwell* Armyes fright.   280
As long as Rivers to the Seas shall runne,
As long as *Cynthia* shall relieve the Sunne,
While Staggs shall fly unto the Forests thick,
While Sheep delight the grassy Downs to pick,
As long as Future Time succeeds the Past,
Always thy Honour, Praise and Name shall last.
   Thou in a pitch how farre beyond the sphere
Of humane Glory towr'st, and, raigning there,
Despoyld of mortall robes, in seas of Blisse

259. *faigne:* Imagine.

Plunging dost bathe, and tread a bright Abysse: 290
There thy greate soule yet once a world does see
Spacious enough and pure enough for thee.
How soon thou *Moses* hast and *Joshua* found
And *David* for the Sword and harpe renown'd!
How streight canst to each happy Mansion goe!
(Farr better known above than here below)
And in these joyes dost spend the endlesse Day
Which in expressing we our selves betray.

    For we, since thou art gone, with heavy Doome
Wander like Ghosts about thy loved Tombe,   300
And lost in tears have neither sight nor minde
To guide us upward through this Region blinde.
Since thou art gone, who best that Way could'st teach,
Onely our Sighs perhaps may thither reach.

    And *Richard* yet, where his great *Parent* led,
Beats on the rugged track: he Vertue dead
Revives, and by his milder beams assures,
And yet how much of them his griefe obscures?

    He, as his Father, long was kept from sight,
In private to be view'd by better light;   310
But open'd once, what splendour does he throw:
A *Cromwell* in an houre a Prince will grow!
How he becomes that Seat, how strongly streins,
How gently winds at once the ruling Reins!
Heav'n to this choise prepar'd a Diadem
Richer than any Eastern silk or gemme:
A pearly rainbow, where the Sun inchas'd
His brows like an Imperiall Jewell grac'd.

    We find already what those Omens mean,
Earth nere more glad, nor *Heaven* more serene: 320
Cease now our griefs, Calme Peace succeeds a War;
Rainbows to storms, *Richard* to *Oliver*.
Tempt not his Clemency to try his pow'r
He threats no Deluge, yet foretells a Showre.

305: Richard Cromwell (1626-1712) was proclaimed Protector on the day of his father's death, but resigned the title in April 1659.
324: Compare "First Anniversary," II. 236-238, p. 100.

The Era of Charles II

The Second Advice to a Painter for drawing the History of our navall busynesse. In Imitation of Mr. Waller

Navem si poscat sibi peronatus arator
Luciferi rudis, exclamet Melicerta perisse
Frontem de rebus.

Pers: Sat. 5.

London, Aprill 1666

Nay *Painter*, if thou dar'st designe that Fight
Which *Waller* only Courage had to write;
If thy bold hand can without shaking draw
What ev'n the Actors trembled when they saw;
Enough to make thy colours change, like theirs,
And all thy Pencills bristle like their haires;
First, in fit distance of the Prospect vain,

The Second Advice to a Painter: Parodies an encomiastic poem by Edmund Waller on the engagements between the British fleet under the command of James, Duke of York, and the Dutch in the summer of 1665. Waller's poem, which purported to instruct a painter in depicting the Duke's triumphs, was entitled "Instructions to a Painter for the Drawing of the Posture and Progress of His Majesty's Forces at Sea, under the Command of His Highness-Royal; together with the Battle and Victory Obtained over the Dutch. June 3, 1665." "The Second Advice" supplies many details which show that this first summer of the war was far from being the triumph of British arms which Waller had described. It reveals many instances of venality and cowardice in the navy.

The epigraph is from Persius' fifth satire (ll. 102–104), and Dryden translated it as follows:

The high-sho'd plowman, should he quit the land,
To take the pilot's rudder in his hand,
Artless of stars, and of the moving sand,
The gods would leave him to the waves and wind
And think all shame was lost in humankind.

4. *trembled:* Trembled at.   6. *Pencills:* Brushes.

7–12: Before war was declared a British squadron under Sir Thomas Allin made an unsuccessful attack on Dutch merchantmen from Smyrna near the straits of Gibraltar. Two British warships ran aground, and the poet pretends that Allin left them to waft (convoy) the Pillars of Hercules as sea-marks between Dover and Calais.

Paint *Allen* tilting at the coast of *Spain*:
Heroick act, and never heard till now,
Stemming of *Herc'les Pillars* with his Prow!   10
And how two Ships he left the Hills to waft
And with new Sea-marks *Dov'r* and *Calais* graft;
Next, let the flaming *London* come in view
Like *Nero's Rome*, burnt to rebuild it new.
What lesser Sacrifice than this was meet
To offer for the safety of the Fleet?
Blow one Ship up, another thence does grow:
See what free Cityes and wise Courts can do!
So some old Merchant, to ensure his Name
Marries afresh, and Courtiers share the Dame.   20
So whatsoere is broke the Servants pay't;
And Glasses are more durable than Plate.
No May'r till now so rich a Pageant feign'd
Nor one Barge all the Companyes contain'd.
    Then, *Painter*, draw cerulean *Coventry*,
Keeper, or rather Chanc'lour of the Sea:
And more exactly to expresse his hew,
Use nothing but ultramarinish blew.
To pay his Fees the silver Trumpet spends:
And Boatswains whistle for his Place depends: 30
Pilots in vain repeat the Compasse ore
Untill of him they learn that one point more.
The constant Magnet to the Pole does hold,
Steele to the Magnet, *Coventry* to Gold.
Muscovy sells up hemp and pitch and tarre;

13-16: The frigate *London* blew up accidentally in March 1665 and was replaced by a voluntary gift from the merchants of the City.

19-22: The old merchant corresponds to the mercantile City which "insures its name" by giving a new frigate, the *Loyal London*, to replace the lost one. The traditional comic figure of the City merchant cuckolded by courtiers is here applied to the manning of the ship by gentlemen volunteers. The citizens who pay for the ship through "voluntary" subscriptions of silver plate are then in the strange position of servants who must pay for the guests' breakage, and *glasses prove more durable than plate* because exempt from such drives for "contributions."

23-24: The warships are compared to the floats or barges of the various merchant companies in the processions which took place annually in the City on Lord Mayor's day.

25-38: Sir William Coventry (1628-86) was noted for his venality in selling offices in the navy.

Iron and copper *Sweden*, *Münster* Warre,
Ashley, prize, Warwick, customs, Cart'ret, pay;
But Coventry sells the whole Fleet away.
   Now let our navy stretch its canvas Wings
Swoln like his Purse, with tackling like its strings,   40
By slow degrees of the increasing gaile,
First under Sale, and after under Saile.
Then, in kind visit unto *Opdams* Gout,
Hedge the *Dutch* in only to let them out.
(So Huntsmen faire unto the Hares give Law,
First find them, and then civilly withdraw)
That the blind *Archer*, when they take the Seas,
The Hamburgh Convoy may betray at ease.
(So that the fish may more securely bite
The Fisher baits the River over night.)   50
   But *Painter* now prepare, t'inrich thy Piece,
Pencill of Ermins, Oyle of Ambergris.
See where the *Dutchesse*, with triumphant taile
Of num'rous Coaches *Harwich* does assaile.
So the Land-Crabbs at Natures kindly call,
Down to engender at the Sea do crawle.
See then the Admirall, with navy whole
To Harwich through the Ocean caracole.
So Swallows bury'd in the Sea, at Spring
Returne to Land with Summer in their Wing.   60
   One thrifty Ferry-boat of Mother-Pearl
Suffic'd of old the *Cytherean Girle*.

36. *Münster:* A bishop with a large mercenary army who signed an alliance with England in return for Dutch territories to which he had a dubious claim.
37. *Ashley:* Antony Ashley Cooper, later first Earl of Shaftesbury, was treasurer of prizes. *Warwick:* Sir Philip Warwick, an official in the office of the treasury. *Carteret:* Sir George Carteret, treasurer of the navy.
43. *Opdam:* Jacob Wassenaer, Baron von Opdam, commander of the Dutch fleet.
47–48: British merchantmen from Hamburg were captured by the Dutch through the carelessness of the convoy commander, Captain Archer.
51–72: A burlesque account of the Duchess of York's visit to the fleet at Harwich in May.
59–60: An allusion to the discredited theory that swallows are torpid in winter.
61–62: After her birth from sea-foam Venus was borne on a seashell to the island of Cytherea.

Yet Navys are but Properties when here,
A small Sea-masque, and built to court you, Dear;
Three Goddesses in one: *Pallas* for Art,
Venus for sport, and *Juno* in your Heart.

　　O *Dutchesse*, if thy nuptiall Pomp were mean,
Tis payd with intrest in this navall Scene!
Never did *Roman Mark*, within the *Nile*,
So feast the faire *Egiptian Crocodile*,   70
Nor the *Venetian Duke*, with such a State,
The *Adriatick* marry at that rate.

　　Now, *Painter*, spare thy weaker art, forbear
To draw her parting Passions and each Tear;
For Love, alas, has but a short delight:
The Winds, the *Dutch*, the *King*, all call to fight.
She therefore the *Dukes* person recommends
To *Bronkard*, *Pen*, and *Coventry*, as Freinds:
(*Pen* much, more *Bronkard*, most to *Coventry*)
For they, she knew, were all more 'fraid than shee.   80

　　Of flying Fishes one had sav'd the finne,
And hop'd with these he through the Aire might spinne,
The other thought he might avoid his Knell
In the invention of the diving Bell,
The third had try'd it and affirm'd a Cable
Coyl'd round about men was impenetrable.
But these the *Duke* rejected, only chose
To keep far off, and others interpose.

　　Rupert, that knew not fear but health did want,

63. *Properties:* Stage properties.
67: The Duchess, the former Anne Hyde, daughter of the Lord Chancellor
Clarendon, was pregnant when she was secretly married in her father's house on
September 3, 1660.
69–70: Compare the refrain to Cleveland's "Mark Antony" (1647): "Never Mark
Antony/Dalli'd more wantonly/With the fair Egyptian Queen."
71–72: The ritual wedding of Venice to the Adriatic on Ascension Day still
commemorates that city's maritime importance.
78. *Coventry:* Sir William, secretary to the Duke of York. *Bronkard:* William, second
Lord Brouncker, a navy commissioner. *Pen:* Sir William Penn, a navy
commissioner and admiral of the Duke of York's flagship. He was severely
criticized for taking refuge in a coil of cable during the battle.
81–86: Allusions to flying fish and the diving bell (introduced from Sweden in
1661) are of course fanciful.
89. *Rupert:* Prince Rupert, Count Palatine of the Rhine and Duke of Bavaria, had
been a distinguished royalist officer in the Civil Wars. He was ill at this time

Kept State suspended in a *Chais-volant*.   90
All, save his head, shut in that wooden case,
He show'd but like a broken Weather-glasse:
But arm'd in a whole Lion Cap-a-chin,
Did represent the *Hercules* within.
Dear shall the *Dutch* his twinging anguish know
And feele what Valour, whet with Pain, can do.
Curst in the mean time be the Traitresse *Jael*
That through his Princely Temples drove the Naile.
  Rupert resolv'd to fight it like a Lyon.
But *Sandwich* hop'd to fight it like *Arion*:   100
He, to prolong his Life in the dispute,
And charm the *Holland* Pirats, tun'd his Lute:
Till some judicious Dolphin might approach,
And land him safe and sound as any Roach.
  Now *Painter* reassume thy Pencill's care,
It hath but skirmisht yet, now Fight prepare,
And draw the Battell terribler to show
Than the *Last Judgment* was of *Angelo*.
  First, let our Navy scowr through Silver Froath,
The Ocean's burthen, and the Kingdomes both: 110
Whose ev'ry Bulk may represent its Birth
From *Hide*, and *Paston*, Burthens of the Earth:
Hide, whose transcendent Paunch so swells of late,
That he the Rupture seems of Law, and State;
Paston, whose Belly bears more Millions
Than *Indian* Caricks, and contains more Tunns.
  Let sholes of Porpisses on evry side
Wonder in swimming by our Oakes outvy'd:
And the Sea Fowle at gaze behold a thing
So vast, more strong, and swift than they of Wing: 120

(of venereal disease, the poem suggests) and used a *Chais-volant*, some type of
enclosed and suspended chair.
93. *Lion:* The symbol of the Palatine. Hercules wore the skin of the Nemean lion he
had slain. *Cap-a-chin*: Head-to-chine (chine = backbone).
97. *Jael:* Slew Sisera by driving a nail into his head while he slept. See Judges 4.
100. *Sandwich:* Edward Montagu, Earl of Sandwich, admiral of the Blue squadron
at the Battle of Lowestoft. *Arion* was a Greek poet of the seventh century B.C. who
was supposed to have been rescued at sea by a dolphin.
112. *Hide:* Edward Hyde, Lord Chancellor Clarendon. *Paston:* Sir Robert Paston,
M.P. from Norfolk, who on February 9, 1665 moved the unprecedented sum of
£2,500,000 for the war.   116. *Caricks:* Carracks.

But with presaging Gorge yet keep in sight,
And follow for the Relicks of a Fight.
   Then let the *Dutch* with well dissembled Fear
Or bold Despaire, more than we wish draw near.
At which our Gallants, to the Sea but tender,
And more to fight, their easy Stomachs render:
With Breast so panting that at evry stroke
You might have felt their Hearts beat through the Oake.
While one, concern'd most, in the intervall
Of straining Choler, thus did cast his Gall.   130
   "*Noah* be damn'd and all his Race accurst,
That in Sea brine did pickle Timber first.
What though he planted Vines! he Pines cut down.
He taught us how to drink, and how to drown.
He first built ships, and in the wooden Wall
Saving but Eight, ere since indangers all.
And thou *Dutch* necromantic Friar, damn'd
And in thine own first Mortar-piece be ram'd,
Who first inventedst Cannon in thy Cell,
Nitre from Earth, and Brimstone fetcht from hell,   140
But damn'd and treble damn'd be *Clarendine*
Our Seventh *Edward* and his House and Line,
Who, to divert the danger of the Warre
With *Bristoll*, hounds us on the *Hollander*;
Foole-coated Gown-man, sells, to fight with *Hans*,
Dunkirk; dismantling *Scotland* quarrels *France*,
And hopes he now hath bus'nesse shap't and Pow'r
T'outlast his Life or ours, and scape the *Tow'r*:

---

137. *Dutch necromantic Friar:* Berthold Schwartz, a fourteenth-century German, who helped to develop gunpowder and adapt it to military uses.

141-142: The poet sarcastically places the Earl of Clarendon as seventh in England's royal line of Edwards.

143-144: The Earl of Bristol brought a charge of treason against Clarendon in the House of Lords in 1663. Bristol was banished for two years.

145. *Gown-man:* A civilian as distinguished from a soldier. *Hans:* A Dutchman.

145-146: In 1662 Clarendon negotiated the sale of Dunkirk to France on the grounds that it was inadequate as a harbor and that its continued possession might provoke a war with France. He then dismantled forts which Cromwell had built in Scotland and in 1665 rejected France's attempted mediation between England and Holland.

And that he yet may see, ere he go down,
His dear *Clarinda* circled in a Crown." 150
   By this time both the Fleets in reach debute
And each the other mortally salute.
Draw pensive *Neptune* biting of his Thumms,
To think himself a Slave whos'ere orecomes,
The frighted Nymphs retreating to the Rocks,
Beating their blew Breasts, tearing their green Locks;
Paint *Echo* slain: only th' alternate Sound
From the repeating Canon does rebound.
   Opdam sailes in, plac'd in his navall Throne,
Assuming Courage greater than his own; 160
Makes to the *Duke*, and threatens him from farr
To naile himself to's Board like a Petarre:
But in the vain attempt takes Fire too soon,
And flyes up in his Ship to catch the Moon.
Monsieurs like Rockets mount aloft, and crack
In thousand Sparks, then dansingly fall back.
   Yet ere this happen'd Destiny allow'd
Him his Revenge, to make his Death more proud.
A fatall Bullet from his Side did range,
And batter'd *Lawson*, O too dear Exchange! 170
He led our Fleet that Day, too short a Space,
But lost his Knee, (dy'd since) in Gloryes Race,
Lawson, whose Valour beyond Fate did go
And still fights *Opdam* through the Lakes below.
   The *Duke* himself, though *Pen* did not forget,
Yet was not out of dangers random set.
Falmouth was there, I know not what to act
(Some say 'twas to grow Duke too by Contact.)
An untaught Bullet in its wanton Scope
Quashes him all to pieces, and his Hope. 180
Such as his Rise such was his Fall, unprais'd;

149-150: Clarendon was often charged by satirists with dynastic ambitions in promoting his daughter's marriage to the Duke of York.
162. *Petarre*: A petard, a small explosive charge for breaching walls or gates, etc.
170. *Lawson*: Sir John Lawson, a vice-admiral who died of wounds.
177. *Falmouth*: Charles Berkeley, Earl of Falmouth, Lord Fitzharding, whose death deeply affected the King and the Duke of York.

A Chance-shot sooner took than Chance him rais'd:
His Shatterd Head the fearlesse *Duke* distains,
And gave the last first proof that he had Brains.
　Barkley had heard it soon, and thought not good
To venture more of Royall *Harding's* Blood.
To be immortall he was not of Age
(And did ev'n now the *Indian* Prize presage),
But judg'd it safe and decent, cost what cost,
To lose the Day, since his Dear Brother's lost.　　　190
With his whole Squadron streight away he bore
And, like good Boy, promist to fight no more.
　The *Dutch Urania* carelesse at us saild,
And promises to do what *Opdam* faild.
Smith to the *Duke* does intercept her Way
And cleaves t' her closer than the *Remora*.
The Captaine wonder'd, and withall disdain'd
So strongly by a thing so small detain'd:
And in a raging Brav'ry to him runs.
They stab their Ships with one anothers Guns,　　　200
They fight so near it seems to be on Ground,
And ev'n the Bullets meeting Bullets wound.
The Noise, the Smoak, the Sweat, the Fire, the Blood
Is not to be exprest nor understood.
Each Captaine from the Quarter-deck commands,
They wave their bright Swords glitt'ring in their hands;
All Luxury of Warre, all Man can do
In a Sea-fight, did passe betwixt them two.
But one must conquer whosoever fight:
Smith tooke the Giant, and is since made Knight.　　　210
　Marleburgh, that knew and dar'd too more than all,

---

185. *Barkley*: William Berkeley, second Viscount Fitzharding, Falmouth's younger
brother. His conduct in the battle was condemned as cowardly.
188: That is, anticipate the capture and illegal sharing of prizes from the captured
Dutch East Indiaman as described in ll. 291–306.
193–210: Capt. Sebastian Senten commanding the *Urania* had sworn to board the
Duke of York's ship, but Capt. Jeremy Smith intervened and captured the *Urania*
and 200 men. Smith was knighted for this exploit.
196. *Remora*: A sucking fish which attaches itself to larger fish.
211–222: James Ley, third Earl of Marlborough, expressed his strong
presentiment of death in a letter to a friend written aboard the *James* near the coast
of Holland, May 27, 1665.

Falls undistinguisht by an Iron Ball.
Dear Lord, but born under a Starre ingrate!
No Soule so clear, and no more gloomy Fate.
Who would set up Warr's Trade that meant to thrive?
Death picks the Valiant out, the Cow'rds survive.
What the Brave merit th'Impudent do vaunt,
And none's rewarded but the Sycophant.
Hence, all his Life he against Fortune fenc'd;
Or not well known, or not well recompens'd.   220
But envy not this Praise to's Memory:
None more prepar'd was or lesse fit to dye.
  Rupert did others and himself excell:
Holmes, Teddyman, Minns; bravely *Samson* fell.
What others did let none omitted blame:
I shall record whos'ere brings in his Name.
But unlesse after Storyes disagree,
Nine onely came to fight, the rest to see.
  Now all conspires unto the Dutchmen's Losse:
The Wind, the Fire, we, they themselves do crosse.   230
When a Sweet Sleep the *Duke* began to drown,
And with soft Diadem his Temples crown.
But first he orders all beside to watch;
And they the Foe while he a Nap should catch.
  But *Bronkard*, by a secreter instinct,
Slept not, nor needs it; he all Day had wink't.
The *Duke* in Bed, he then first draws his Steele,
Whose Virtue makes the misled Compasse wheele:
So ere he wak'd, both Fleets were innocent,
And *Bronkard* Member is of Parliament.   240
  And now, dear *Painter*, after pains like those

---

224. *Holms, Teddyman, Minns:* Naval captains. Robert *Sansom*, rear-admiral of
Prince Rupert's squadron, was killed in the battle.
229–240: Henry Brouncker, confidant of the Duke of York, gave orders to
Harman, the flagship's captain, to shorten sail. At that time the Duke was napping
after the engagement and the Dutch were fleeing toward their coasts. Harman,
accepting the orders as authorized by the Duke, allowed the enemy fleet to escape.
Brouncker seems to have been terrified of another battle. After a Parliamentary
investigation he was expelled from his recently-won seat in the House of
Commons.

'Twere time that thou and I too should repose.
But all our Navy scap'd so sound of Limm
That a small space serv'd to refresh its trimm.
And a tame Fleet of theirs does Convoy want,
Laden with both the *Indyes* and *Levant*.
Paint but this one Scene more, the world's our own:
The *Halcyon Sandwich* does command alone.

    To *Bergen* now with better Maw we haste,
And the sweet spoyles in Hope already taste,   250
Though *Clifford* in the Character appears
Of *Supracargo* to our Fleet and theirs,
Wearing a signet ready to clap on,
And seize all for his Master *Arlington*.

    Ruyter, whose little Squadron skim'd the Seas
And wasted our remotest Colonyes,
With Ships all foule return'd upon our Way;
Sandwich would not disperse, nor yet delay,
And therefore, like Commander grave and wise,
To scape his Sight and Fight, shut both his Eyes,   260
And, for more State and surenesse, *Cuttins* true
The left Eye closes, the right *Montague*,
And even *Clifford* profer'd, in his Zeale
To make all safe, t'apply to both his Seale.
Ulisses so, till he the *Syrens* past,
Would by his Mates be pinion'd to the Mast.

    Now may our Navy view the wished Port
But there too (see the Fortune!) was a Fort.
Sandwich would not be beaten, nor yet beat:
Fooles only fight, the Prudent use to treat.   270
His Cousin *Montague*, by Court disaster

245. *tame Fleet:* Rich Dutch merchantmen returning from the East Indies which the English intended to capture or destroy.

249-254: Sir Gilbert Talbot, English envoy at Copenhagen, was negotiating with the King of Denmark a joint attack on the Dutch merchantmen which had taken refuge in neutral Danish harbors. *better Maw:* Better appetite. *Clifford:* Sir Thomas Clifford, confidential agent of Arlington, the secretary of state, who was involved in the scheme to attack the Dutch ships at Bergen.

255-266: The Dutch admiral Michael de Ruyter, homeward bound from harrying the English in Guinea, managed to elude a fleet under the command of Sandwich (and Cuttins, his captain) by hugging the Danish coast.

271-282: Edward Montague, Sandwich's cousin, dismissed from his post as Master of the Horse to the Queen, now master of the wooden horse contrived against the Dutch at Bergen. The Bod. MS. has a marginal note: "Montagu

Dwindled into the wooden Horse's Master,
To speak of Peace seem'd among all most proper,
Had *Talbot* then treated of nought but Copper,
For what are Forts when void of Ammunition?
With Freind or Foe what would we more condition?
Yet we three dayes, till the *Dutch* furnisht all—
Men, Powder, Cannon, Money—treat with *Wall*.
Then *Teddy*, finding that the *Dane* would not,
Sends in Six Captains bravely to be shot.   280
And *Montague*, though drest like any Bride,
Though aboard him too, yet was reacht and dy'd.
    Sad was this Chance, and yet a deeper Care
Wrinkles our Membranes under Forehead faire.
The *Dutch Armada* yet had th' Impudence
To put to Sea, to waft their Merchants hence.
For, as if all their Ships of Wall-nut were,
The more we beat them, still the more they bear.
But a good Pilot and a fav'ring Winde
Bring *Sandwich* back, and once again did blind.   290
    Now gentle *Painter*, ere we leap on Shore,
With thy last strokes ruffle a Tempest o'er:
As if in our Reproach, the Winds and Seas
Would undertake the *Dutch* while we take Ease,
The Seas their Spoiles within our Hatches throw,
The Winds both Fleets into our Mouthes do blow,
Strew all their Ships along the Coast by ours,
As easy to be gather'd up as Flow'rs.

---

was Master of the Horse to the Queen. One day, as he led her, he tickled her palm.
She asked the King what that meant. The King by this means getting knowledge
of it, turned Montagu out of his place."

    The rest of this difficult passage seems to mean that if Talbot had not
prolonged negotiations by insisting on a Danish declaration of war the Dutch ships
could have been captured while there were no arms or ammunition to defend
them. *Wall* personifies Danish intransigence. *Teddy*, Sir Thomas Tyddiman,
commander of the British squadron.

287–288: An allusion to the old saying, "A woman, ass, and walnut tree, the more
you beat the better be."

291–306: A violent storm early in September dispersed the heavily laden East
Indiamen. Sandwich was criticized for his failure to attack and win a decisive
victory, although this would have entailed a night battle in rough weather on a lee
shore. He contented himself with distributing prizes from the *Phoenix* and *Slothony*
among his officers. Because the distribution was made without a warrant from the
prize commission, Sandwich was removed from his command and sent on an
embassy to Spain.

But *Sandwich* fears for Merchants to mistake
A Man of Warre, and among Flow'rs a Snake.   300
Two *Indian* Ships pregnant with Eastern Pearle
And Di'monds sate the Officers and *Earle*;
Then warning of our Fleet, he it divides
Into the Ports, and he to *Oxford* rides,
While the *Dutch* reuniting, to our Shames,
Ride all insulting o'er the *Downs* and *Thames*.
　　Now treating *Sandwich* seems the fittest choice
For *Spain*, there to condole and to rejoyce.
He meets the *French*, but, to avoyd all harms,
Slips to the *Groyne* (Embassyes bear not Arms!)   310
There let him languish a long *Quarantain*,
And ne'er to *England* come till he be clean.
　　Thus having fought we know not why, as yet,
We've done we know not what, nor what we get.
If to espouse the Ocean all this paines,
Princes unite and will forbid the Baines;
If to discharge Fanaticks, this makes more,
For all Fanatick turn when sick or poore;
Or if the *House of Commons* to repay,
Their Prize Commissions are transfer'd away;   320
But for triumphant Checkstones, if, and Shell
For *Dutchesse*' Closet, 't has succeeded well.
If to make Parliaments all odious passe,
If to reserve a Standing Force, alas,
Or if, as just, *Orange* to reinstate,
Instead of that, he is regenerate;
And with four Millions vainly giv'n, as spent,
And with five Millions more of detriment,
Our Summe amounts yet only to have won
A Bastard *Orange* for Pimp *Arlington*.   330
　　Now may Historians argue Con and Pro:

307–312: En route to Spain, Sandwich was forced by a storm to take shelter in
Corunna (the *Groyne*) where, in violation of his diplomatic mission, he seized a
Dutch merchantman.　　316. *Baines:* Banns.
321–322: The Duchess of York, the poet suggests, was one of the few beneficiaries
of this costly naval war. *Checkstones:* Counters used in a children's game. *Shell*: Cant
word for money.
330. *Bastard Orange:* Arlington was married to the daughter of Louis of Nassau,
illegitimate son of Prince Maurice. As *pimp* he induced Louise de Kéroualle, later
Duchess of Portsmouth, to become Charles' mistress.

Denham saith thus, though *Waller* always so,
But he, good Man, in his long Sheet and Staffe
This Penance did for *Cromwell's* Epitaph.
And his next Theme must be of *th' Duke's Maistress*:
Advice to draw *Madam Edificatresse*.
    Henceforth, O Gemini! two *Dukes* command:
Castor and *Pollux, Aumarle, Cumberland*.
Since in one Ship, it had been fit they went
In *Petty's* double-keel'd *Experiment*.   340

To the King
    Imperiall *Prince*, King of the Seas and Isles,
Dear Object of our Joys and Heaven's Smiles,
What boots it that thy Light does guild our Dayes
And we lye basking by thy milder Rayes,
While Swarms of Insects, from thy warmth begun,
Our Land devour, and intercept our Sunn?
    Thou, like *Jove's Minos*, rul'st a greater *Crete*
(And for its hundred Cityes count thy Fleet.)
Why wilt thou that *State-Dedalus* allow,
Who builds thee but a Lab'rinth and a Cow?   350
If thou art *Minos*, be a Judge Severe,
And in's own Maze confine the Engineer,
Or if our Sunn, since he so near presumes,
Melt the soft wax with which he imps his Plumes,
And let him falling leave his hated Name
Unto those Seas his Warre hath set on Flame.
From that Enchanter having clear'd thine Eyes,

332. *Denham*: The poet pretends that the poem was written by Sir John Denham, who was known at this time to be insane. Denham's friend, Edmund Waller, had written an elegy on Cromwell.   335-336: "Denham's" next assignment will be to write a poem about the Duke of York's mistress who happened to be the wife of the royal architect, the real Sir John Denham (hence her title, *Madam Edificatresse*). The subject is in contrast to Waller's fulsome eulogy on the Duke's wife in "Instructions to a Painter."   338. *Aumarle*: George Monck, Duke of Albemarle, the remarkable soldier, sailor and statesman who was the architect of the Restoration. *Cumberland*: Prince Rupert, who also held the title of Duke of Cumberland.   340: Sir William Petty designed a double-keeled ship, the *Experiment*.   349-350. *State-Dedalus*: Refers to Clarendon, the chief architect of English policy, and the lines parody Waller's comparison of Charles to Minos at the end of "Instructions to a Painter." Where Daedalus built a labyrinth for the Minotaur, Clarendon, by his evil policies, has confined Charles himself in a labyrinth and provided him with a cow (the barren Queen?).

Thy Native Sight will pierce within the Skyes,
And view those Kingdomes calm of Joy and Light
Where's universall Triumph but no Fight,   360
Since both from Heav'n thy Race and Pow'r descend,
Rule by its pattern, there to reascend.
Let Justice only draw: and Battell cease.
Kings are in War but Cards: they're Gods in Peace.

The third Advice to a Painter
London. October 1st 1666

　　Sandwich in *Spain* now, and the *Duke* in Love,
Let's with new *Gen'ralls* a new *Painter* prove.
Lilly's a *Dutchman*, danger in his Art:
His Pencills may intelligence impart.
Thou *Gibson*, that among thy Navy small
Of marshall'd Shells commandest Admirall,
Thy self so Slender that thou show'st no more
Than Barnacle new hatcht of them before,

364: In war kings are but playing-cards, powerless instruments of their ministers. *The third Advice to a Painter*: After the royal family had compelled the Duke of York to avoid the risks entailed in the position of Lord High Admiral, and his successor, the Earl of Sandwich, had been cashiered for misappropriating prizes, command of the navy was vested jointly in the versatile George Monck, Duke of Albemarle, and the aging, ailing Prince Rupert. "The Third Advice" picks up the story of the naval war against Holland early in the summer of its second year (1666) when the fleet was divided and that portion of it under Albemarle was only saved from total destruction in the Four Days' Battle (June 1–4) by Rupert's last-minute appearance.

　　"The Third Advice" introduces a new feature into the painter poem convention by entrusting most of the narrative (ll. 201–434) to Albermarle's plain-spoken and viraginous lady: as the poet says to the painter, "Paint thou but her, and she will paint the rest" (l. 172). The device permits Marvell to criticize the conniving and opportunistic politicians who feared the Presbyterian Monck while they were forced to use him and at the same time to expose the reckless bravado of Albemarle and the coarseness of his low-born wife. This technique results in portraits that are unusually well-balanced: satire does not obliterate a lingering respect for the indomitable leader or even for his crude and ill-mannered wife.　　1: Sandwich was in Spain from May 1666 to September 1668. The Duke of York was in love with the young wife whom Sir John Denham had married in May 1665.　　2. *Gen'ralls:* Commanding officers at sea.

3. *Lilly:* Sir Peter Lely, a famous court painter.

5. *Gibson:* Richard Gibson, a dwarf who painted miniatures.

Come, mix thy water colours, and expresse,
Drawing in little, how we do yet lesse.   10
    First, paint me *George* and *Rupert*, ratling far
Within one box, like the two Dice of War:
And let the terrour of their linked Name
Fly through the aire like chainshot, tearing Fame.
Jove in one cloud did scarsely ever wrap
Lightning so fierce, but never such a Clap.
United *Gen'ralls!* sure the only spell
Wherewith *United Provinces* to quell.
Alas, ev'n they, though shell'd in treble Oake
Will prove an addle Egge with double Yolke.   20
    And therefore next uncouple either Hound,
And loo them at two Hares ere one be found.
Rupert to *Beaufort* hollow: "Ay there, *Rupert!*"
Like the phantastick hunting of *St. Hubert*,
When he with airy Hounds, and Horn of aire,
Pursues by *Fountainbleau* the witchy Hare.
Deep Providence of State, that could so soon
Fight *Beaufort* here ere he had quit *Toulon!*
So have I seen, ere humane quarrells rise,
Foreboding Meteors combate with the Skyes.   30
    But let the *Prince* to fight with rumour goe:
The *Gen'rall* meets a more substantiall Foe.
Ruyter he spyes, and, full of youthful heat,
Though half their Number, thinks his odds too great.
The Fowler so watches the watry spot
And, more the Fowle, hopes for the better shot.
Though such a Limbe were from his Navy torn,
He found no weaknesse yet, like *Samson* shorn,
But swoln with sense of former Glory won,
Thought *Monk* must be by *Albemarle* outdon.   40
Little he knew, with the Same Arm and Sword,
How far the Gentleman outcuts the Lord.
    Ruyter, inferior unto none for Heart,
Superior now in Number and in Art,

---

18. *United Provinces:* Holland.
23–28: In May 1666 a squadron of twenty ships under Rupert was detached to
attack French warships commanded by the duc de Beaufort reported to be in the
Bay of Biscay. Beaufort was actually still in the Mediterranean.

Askt if he thought (as once our rebell Nation)
To conquer theirs too by a Declaration.
And threatens, though he now so proudly saile,
He shall tread back his *Iter Boreale*.
This said, he the short Period, ere it ends,
With iron words from brazen mouths extends.   50
   Monk yet prevents him ere the Navyes meet,
And charges in, himself alone a Fleet.
And with so quick and frequent motion wound
His murd'ring sides about, the Ship seem'd round,
And the Exchanges of his circling Tire
Like Whirling hoopes show'd of triumphall Fire.
Single he does at their whole Navy aime,
And shoots them through, a Porcupine of Flame.
He plays with danger, and his Bullets trowles,
As 'twere at *Trou Madam*, through all their Howles.   60
In noyse so regular his Cannon met,
You'd think that Thunder were to Musick set.
Ah, had the rest but kept a time as true,
What Age could such a Martiall Consort shew?
   The listning aire, unto the distant shoare,
Through secret Pipes conveys the tuned roare:
Till, as the Echoes vanishing abate,
Men feel a deaf sound, like the Pulse of Fate.
If Fate expire, let *Monk* her place supply:
His Gunns determine who shall live or dye.   70
   But Victory does always hate a Rant:
Valour her Brave, but Skill is her Galant.
Ruyter no lesse with virtuous envy burns,
And Prodigyes for Miracles returns.
Yet Shee observ'd how still his iron Balls
Bricold in vain against our oaken Walls,
And the hard Pellets fell away, as dead,
Which our enchanted timber fillipped.
"Leave then," said she, "th' invulnerable Keele:
We'll find their foible, like *Achilles'* heele."   80
   He, quickly taught, pours in continuall clowds

48. *Iter Boreale:* The northern journey which Monck took from Scotland which led
to the restoration of Charles II.
60. *Trou Madam:* A game in which balls were rolled into holes.
76. *Bricold:* Recoiled.   78. *fillipped:* Struck smartly.

Of chaind Dilemmas through our sinewy Shrowds.
Forrests of Masts fall with their rude embrace:
Our stiffe Sailes masht are netted into Lace,
Till our whole Navy lay their wanton Marke,
Nor any Ship could saile but as the Arke.
Shot in the wing, so, at the Powders call
The disappointed Bird does flutt'ring fall.
Yet *Monk*, disabled, still such Courage shows
That none into his mortall gripe durst close.   90
So an old Bustard, maim'd, yet loath to yeild,
Duells the Fowler in *Newmarket Field*.
But soon he found 'twas now in vain to fight
And imps his Plumes the best he may for Flight.
    This, *Painter*, were a noble task, to tell
What indignation his great Breast did swell.
Not vertuous Men unworthily abus'd,
Not constant Lovers without cause refus'd,
Not honest Merchant broke, not skillfull Play'r
Hist off the Stage, not Sinner in despayre,   100
Not losing Rookes, not Favourites disgrac't,
Not *Rump* by *Oliver* or *Monk* displac't,
Not Kings depos'd, not Prelates ere they dye,
Feele half the rage of Gen'ralls when they fly.
    Ah, rather than transmit our scorn to Fame
Draw Curtains, gentle *Artist*, o'er this Shame.
Cashiere the Mem'ry of *Dutell*, raisd up
To taste in stead of Death's, his *Highnesse*' Cup.
And, if the thing were true, yet paint it not:
How *Barclay*, as he long deserv'd, was shot,   110
Though others, that surveyd the Corpse so clear,
Say he was only petrify'd with Fear,
And the hard Statue, mummy'd without Gumme,

---

88. *disappointed:* Unprepared.   91. *Bustard:* A large bird.

102. *Rump:* The Parliamentary remnant after Pride's Purge (sixteen who were
displaced by Cromwell when he assumed the Protectorate and restored after the
fall of Richard Cromwell only to be displaced a second time by Monck).

107-108. *Dutell:* A Frenchman dismissed by Albemarle because, in the words of
Lady Albemarle, he "fired more shot into the Prince's ship and others of the king's
ships than of the enemy." The Duke of York employed him as cupbearer.

110. *Barclay:* William Berkeley, censured for cowardice at the Battle of Lowestoft.
Compare "The Second Advice," ll. 185-192, p. 124.

Might the *Dutch* Balm have spar'd and *English* Tombe.
Yet if thou wilt, paint *Mings* turn'd all to Soule;
And the great *Harman* chark'd almost to coale:
And *Jordan* old, thy Pencills worthy paine,
Who all the way held up the *Ducall* Traine.
But in a dark cloud cover *Askue*, when
He quit the Prince t' imbarke in *Loovesten*,   120
And wounded Ships, which we immortall Boast,
Now first led captive to an hostile Coast.
   But most, with story of his Hand or Thum,
Conceale, as honour would, his *Grace's* Bum.
When the rude Bullet a large Collop tore
Out of that Buttock, never turn'd before.
Fortune it seem'd would give him, by that lash,
Gentle correction for his Fight so rash.
But should the *Rump* perceive't, they'd say that *Mars*
Had now reveng'd them upon *Aumarle's* Arse.   130
   The long disaster better o're to veile,
Paint only *Jonas* three days in the Whale,
Then draw the youthfull *Perseus*, all in haste,
From a Sea-Beast to free the Virgin chaste:
But neither riding *Pegasus* for speed,
Nor with the *Gorgon* sheilded at his need.
For no lesse time did conqu'ring *Ruyter* chaw
Our flying Gen'rall in his spungy Jaw.
So *Rupert* the Sea-dragon did invade,
But to save *George* himself, and not the Maid,   140
And so, arriving late, he quickly mist
Ev'n Sailes to fly, unable to resist.
   Not *Greenland* Seamen, that survive the fright

115. *Mings:* Sir Christopher Myngs, leading the van, was shot in the throat on the fourth day of the battle. He stopped the wound with his fingers and continued to give orders. He died a few days after the battle.
116. *Harman:* Sir John Harman, rear-admiral of the White. The Dutch set fire to his ship, many of his men deserted him, and he was pinned by a falling mast, but nevertheless managed to extinguish the fire and refit during the night.
117. *Jordan:* Capt. Sir Joseph Jordan, knighted for his bravery at Lowestoft, commander of the *Royal Oak*, covered Albemarle's retreat.
119-120: Sir George Ayscue, admiral of the White, ran the *Royal Prince* aground on Galloper Sands. He was captured by the Dutch who treated him ignominiously and imprisoned him in the Castle of Lowestein.

Of the cold Chaos, and half-eternall Night,
So gladly the returning Sun adore,
Or run to spy their next years Fleet from Shoare,
Hoping, yet once, within the oyly side
Of the fat Whale againe their Spears to hide,
As our glad Fleet, with universall shout,
Salute the *Prince*, and wish the second bout.   150
Nor Winds, long Pris'ners in Earth's hollow Vault,
The fallow Seas so eagerly assault,
As firy *Rupert*, with revengefull Joy,
Does on the *Dutch* his hungry Courage cloy.
But, soon unrigg'd, lay like an uselesse board,
As wounded in the wrist men drop the Sword;
When a propitious Clowd betwixt us stept
And in our aid did *Ruyter* intercept.
Old *Homer* yet did never introduce,
To save his Heroes, Mist of better use.   160
Worship the Sun, who dwell where he does rise:
This Mist does more deserve our Sacrifice.

Now joyfull Fires, and the exalted Bell,
And Court-gazets our empty Triumph tell;
Alas: the time draws near, when overturn'd
The lying Bells shall through the tongue be burn'd;
Paper shall want to print that Lye of State,
And our false Fires true Fires shall expiate.

Stay, *Painter*, here awhile, and I will stay:
Nor vex the future Times with nice survey.   170
Sees't not the *Monkey Dutchesse*, all undrest?
Paint thou but her, and she will paint the rest.

The sad Tale found her in her outer Roome
Nailing up Hangings, not of *Persian* loome,
Like chaste *Penelope*, that ne'r did rome,
But made all fine against her *George* came home;
Upon a Ladder, in her coat most shorter,
She stood, with Groome and Porter for Supporter.
And carelesse what they saw, or what they thought,
With *Hony pensy* honestly shee wrought.   180

165–168: An allusion to the Great Fire of London, which broke out in September.
171. *all undrest:* En *déshabillé*.
180. *Hony pensy:* Albemarle was a member of the Order of the Garter, whose motto
is *Honi soit qui mal y pense*.

For in She-Gen'rall's Britch, none could (she knows)
Carry away the piece with Eyes or Nose.
One Tenter drove, to lose no time nor place,
At once the Ladder they remove and *Grace*.
While thus they her translate from North to East,
In posture just of a foure-footed Beast,
She heard the News: but alter'd yet no more
Than that what was behind she turn'd before;
Nor would come down; but with an hankecher,
Which pocket foule did to her neck prefer,   190
She dry'd no Tears, for she was too viraginous:
But only snuffing her Trunk cartilaginous,
From scaling Ladder she began a Story,
Worthy to be had in me(mento)mory,
Arraigning past, and present, and futury;
With a prophetick (if not spirit) Fury.
Her Haire began to creep, her Belly sound,
Her Eyes to startle, and her Udder bound.
Half Witch, half Prophet, thus *she-Albermarle*,
Like *Presbyterian Sibyll*, out did Snarle.   200
    "Traytors both to my *Lord* and to the *King*,
Nay now it grows beyond all suffering:
One valiant Man on land, and he must be
Commanded out to stop their leaks at Sea!
Yet send him *Rupert*, as an helper meet:
First the command dividing, ere the Fleet.
One may, if they be beat, or both be hit,
Or if they overcome, yet Honour's split;
But reck'ning *George* already knockt o' th' head,
They cut him out like Beef, ere he be dead.   210
Each for a quarter hopes: the first does skip,
But shall snap short though, at the *Gen'ralship*:
Next they for *Master of the Horse* agree:
A third the *Cockpit* begs; not any mee.
But they shall know, ay, marry shall they do,
That who the *Cockpit* has shall have me too.

183. *Tenter:* Tenter-hook, for fastening the hangings.
213: Albemarle had been Master of the Horse to the King since 1660.
214. *Cockpit:* Albemarle's lodgings in the palace at Whitehall.

"I told *George* first, as *Calamy* did me,
If the *King* these brought over, how 'twould be:
Men, that there pickt his Pocket to his Face,
To sell intelligence or buy a Place, 220
That their Religion pawn'd for Clothes; nor care
('T has run so long) now to redeem't, nor dare.
O what egregious Loyalty to cheat!
O what Fidelity it was to eat!
While *Langdales, Hoptons, Glenhams* Starv'd abroad,
And here true *Royalists* sunk beneath the load.
Men that did there affront, defame, betray
The *King*, and do so here, now who but they?
What, say I Men? nay rather Monsters: Men
Only in Bed, nor (to my knowledge) then. 230
    "See how they home return, in revell rout,
With the same Measures that they first went out.
Nor better grown, nor wiser all this while,
Renew the causes of their first Exile,
As if (to show you Fooles what 'tis I mean)
I chose a foule Smock, when I might have clean.
    "First, they for Fear disband the Army tame
And leave good *George* a *Gen'ralls* empty Name,
Then Bishops must revive, and all unfix
With discontent to content twenty six. 240
The *Lords House* drains the Houses of the Lord,
For Bishops voices silencing the *Word*.
O *Bartlemew*, Saint of their Calender!
What's worse? thy *Ejection* or thy *Massacre*?
Then *Culp'per, Gloster*, ere the *Princesse*, dy'd:

217. *Calamy:* Edmund Calamy, celebrated Puritan divine, had been appointed one of Charles II's chaplains in 1660, a post which he quickly resigned.
225. *Langdales, Hoptons, Glenhams:* Devoted royalists.
237-238: Most of the army was disbanded as an economy measure after the Restoration.
239-242: Bishops again sat in the House of Lords after the Restoration. In 1660 a bill to modify the rigid Anglican service and extend indulgences to Nonconformists was defeated in the Commons by 26 votes.
243-244. *Bartlemew:* The Act of Uniformity under which Nonconformist ministers were expelled from their churches took effect on August 24, 1662, the anniversary of the St. Bartholomew's Day Massacre (1572).
245. *Culp'per:* Sir John Culpeper, who helped bring about the King's restoration, died in the summer of 1660. *Gloster:* Henry, Duke of Gloucester, and Princess

Nothing can live that interrupts an *Hide*.
O more than human *Gloster*! Fate did shew
Thee but to Earth, and back againe withdrew.
Then the fat *Scriv'ner* durst begin to think
'Twas time to mix the royall Blood with ink.   250
Barclay, that swore, as oft as she had Toes
Does, kneeling, now her chastity depose,
Just as the first *French Card'nall* could restore
Maidenhead to his Widdow-Niece and Whore.
For Portion, if she should prove light when weigh'd,
Four Millions shall within three years be paid.
To raise it, we must have a Navall War:
As if 'twere nothing but Tara-tan-tar.
Abroad all Princes disobliging first,
At home, all Partyes but the very worst.   260
    "To tell of *Ireland*, *Scotland*, *Dunkirk's* sad,
Or the *Kings* Marriage; but he thinks I'm mad.
And sweeter creature never saw the Sun,
If we the *King* wisht Monk, or *Queen* a Nun.
But a *Dutch* war shall all these rumours still,
Bleed out these Humours, and our Purses spill.
Yet, after one Dayes trembling Fight, they saw
'Twas too much danger for a Son-in-Law.

Mary, brother and sister to Charles II, both died in the same year.

246. *an Hide:* A punning reference to the Duchess of York, insinuating that she tried to ensure her husband's succession to the throne by eliminating the immediate heirs.

249-252: An allusion to the alleged dynastic ambitions of Anne's father, the Earl of Clarendon. Sir Charles Berkeley, later Lord Falmouth, who had repeatedly sworn that Anne was an immoral woman, subsequently denied these oaths. He was a close friend of the King and the Duke and was killed in the Battle of Lowestoft. Compare "The Second Advice," ll. 177-184, pp. 123-124.

253-254: Possibly a covert allusion to the representation of clerics' mistresses as nieces.

261: See "The Second Advice," ll. 141-146 and note, p. 122. The reference to Ireland has to do with the release of restrictions on the Irish Catholics.

262. *the Kings Marriage:* To the barren Catherine de Braganza. *but he thinks I'm mad:* The poet has momentarily forgotten that not Denham but the Duchess of Albemarle is speaking. See introductory note.

267-270: After Lowestoft, Parliament voted James £120,000 "in token of the great sense they had of his conduct and bravery in the late engagement." They followed this up with a humble address to the King asking him not to allow James to risk his life again. Charles readily acceded to this appeal.

Hire him to leave with six score thousand pound;
As with the *Kings* Drumms men for sleep compound.   270
Then modest *Sandwich* thought it might agree
With the State-prudence, to do lesse than he,
And, to excuse their timrousnesse and sloth,
They've found how *George* might now do lesse than both.
   "First, *Smith* must for *Legorn*, with Force enough
To venture back againe, but not go through.
Beaufort is there, and, to their dazeling Eyes,
The distance more the object magnifyes.
Yet this they gain, that *Smith* his time shall lose
Herewith assembles the supream *Divan*,
   "But fearing that our Navy, *George* to break,
Might yet not be sufficiently weake,
The *Secretary* that had never yet
Intelligence but from his own gazett,
Discovers a great secret, fit to sell,
And pays himself for't ere he would it tell.
Beaufort is in the *Chanell*. Hixy, here:
Doxy, *Toulon: Beaufort* is ev'ry where!
Herewith assembles the supream *Divan*,
Where enters none but *Devill, Ned*, and *Nan*:   290
And, upon this pretence, they streight design'd
The Fleet to sep'rate, and the world to blind.
Monk to the *Dutch*, and *Rupert* (here the Wench
Could not but smile) is destin'd to the *French*.
To write the order *Bristoll's Clerke* they chose;
(One slit in's Pen, another in his Nose)
For he first brought the News, and 'tis his Place:
He'll see the Fleet devided like his Face,

275–280: Sir Jeremy Smith was dispatched to the Straits of Gibraltar to protect the Levant trade and then recalled too late to help Albemarle.
281–314: The intelligence service was operated by Arlington, the secretary of state. The only licensed newspaper, the *London Gazette*, drew its news from this source and reported in May that Beaufort was in the Channel. *Hixy* and *Doxy*: Juggler's patter. The whole passage sees the division of the fleet as a plot by the Duchess of York, Clarendon, and Arlington to destroy Albemarle.
295–300: Arlington had been secretary to the Earl of Bristol. In the Civil War he had suffered a cut on the nose which he accentuated with a strip of black plaster. *The Dutch chink* refers to his wife.

And through that cranny in his gristly part,
To the *Dutch* chink intelligence may start.   300
The Plot succeeds: the *Dutch* in haste prepare,
And poore pilgarlick *George's* Arse they share.
And now, presuming of his certaine wrack,
To help him late they write for *Rupert* back.
Officious *Will* seem'd fittest, as afraid
Lest *George* should looke too far into his Trade.
On the first draught they pause with Statesmen's care,
Then write it faire, then copy't out as faire,
Then they compare them; when at last 'tis sign'd,
Will soon his purstrings but no seale could find.   310
At night he sends it by the common Post
To save the *King* of an Expresse the cost.
Lord what adoe to pack one letter hence!
Some Patents passe with lesse circumference.
    "Well, *George*, in spight of them thou safe dost ride,
Lessen'd, I hope, in nought but thy Back-side.
For as to reputation, this retreat
Of thine exceeds their Victoryes so great.
Nor shalt thou stirre from thence, by my consent,
Till thou hast made the *Dutch* and them repent.   320
'Tis true I want so long the nuptiall gift,
But, as I oft have don, I'l make a Shift.
Nor with vain Pomp will I accost the Shore
To try thy Valour at the *Buoy-i'th'-nore*.
Fall to thy worke there, *George*, as I do here:
Cherish the valiant up, the cow'rd cashiere.
See that the Men have Pay and Beef and Beere;
Find out the cheats of the foure-millioneer.
Out of the very Beer they steale the Malt,
Powder out of Powder, from powder'd Beef the Salt.   330
Put thy hand to the Tub: instead of Ox,
They victuall with *French* Pork that has the Pox.

---

302. *pilgarlick:* An expression of mock pity.
305. *Officious Will:* The venal Sir William Coventry. See "The Second Advice,"
ll. 25–38 and notes, pp. 118–119.
322: A pun on Lady Albemarle's former occupation as seamstress.

Never such Cotqueans by small arts to wring:
Ne'r such ill Huswives in the managing.
Pursers at Sea know fewer cheats than they:
Mar'ners on Shore lesse madly spend their Pay.
See that thou hast new Sailes thy self, and spoyle
All their Sea-market and their cable-coyle.
Tell the *King* all, how him they countermine;
Trust not, till don, him with thy own designe.   340
Looke that good Chaplains on each Ship do wait,
Nor the Sea-Diocesse be impropriate.
Looke to the Pris'ners, sick, and wounded; all
Is Prize: they rob even the Hospitall.
Recover back the Prizes too: in vain
Wee fight if all be taken that is ta'en.

    "Now by our Coast the *Dutchmen*, like a flight
Of feeding Ducks, morning and ev'ning light.
How our *Land Hectors* tremble, voyd of sense!
As if they came streight to transport them hence.   350
Some Sheep are stoln, the Kingdome's all array'd:
And ev'n *Presbit'ry's* now call'd out for aid.
They wish ev'n *George* divided to command;
One half of him the Sea, and one the Land.

    "What's that I see? ha! 'tis my *George* agen:
It seems they in sev'n weeks have rigg'd him then.
The curious Heav'n with Lightning him surrounds
To view him, and his name in Thunder sounds,
But with the same shaft gores their Navy near,
As ere we hunt, the Keeper shoots the Deere.   360
Stay Heav'n a while, and thou shalt see him saile,
And how *George* too can lighten, thunder, haile.
Happy the time that I thee wedded, *George*,
The Sword of *England*, and of *Holland* scourge.
Avant *Rotterdam-dog*, *Ruyter*, avant!
Thou Water-rat, thou shark, thou Cormorant:
I'll teach thee to shoot scizzers! I'll repaire
Each rope thou losest, *George*, out of this haire.
Ere thou shalt lack a saile and lye a drift
('Tis strong and course enough) I'll cut this Shift.   370
Bring home the old ones, I again will sew,

342. *impropriate:* Annexed. Used particularly of ecclesiastical benefices.
367. *scizzers:* Chain-shot, used against rigging.

And darn them up to be as good as new.
What twice disabled? Never such a thing!
Now, *Souveraigne*, help him that brought in the *King*;
Guard thy Posteriour left, lest all be gone:
Though Jury-Masts, th' hast Jury-buttocks none.
Courage! How bravely, whet with this disgrace,
He turns, and Bullets spits in *Ruyter's* Face!
They fly, they fly! Their Fleet does now divide:
But they discard their *Trump*; our *Trump* is *Hide*.   380
    "Where are you now, *De Ruyter*, with your bears?
See how your Merchants burn about your ears.
Fire out the wasps, George, from their hollow trees,
Cramm'd with the honey of our *English* Bees.
Ay, now they're paid for *Guiny*: ere they steere
To the gold coast, they find it hotter here.
Turn theyr ships all to Stoves, ere they set forth
To warm their traffick in the frozen North.
Ah *Sandwich!* had thy conduct been the same,
Bergen had seen a lesse, but richer Flame,   390
Nor *Ruyter* liv'd new Battell to repeat,
And oftner beaten be than we can beat.
    "Scarse has *George* leisure, after all this pain,
To tye his Briches: *Ruyter's* out againe.
Thrice in one year! why sure the man is wood:
Beat him like Stockfish, or he'll ne'r be good.
I see them both prepar'd againe to try:
They first shoot through each other with the Eye;
Then—But that ruling Providence that must
With humane Projects play as Winds with dust,   400
Raises a Storm, (so Constables a fray
Knock down) and sends them both well cuft away.

373–376: The *Gazette* for June 4–7, 1666, reported with rare humor: "The Duke had all his tackle taken off by chain shot, and his breeches to the skin were shot off, but he rigged again with jury masts, and fell into the body of the Dutch fleet, where he attacked de Ruyter."

380: Admiral Tromp was drawn off in a separate action from the main engagement. The poet makes the far-fetched suggestion that the English follow the Dutch example by discarding Clarendon.

385: De Ruyter's fleet had returned the year before from harassing English settlements in Guinea. Compare "The Second Advice," ll. 255–266 and note, p. 126.

396. *Stockfish:* Dried salted fish that must be pounded before cooking.

Plant now *Virginian* Firrs in *English* Oke,
Build your Ship-ribbs proof to the Cannon's stroke,
To get a Fleet to Sea, exhaust the Land,
Let longing Princes pine for the Command:
Strong Marchpanes! Wafers light! so thin a puffe
Of angry aire can ruine all that huffe!
So Champions having shar'd the Lists and Sun,
The Judge throws down his Warder and they've done.   410
For shame come home, *George*: 'tis, for thee, too much
To fight at once with *Heaven* and the *Dutch*.

"Woe's me, what see I next? Alas the Fate
I see of *England*, and its utmost date.
Those flames of theirs, at which we fondly smile,
Kindled, like Torches, our Sepulchrall Pile.
Warre, Fire, and Plague against us all conspire:
We the Warre, *God* the Plague, who rais'd the Fire?
See how Men all, like Ghosts, while *London* burns,
Wander and each over his ashes mourns!   420
Dear *George*, sad Fate, vain Mind that me didst please
To meet thine with far other Flames than these!

"Curst be the Man that first begot this Warre,
In an ill houre, under a blazing Starre.
For other's sport, two Nations fight a Prize:
Between them both Religion wounded dyes.
So of first *Troy*, the angry Gods unpaid,
Ras'd the foundations which themselves had lay'd.

"Welcome, though late, dear *George:* here hadst thou been,
We'd scap'd (let *Rupert* bring the Navy in!)   430
Thou still must help them out when in the mire:
Gen'rall at Land, at Sea, at Plague, at Fire.
Now thou art gone, see, *Beaufort* dares approach:
And our whole Fleet, angling, has catcht a Roach."

Gibson, farewell, till next we put to Sea:
Faith thou hast drawn her in effigie!

407. *Marchpanes:* Marzipan, a light confectionery.

To the King
  Great *Prince*, and so much greater as more wise,
Sweet as our Life, and dearer than our Eyes:
What Servants will conceale, and Couns'lours spare
To tell, the Painter and the Poet dare.   440
And the assistance of an heavn'ly Muse
And Pencill represents the Crimes abstruse.
  Here needs no Sword, no Fleet, no foraine Foe;
Only let Vice be damm'd, and Justice flow.
Shake but like *Jove*, thy locks divine, and frowne;
Thy Scepter will suffice to guard thy Crowne.
Hark to *Cassandra's* Song, ere Fate destroy,
By thy own Navy's wooden horse, thy *Troy*.
Us our *Apollo*, from the Tumult's wave,
And gentle gales, though but in Oares, will save.   450
  So *Philomel* her sad embroyd'ry strung,
And vocall silks tun'd with her Needle's tongue.
(The Picture dumbe, in colours lowd, reveal'd
The tragedy's of *Court*, so long conceal'd.)
But, when restor'd to voice, increas'd with Wings,
To Woods and Groves what once she painted sings.

Clarindon's *House-warming*

  i
When *Clarindon* had discern'd before hand
(As the Cause can eas'ly foretell the Effect)

449–450: Apollo was a patron deity of Troy. According to legend, England was
Troynovant. *Oares* here are small boats as opposed to men-of-war.
451–456: The Duchess of Albemarle is compared to Philomel, who was raped by
Tereus and had her tongue cut out. She resorted to needlework to reveal the crime.
Clarindon's House-warming: From the Restoration to 1666, the Lord Chancellor
Clarendon moved from one rented house to another until, with the King's
encouragement, he commissioned an enormous and ostentatious building in Hyde
Park. Completed when London was suffering from the disastrous effects of war,
plague, and fire, it immediately became the focal point of public resentment and
was known as Dunkirk House on the assumption that it was financed out of
Clarendon's unpopular sale of Dunkirk to the French in 1662. In "Clarendon's
House-warming" Marvell converts to satiric use the architectural motif which
plays a key role in "Upon Appleton House" and "The First Anniversary."

At once three deluges threatning our land,
'Twas the season, he thought, to turn Architect.

ii

Us *Mars* and *Apollo* and *Vulcan* consume,
While he, the betrayer of *England* and *Flander*,
Like the Kings-fisher chuses to build in the brume,
And nestles in flames like the Salamander.

iii

But (observing that Mortalls run often behind,
So unreasonable are the rates that they buy at)   10
His omnipotence, therefore, much rather design'd
How he might create an House with a fiat.

iv

He had read of *Rhodopis*, a Lady of *Thrace*,
That was digg'd up so often ere she did marry:
And wisht that his Daughter had had as much Grace
To erect him a Pyramid out of her Quarry:

v

But then (recollecting how harper *Amphion*
Made *Thebes* danse aloft while he fidled and sung)
He thought (as an instrument he was most free on)
To build with the Jews-trump of his own toungue.   20

vi

Yet a Precedent fitter in *Virgil* he found
Of *African Poltney* and *Tyrian Dide*

5. *Mars, Apollo, Vulcan:* War, plague, fire.   6. *Flander:* Holland.
7. *brume:* Winter, when the kingfisher was believed to build its nest.
13-16. *Rhodopis:* A celebrated courtesan who built a pyramid out of her earnings.
The allusion is to the alleged pre-marital love affairs of the Duchess of York.
Compare "Third Advice," ll. 251-254, p. 138, and "Last Instructions," ll. 49-54,
p. 153.
17-18: Amphion built the walls of Thebes with stones miraculously fitted together
by the music of his lyre.   20. *Jews-trump:* Jews' harp.
21-24: King Iarbas of Carthage granted Dido as much land as might be enclosed
with the hide of an ox. Dido cut the hide into fine strips and thus acquired a much
larger site than Iarbas had intended to give her (*Aeneid*, I, 367).
22. *Poltney:* One of the original owners of the land acquired by Clarendon.
(Margoliouth)

That she begg'd, for a Palace, so much of his ground
As might carry the measure and name of an Hide.

vii

Thus daily his gowty invention he paind;
And all for to save the expense of brick-bat,
That Engine so fatall which *Denham* had brain'd
And too much resembled his Wife's Chocolatt.

viii

But while these devices he all does compare
None solid enough seem'd for this Thong-caster: 30
He himself would not dwell in a Castle of aire,
Though he'd built full many an one for his *Master*.

ix

Already he'd got all our money and cattell
To buy us for slaves and to purchase our lands:
What *Joseph* by famine, he wrought by Sea-battell;
Nay scarce the Priests portion could scape from his hands.

x

And, hence-forth, like *Pharao*, that Israel prest
To make mortar and brick yet allow'd 'm no straw,
He car'd not though *Egypt's* ten Plagues us infest,
So he could but to build make that Policy Law.   40

24: Compare the pun on Anne Hyde's name in "Third Advice," l. 246, p. 138.
26. *brick-bat:* Bricks.
27-28: Allusions to the madness of Sir John Denham in 1666, here ascribed to an accident befalling him in the course of his duties as surveyor of the King's Works, and to the death of Lady Denham, mistress of the Duke of York, in January 1667. Lady Denham believed she had been poisoned by a cup of chocolate.
30. *Thong-caster:* The castle (Latin *caster*) built on land enclosed by the oxhide thong.
35-36: Joseph bought up land in Egypt during the famine with corn he had stored up in the years of good harvests (Genesis 47:13-26) and Clarendon is seen as using the war with Holland for the same purpose.

xi

The *Scotch-forts* and *Dunkirke*, but that they were sold,
He would have demolisht to raise up his Walls;
Nay even from *Tangier* sent back for the Mold,
But that he had nearer the Stone of *St. Pauls*.

xii

His wood would come in at the easyest rate,
As long as the yards had a deale or a sparre:
His freind in the Navy would not be ingrate
To grudge him for timber, who fram'd him the War.

xiii

To proceed on this Moddell, he call'd in his *Allans*—
The two *Allans* when joviall that ply him with galons,   50
The two *Allans* that serve his blind justice for balance,
The two *Allans* that serve his injustice for talons.

xiv

They approv'd it thus far and said it was fine,
Yet his *Lordship* to finish it would be unable
Unlesse all abroad he divulg'd the designe:
But his House then would grow like a vegetable.

41: In Clarendon's administration four forts which Cromwell had built in
Scotland were dismantled and Dunkirk was sold to the French. Compare "Second
Advice," ll. 145-146, p. 122.
43. *Tangier:* Part of Queen Catherine's dowry. England constructed a large mole
(mold) there in the hope of making it a major naval station.
44: Clarendon bought the stones of old St. Paul's, which had burned down in the
Great Fire, to complete his house.
49-52: Sir Allen Apsley and Sir Allen Broderick were liberally rewarded by
Charles II and James II for their loyalty to the Stuart cause. Broderick was
described as "bribe-broker for his master the Chancellor." They were heavy
drinkers and boon companions.

xv

His rent would no more in arreare run to *Worster;*
He should dwell more nobly and cheaper too at home,
While into a fabrick the presents would muster,
As by hooke and by crooke the world clustered of Atome.   60

xvi

He lik'd the advice and they soon it assay'd;
And presents crowd headlong to give good example;
So the Bribes overlayd her that *Rome* once betrayd;
The Tribes ne'r contributed so to the Temple.

xvii

Streight Judges, Priests, Bishops (true sons of the *Seale*)
Sinners, Governors, Farmers, Banquiers, Patentees
Bring in the whole milk of a yeare at a meale:
As all *Chedder* Dairies club to th' incorporate Cheese.

xviii

Bulteale's, *Bealin's*, *Morley's*, *Wren's* fingers with telling
Were shrivled, and *Clutterbook's*, *Eager's*, and *Kipps*:   70
Since the *Act of Oblivion* was never such selling
As at this benevolence out of the snipps.

57. *Worster:* Clarendon had rented Worcester House for £500 a year.
60: According to Epicurean science atoms clung together as if by hooks.
63: The daughter of Tarpeius, commander of a Roman citadel, offered to betray the citadel to the Sabines in exchange for what they had on their left arms, meaning their gold bracelets, but they crushed her to death under their shields. (Margoliouth)
65: Clarendon was Keeper of the Great Seal and took the lead in restoring episcopacy.   66. *Farmers:* Tax-farmers. *Patentees:* Holders of monopolies.
68: Milk from a number of dairies was pooled to make Cheddar cheese.
69–70: All these names refer to underlings of Clarendon whom Marvell imagines to be employed in telling the "contributions."
71. *Act of Oblivion:* Passed after the Restoration, confirming the validity of sales of land made voluntarily during the Interregnum. Many new owners made haste to sell their holdings.
72. *benevolence:* A voluntary contribution to the revenue. *snipps:* Perquisites.

xix

'Twas then that the Chimney contractors he smok'd
Nor would take his belov'd Canary in kind:
But he swore that the Patent should ne'r be revok'd,
Not, would the whole *Parliament* kisse him behind.

xx

Like *Jove* under *Ætna* orewhelming the *Giant*,
For foundation he *Bristoll* sunk in the earth's bowell;
And *St. John* must now for the Leads be complaint,
Or his right hand shall else be hackt off with a trowell.   80

xxi

For surveying the building *Prat* did the feate;
But for the expense he rely'd upon *Wost'holme*,
Who sat heretofore at the *Kings* receit,
But receiv'd now and paid the *Chancellor's* Custome.

xxii

By subsidyes thus both clerick and laick,
And of matter profane cemented with holy,
He finisht at last his Palace mosaick;
By a modell more excellent than *Leslye's-folly*.

73. *Chimney contractors:* Collectors of the chimney money or hearth tax, a form of revenue that was widely resented. *smok'd:* Took note of.

74-75: Clarendon is accused of extorting money from merchants who had a monopoly in trade with the Canary islands, chiefly in Canary wine.

78. *Bristoll:* After an unsuccessful attempt to impeach Clarendon in 1663, Bristol went into hiding to avoid arrest. See "Last Instructions," l. 933, p. 184.

79. *St. John:* Charles Paulet, Lord St. John of Basing, one of the farmers of the customs.

81. *Prat:* Roger Pratt, the architect, who greatly underestimated the cost of the house.

82. *Wost'holme:* Sir John Wostenholm, a farmer of the customs.

88. *Leslye's-folly:* A fortified palace built by Dr. John Leslie, Bishop of Orkney. (Margoliouth)

xxiii

And upon the Tarras to consummate all,
A Lantern, like *Fauxe's*, surveys the burnt town;   90
And shows, on the top, by the regall gold ball,
Where you are to expect the Scepter and Crowne.

xxiv

Fond City its rubbish and ruines that builds,
Like vain Chymists, a flowr from its ashes returning;
Your Metropolis-house is in St. James's feilds
And till there you remove you shall never leave burning.

xxv

This Temple of Warre and of Peace is the shrine
Where our *Idoll of State* sits ador'd and accurst:
And to hansell his Altar and nostrills divine
Greate *Buckingham's* Sacrifice must be the first.   100

xxvi

Now some, as all Builders must censure abide,
Throw dust on its front and blame situation:
And others as much reprehend his backside,
As too narrow by farre for his expatiation.

xxvii

But do not consider, in processe of times,
That, for name's sake, he may with *Hide-park* it enlarge;
And with what convenience he hence for his crimes
At *Tyburn* may land, and spare the *Tow'r-barge*.

---

89. *Tarras:* Terrace.
90. *Fauxe's*: Guy Fawkes, architect of the Gunpowder Plot, was captured with a dark-lantern, gunpowder, and matches in his possession. Clarendon's *lantern* was the cupola atop his house.   99. *hansell:* Inaugurate the use of.
100: George Villiers, second Duke of Buckingham, one of the richest and most powerful nobles of the period, had lost favor at court partly through his inveterate hostility to Clarendon.
104. *expatiation:* Expansion, with a reflection on Clarendon's corpulence.
108. *Tyburn:* With its celebrated gallows-tree, Tyburn was at the northeast corner of Hyde Park. The suggestion is that Clarendon may be taken more conveniently to Tyburn than down the Thames to the Tower where great malefactors were usually imprisoned or executed.

xxviii

Or rather, how wisely his Stall was built near,
Lest with driving too farre, his tallow impaire;   110
When like the whole Ox, for publick good cheare
He comes to be roasted next St. James's Faire.

The last Instructions to a Painter
London. September 4th, 1667

After two sittings, now, our Lady State,
To end her Picture, does the third time waite.
But ere thou falst to worke, first, *Painter*, see
It be'nt too slight grown or too hard for thee.
Canst thou paint without colors? Then 'tis right:
For so wee too without a Fleet can fight.
Or canst thou dawb a sign-post, and that ill?
'Twill suit our great debauch and little skill.
Or hast thou mark'd how antique Masters limn
The Aly roof with Snuffe of Candle dimme,   10
Sketching in shady smoke prodigious tooles?
'Twill serve this race of Drunkards, Pimps, and Fooles.
But if to match our crimes thy skill presumes,
As *th' Indians*, draw our Luxury in Plumes;
Or if to score out our compendious Fame,
With *Hooke*, then, through the *Microscope* take aim,

112. *St James's Faire:* That is, at the next meeting of Parliament fixed for St. James's Day, July 25, 1667.
1–2: Three sittings was the usual number for "limning" a portrait. The first two, of course, were described in the second and third "Advices."
6. *without a Fleet:* The fleet was laid up in May 1667.
9. *antique Masters:* Masters of grotesque painting.
10. *Aly roof:* Ceiling of an alehouse or tavern.
14: The Indians of Florida and the Caribbean developed the art of "painting" by arranging various colors and sizes of feathers and gluing them together. Such paintings were necessarily on a large scale. *Plumes* would also represent fittingly the luxury of the court.
15. *score out:* Sketch in outline. *compendious:* Minute.
16–18: Robert Hooke (1634–1703) was an experimental philosopher and fellow of the Royal Society. In his *Micrographia* (1665) he depicted various objects seen

Where, like the new *Controller*, all men laugh
To see a tall Lowse brandish the white staffe.
Else shalt thou oft thy guiltlesse Pencill curse,
Stamp on thy Pallat, nor perhaps the worse.   20
The Painter so, long having vext his cloth,
Of his Hound's mouth to feign the raging froth,
His desp'rate Pencill at the work did dart:
His Anger reacht that rage which past his Art;
Chance finisht that which Art could but begin,
And he sat smiling how his Dog did grin.
So mayst thou perfect, by a lucky blow,
What all thy softest touches can not do.
   Paint then *St. Albans*, full of soup and gold,
The new *Court's* patern, Stallion of the old.   30
Him neither Wit nor Courage did exalt,
But Fortune chose him for her pleasure Salt.
Paint him with Dray-man's shoulders, Butcher's Mien,
Member'd like Mules, with elephantine Chine.
Well he the title of *St. Albans* bore,
For *Bacon* never study'd Nature more.
But Age, allaying now that youthful heat,
Fits him in *France* to play at Cards and treat.
Draw no Commission, lest the *Court* should lie,

---

under the microscope, among which was a louse climbing a human hair, which
Marvell here compares to the new comptroller of the Household, Lord Clifford of
Chudleigh, who took office in November 1666. The comptroller carried a white
staff as the emblem of his office. (Margoliouth)

29. *St. Albans:* Henry Jermyn, Earl of St. Albans (d. 1684), was ambassador at the
French court at the beginning of Charles II's reign. He was sent to France in
January 1667 to negotiate a treaty with Louis XIV. In his youth he acquired the
reputation of a rake and was once banished from court for seducing Eleanor
Villiers, a Lady of Honor. He was rumored to have married Queen Henrietta
Maria and devoted his old age to the pleasures of the table and to cards.

35-36: In this couplet Marvell wrily compares the lecherous Earl of St. Albans
with the great exponent of the inductive approach to nature, Francis Bacon, first
Baron Verulam and Viscount St. Albans (1561-1626).

38. *treat*: (1) to entertain; (2) to negotiate a treaty.

39: The negotiations undertaken by St. Albans were at first informal and
unofficial, and Marvell attributes this failure to send a duly-authorized
ambassador with commission and seal to the court's desire for a large grant from
Parliament. Parliament did in fact vote £1,800,000, but there was much
resentment about alleged waste in the expenditure of earlier grants.

That disavowing Treaty asks supply.   40
He needs no Seale, but to *St. James's* Lease,
Whose briches wear the Instrument of Peace;
Who, if the *French* dispute his Pow'r, from thence
Can streight produce them a Plenipotence.
Nor fears he *The most Christian* should trepan
Two Saints at once, *St. Germain, St. Alban,*
But thought the golden Age was now restor'd,
When Men and Women took each others Word.
      Paint then again *Her Highnesse* to the life,
Philosopher beyond *Newcastle's* Wife.   50
She, nak'd, can *Archimedes* self put down,
For an experiment upon the Crown.
She perfected that Engine, oft assayd,
How after childbirth to renew a Maid,

41. *St. James's Lease:* St. Albans obtained a large grant of land in Pall Mall and planned St. James's Square.

42: This line seems to refer somewhat obscurely to St. Albans' widely-rumored affair with Henrietta Maria. Whether or not such an affair took place, his influence with the Queen Mother was great, and it was through her that Louis XIV was persuaded to consider negotiations for peace between Holland and Britain.

43-44: These lines carry on the suggestion of l. 42 about the source of St. Albans' authority to negotiate. "St. Albans' instructions, drafted by Clarendon, did not empower him even to sign preliminaries" (Keith Feiling, *British Foreign Policy, 1660-1672*).

45. *The most Christian*: Louis XIV. *trepan*: Entrap.

46. *St. Germain, St. Alban:* A play on the ambassador's name and title and on the quarter of Paris in which he resided.

49-78: Much popular gossip about Anne Hyde, Duchess of York, is assembled in this passage. She was secretly married to York on September 3, 1660, and gave birth to the short-lived Charles, Duke of Cambridge, less than two months after the ceremony (ll. 55-56), which was performed by Dr. Joseph Crowther, the Duke's chaplain. Lines 49-58 refer to the allegations against her chastity made by two of the Duke's friends, Sir Charles Berkeley and Henry Jermyn (St. Albans' nephew), who wished to prevent the recognition of the marriage. For further details see "Third Advice," ll. 251-254 and notes, p. 138.

      Margaret Brooke, Lady Denham, became York's mistress in 1665, and Sir John Denham's madness was widely attributed to grief at this development. She is the "Madam Edificatresse" referred to in "Second Advice," l. 336, p. 129, and is mentioned in the opening line of "Third Advice." Her sudden death on January 6, 1667 was thought, without evidence, to be from poison introduced into her cocoa, and Denham and the Countess of Rochester were both blamed. Marvell, however, introduces the suggestion that the Duchess of York was the culprit, an idea that agrees with the attack on her in "Third Advice," ll. 245-246, pp. 137-138.

53-54: The satirical pretense that the Duchess had discovered "how after childbirth to renew a Maid" appears also in "Third Advice," ll. 253-254

And found how Royall Heirs might be matur'd
In fewer Months than Mothers once indur'd.
Hence *Crowder* made the rare Inventresse free
Of's *Highnesse's* Royall Society:
Happy'st of Women, if she were but able
To make her glassen *Dukes* once malleable!   60
Paint her with Oyster lip, and Breath of Fame,
Wide Mouth, that Sparagus may well proclaime:
With *Chanc'lors* Belly, and so large a Rump
There, not behind the Coach, her Pages jump.
Expresse her studying now, if *China* clay
Can without breaking venom'd Juice convay,
Or how a mortall Poyson she may draw
Out of the cordiall meale of the Cacao.
Witnesse, ye starrs of Night, and thou the pale
Moon, that or'ecome with the sick steam didst faile;   70
Ye neighbring Elms, that your green leavs did shed,
And Fawns, that from the Wombe abortive fled!

---

p. 138, where the renewal of lost virginity is attributed jointly to Berkeley's recantation and, ironically, to the intervention of Cardinal Mazarin, who prevailed on Queen Henrietta Maria to drop her opposition to the marriage. Here Anne is presented as a *philosopher* (natural philosopher or scientist) and *inventress* whose *engine* (device) for restoring virginity makes her superior to her friend the famed bluestocking, Margaret, Duchess of *Newcastle*, and even to *Archimedes*. Archimedes founded the science of hydrostatics, as the well-known legend has it, by discovering the principle of displacement while taking a bath. He applied this principle in answering a question from a prince named Hiero, who feared that his gold crown might be alloyed with silver. In the same manner, Marvell suggests, the Duchess has devised some way of demonstrating that she is not a light woman and thereby could make *an experiment upon the crown*, that is, an attempt upon it, either for herself (as future queen) or through her children. A similar ambitiousness in the Hyde family is attributed to her father in "Second Advice," ll. 153-154, p. 123, and to Anne in "Third Advice," ll. 245-246, pp. 137-138.
58: The Duke of York was a charter member of the Royal Society.
60. *glassen Dukes:* A reference to the other short-lived children of this marriage: James, Duke of Cambridge (born July 12, 1663, died June 20, 1667) and Charles, Duke of Kendal (born July 4, 1666, and died May 22, 1667).
65-68: Margoliouth cites Browne, *Pseudodoxia Epidemica* (1646): "Surely the properties must be verified which by Scaliger and others are ascribed to china dishes, that they admit no poison, that they strike fire ... for such as pass amongst us ... will only strike fire, but not discover aconite, mercury, nor arsenic ..." (2, 5, sec. 7).
69-74: This description of the Duchess' black arts seems indebted in a general way to Ovid's account of Medea's trafficking in sorcery (*Metamorphoses*, 7).

Not unprovok'd, she trys forbidden Arts,
But in her soft Breast Love's hid Cancer smarts,
While she revolves at once *Sidney's* disgrace
And her self scorn'd for emulous *Denham's* Face.
And nightly hears the hated Guards away
Galloping with the *Duke* to other Prey.
    Paint *Castlemain* in Colors that will hold
(Her, not her Picture, for she now grows old).   80
She through her Lackyes drawers, as he ran,
Discern'd Love's cause, and a new Flame began.
Her wonted Joys, thenceforth, and *Court* she shuns,
And still within her Mind the Footman runs:
His brazen Calves, his brawny Thighs (the Face
She slights), his Feet shap'd for a smoother race.
Poring within her Glasse she readjusts
Her Lookes and oft-try'd Beauty now distrusts;
Fears lest he scorn a Woman once assayd,
And now first wisht she e'er had been a Maid.   90
Great Love, how dost thou triumph, and how reigne,
That to a Groom couldst humble her disdaine!
Stript to her Skin, see how shee stooping stands,
Nor scorns to rub him down with those faire Hands,
And washing (lest the Scent her Crime disclose)
His sweaty Hooves, tickles him 'twixt the Toes.
But envious Fame, too soon, begun to note
More gold in's fob, more lace upon his coat:
And he unwary, and of Tongue too fleet,
No longer could conceale his Fortune sweet.   100
Justly the Rogue was whipt in Porters Den,
And *Jermin* streight has leave to come agen.
Ah, *Painter*, now could *Alexander* live,
And this *Campaspe* thee, *Apelles*, give!

75: Henry Sidney (1636–1708), Groom of the Bedchamber to the Duke and
Master of the Horse to the Duchess, was dismissed as a result of the Duke's
jealousy.
79–104: Although most of Lady Castlemaine's many love affairs seem to be
minutely and extensively recorded, this seems to be the only account of her
alliance with the lackey.
104: Apelles was court painter to Alexander of Macedon, and fell in love with
Alexander's mistress, Campaspe.

Draw next a Paire of Tables op'ning, then
The *House of Commons* clat'ring like the Men.
Describe the *Court* and *Country*, both set right,
On opposite points, the black against the white:
Those having lost the Nation at Trick-track,
These now advent'ring how to win it back.   110
The Dice betwixt them must the Fate divide
(As Chance doth still in Multitudes decide).
But here the *Court* does its advantage know,
For the Cheat *Turner* for them both must throw.
As some from Boxes, he so from the Chaire
Can strike the Die and still with them goes share.
        Here, *Painter*, rest a little, and survey
With what small Arts the publick game they play.
For so too *Rubens* with affaires of State
His lab'ring Pencill oft would recreate.   120
        The close *Caball* markt how the Navy eats
And thought all lost that goes not to the cheats;
So therefore secretly for Peace decrees,
Yet as for Warre the *Parlament* would squeeze,
And fix to the Revenue such a summe
Should *Goodrick* silence, and strike *Paston* dumbe,
Should pay land Armyes, should dissolve the vain

109. *Trick-track:* A kind of backgammon on tables. The players (Men) represent
the two Parliamentary parties: the Court party, whose chiefs are enumerated in
ll. 113–238, and the Country party who appear in ll. 239–307. The battle, which is
won by the Country party with which Marvell's sympathies obviously lie, is fought
on the issue of a general excise which the Court party wished to impose in order to
raise the £1,800,000 (l. 332) voted late in 1666. The general excise was defeated on
November 8, 1666.
114. *Turner:* Sir Edward Turner or Turnor (1617–76), Speaker of the House of
Commons, 1661–73. *Cheat* may refer simply to several large gifts bestowed on him
from the treasury through royal favor, though he was later removed as Solicitor-
General, according to Roger North, for having received a trifling gratuity from
the East India Company.
116. *strike the Die:* Throw in some particularly fraudulent manner.
120. *recreate:* Refresh (by a change of occupation). Rubens was occasionally sent
on diplomatic missions.
121. *Caball:* A committee for foreign affairs drawn from the Privy Council.
126. *Goodrick:* Sir John Goodrick, M.P. for the county of York, who sometimes
acted as teller for the Court party during this session. (Margoliouth) Paston first
moved the huge appropriation of £2,500,000 for the war. See "Second Advice,"
ll. 109–116, p. 121.

Commons, and ever such a *Court* maintaine;
Hide's Avarice, *Bennet's* Luxury should suffice:
And what can these defray but the *Excise?*   130
Excise, a Monster worse than ere before
Frighted the Midwife and the Mother tore,
A thousand Hands she has, and thousand Eyes:
Breks into shops and into Cellars pryes,
With hundred rows of teeth the Sharke exceeds,
And on all trade like Casawar shee feeds:
Chops off the piece wheres'ere she close the Jaw,
Else swallows all down her indented maw.
She stalks all day in Streets conceal'd from sight
And flyes like Batts with leathern wings by night,   140
She wastes the Country and on Cityes preys:
Her, of a female *Harpy*, in Dog-dayes,
Black *Birch*, of all the earthborn race most hot
And most rapacious, like himself begot,
And, of his Bratt inamour'd, as't increast,
Bougred in incest with the mungrell Beast.
    Say, *Muse*, for nothing can escape thy Sight
(And, *Painter*, wanting other, draw this Fight)
Who in an *English Senate* fierce debate
Could raise so long for this new whore of State.   150
    Of early Wittalls first the Troop march'd in,
For Diligence renown'd and Discipline:
In loyall haste they left young Wives in Bed,
And *Denham* these by one consent did head.
Of the old Courtiers next a Squadron came,
That sold their *Master*, led by *Ashburnham*.
To them succeeds a despicable Rout,
But know the Word, and well could face about:

---

136. *Casawar:* The omnivorous cassowary.
142–146: In matter and manner this passage seems to be a mock-epic imitation of the incestuous relationship of Satan to his daughter Sin, which produced Death. See *Paradise Lost*, 2: 746–785. Milton's epic was first published in 1667.
143. *Birch:* John Birch (1616–91), excise official under the Protectorate and auditor after the Restoration.
151. *Wittalls:* Cuckolds.
156. *Ashburnham:* John Ashburnham (1603–71), who, with Sir John Berkeley, arranged King Charles I's flight to the Isle of Wight. For a long time he was suspected of having betrayed the King to the governor of the island.

Expectants pale, with hopes of Spoyle allur'd,
Though yet but Pioneers, and led by *Stew'rd*.   160
Then damning Cowards rang'd the vocall Plain:
Wood these commands, Knight of the Horn and Cane.
Still his hook-shoulder seems the blow to dread,
And under's Armpit he defends his Head.
The posture strange men laught at of his Poll,
Hid with his Elbow like the Spice he stole.
Headlesse *St. Dennis* so his Head does beare,
And both of them alike *French Martyrs* were.
Court Officers, as us'd, the next place tooke
And follow'd *Fox*, but with disdainfull looke.   170
His Birth, his Youth, his Brokage all dispraise,
In vain, for always he commands that payes.
Then the Procurers under *Prodgers* fil'd,
Gentlest of men, and his Lieutenant mild,
Bronkard, Love's squire; through all the field array'd
No Troop was better clad, nor so well•pay'd.
Then marcht the Troop of *Clarindon*, all full,
Haters of Fowle, to teale preferring Bull:

160. *Stew'rd:* James Butler, Duke of Ormonde, Lord Steward of the Household.
162. *Wood:* Sir Henry Wood (1597-1671), Clerk of the Spicery to Charles I, M.P. for Hythe, a Clerk Comptroller of the Board of Green Cloth, in which capacity he was responsible for maintaining order in the palace and for examining the accounts.
170. *Fox:* Sir Stephen Fox (1627-1716), M.P. for Salisbury and Paymaster-General. He came from a modest Wiltshire family, and after an early training in bookkeeping was employed by the Percys. In 1654 he took charge of Charles II's household.
171. *Brokage:* The premium or commission of a broker. Fox made a profit on money advanced to pay the soldiers.
173. *Prodgers:* Edward Progers, M.P. for Brecon and one of the King's procurers.
175. *Bronkard:* Henry Brouncker, cofferer to Charles II and Gentleman of the Bedchamber to the Duke of York, whom he served in the same capacity as Progers did Charles. He was dismissed from the court in August 1667 and expelled from Parliament in April 1668 for "bringing pretended orders from the Duke for lowering the sails" of the *Royal Prince* and thereby breaking off the pursuit of the Dutch in the Battle of Lowestoft. Compare "Second Advice," ll. 77ff., p. 120, ll. 233ff., p. 125.
178: A play on the name of John Bulteel, an M.P. for Lostwithiel and secretary to the Earl of Clarendon.

Grosse Bodyes, grosser Minds, and grossest cheats,
And bloated *Wrenn* conducts them to their seats.   180
Charlton advances next, whose coife does aw
The *Miter Troop*, and with his looks gives Law.
He marcht with beaver cockt of Bishop's brimme
And hid much Fraud under an aspect grimme.
Next th' Lawyers mercenary band appeare,
Finch in the Front, and *Thurland* in the reare.
The Troop of Privilege, a Rabble bare
Of Debtors deep, fell to *Trelawny's* care.
Their Fortunes error they supply'd in Rage,
Nor any further would than these ingage.   190
Then march't the Troop whose valiant Acts before
(Their publick Acts) oblig'd them still to more.
For Chimney's sake they all *Sir Poole* obey'd,
Or in his absence him that first it lay'd.
Then comes the thrifty Troop of Privateers,
Whose Horses each with other interferes:
Before them *Higgons* rides with brow compact,

180. *Wrenn:* Matthew Wren (1629–72), original member of the Royal Society and cousin of Christopher, M.P. for St. Michael, secretary to Clarendon, 1660–67, and to York, 1667–72.

181–182. *Charlton:* Sir Job Charlton (1614–97), M.P. for Ludlow and Chief Justice of Chester. *The Miter troop* presumably refers to a group of lawyers associated with Mitre Court, one of the Inns of Court since demolished. Charlton later became Speaker. Roger North described him as "an old Cavalier, loyal, learned, grave, and wise."

186. *Finch:* Heneage Finch (1621–82). Solicitor-General and member for Oxford University, who supported oppressive measures against Dissenters. Compare note to l. 256. *Thurland:* Sir Edward Thurland (1624–85), M.P. for Reigate and solicitor to the Duke of York.

187. *The Troop of Privilege:* Those who relied on the immunity of Parliamentary privilege to avoid arrest for debt.

188. *Trelawny:* Sir Jonathan Trelawny (1624–85) was ruined by sequestration, but, according to *Flagellum Parliamentarium* (1677), later made a fortune as an informer.

193: Sir Courtenay Pool, M.P. for Honiton, proposed the hated hearth tax (chimney money) of two shillings on every hearth in 1662.

195. *thrifty Troop of Privateers:* Those who, like Higgons (see below, l. 197) sought to enrich themselves by the passage of private bills, and whose horses are therefore represented as overriding each other.

197. *Higgons:* Sir Thomas Higgons (1624–91), Court party M.P. for New Windsor, who introduced a bill in the session of 1666–67 for the recovery of £4,500. Marvell reports the defeat of this bill on January 12, 1667. Higgons married the widow of the Earl of Essex and published an oration delivered at her funeral in 1656.

Mourning his *Countesse*, anxious for his *Act*.
Sir Frederick and *Sir Salomon* draw Lotts
For the command of Politicks or Sotts;   200
Thence fell to words, but, quarrell to adjourn,
Their freinds agreed they should command by turn.
Cart'ret the rich did the Accountants guide,
And in ill *English* all the World defy'd.
The *Papists*, but of these the *House* had none;
Else *Talbot* offer'd to have led them on.
Bold *Duncom* next, of the Projectors chief:
And old *Fitzharding* of the *Eaters Beef*.
Late and disorder'd out the Drinkers drew;
Scarce them their Leaders, they their Leaders knew.   210
Before them enter'd, equall in Command,
Apsly and *Brothrick*, marching hand in hand.
Last then but one *Powell*, that could not ride,
Led the *French* Standard, weltring in his stride.
He to excuse his slownesse, truth confest

199. *Sir Frederick and Sir Salomon:* Usually identified as Sir Frederick Hyde (Court party M.P. for Haverfordwest) and Sir Salomon Swale (Court party M.P. for Aldborough). Swale was a Roman Catholic and opposed the bill against recusants at this session.
200. *Politicks:* Politicians. *Sotts:* Drunkards.
203. *Cart'ret:* Sir George Carteret (d. 1680), treasurer of the navy after the Restoration. He served in the navy from childhood (see Samuel Pepys, *Diary*, July 4, 1663, on his lack of education) and resigned his post while the Dutch were in the Medway.
206: There were three Talbots in the Commons at this time, and two of them appear in *Flagellum Parliamentarium*: Sir Gilbert Talbot, "the King's jeweller, a great cheat at bowls and cards, not born to a shilling," and Sir John Talbot, "Commissioner of Prizes and a great cheater therein." The Talbots were an Irish Roman Catholic family.
207. *Duncom:* Sir John Duncombe, a Privy Councillor, once Commissioner of the Ordnance, now of the treasury, and Baptist May's brother-in-law. *Projectors:* Schemers, speculators, cheats.
208. *Fitzharding:* Sir Charles Berkeley (1600–68), second Viscount Fitzhardinge in the Irish peerage and treasurer of the Household, in which capacity he was in charge of the yeomen of the guard. This is the first known instance of their being called Beefeaters.
212. *Apsly:* Sir Allen Apsley (1616–83), treasurer of the Duke of York's household. *Brothrick:* Sir Allen Broderick, M.P. for both Orford and Callington (Cornwall). Compare "Clarindon's House-warming," note to ll. 49–52, p. 147.
213. *Powell:* Sir Richard Powell, Gentleman of the Horse to the Duchess of York. *French Standard* is an allusion to the pox, which caused him to *welter in his stride*.

That 'twas so long before he could be drest.
The Lords' Sons, last, all these did reinforce:
Cornb'ry before them manag'd Hobby-horse.
   Never, before nor since, a Host so steel'd
Troopt on to muster in the *Tuttle-field*.   220
Not the first cock-horse that with cork were shod
To rescue *Albermarle* from the Sea-Cod:
Nor the late Feather-men, whom *Tomkins* fierce
Shall with one Breath, like thistle-down disperse.
All the two *Coventrys* their Gen'ralls chose,
For One had much, the other nought to lose;
Nor better choice all accidents could hit,
While *Hector Harry* steers by *Will the Witt*.
They both accept the Charge with merry glee
To fight a Battell from all Gun-shot free.   230
   Pleas'd with their numbers, yet in Valor wise,
They feigne a Parly better to surprize:
They, that ere long shall the rude *Dutch* upbraid,
Who in a time of Treaty durst invade.
   Thick was the Morning, and the *House* was thin,

---

218. *Cornb'ry*: Henry Hyde, Lord Cornbury (1638-1709), Clarendon's eldest son, Chamberlain to the Queen. *Hobby-horse:* perhaps an allusion to his youth.
220. *Tuttle-field:* Tothill Fields, Westminster, used for drilling troops.
221-222: This obscure couplet alludes to the rescue of Albemarle by Rupert in the Four Days' Fight (June 1-4, 1666). *Sea-Cod* represents De Ruyter, who was prevented from destroying Albemarle's ship by Rupert's intervention. Compare the sea-dragon in "Third Advice," ll. 135-142, p. 134. *Cock-horse* shod with cork may refer obscurely to Rupert's career as a famous cavalry leader in the Civil Wars.
223-224: The *Feather-men* are probably the standing army raised by the government in the spring of 1667 ostensibly to prevent an invasion, which Sir Thomas Tomkins spoke against in the abortive Parliamentary session of July 25-29, 1667.
225-234: The *two Coventrys* are Henry (1619-86) and Sir William (1628?-86), who "practically led the House" (*Dictionary of National Biography*). Henry had "nought to lose" because, having concluded an embassy to Sweden, he was now without an appointment from the government, and Sir William much to lose, because he was commissioner of the treasury and of the navy and could protect the large profits allegedly made from these posts by active leadership of the Court party faction.   230: An allusion to Coventry's alleged cowardice at Lowestoft. See "Second Advice," ll. 77-80. p. 120.
233-234: Henry Coventry was one of the ambassadors who negotiated the Dutch peace, and his brother is held chiefly responsible for having failed to prepare the fleet on the grounds that peace was expected.
235: The Court party M.P.s proposed the grant of £1,800,000 for the King

The *Speaker* early, when they all fell in.
Propitious *Heavens*, had not you them crost,
Excise had got the Day, and all been lost!
For th' other Side all in loose Quarters lay,
Without Intelligence, Command, or Pay: 240
A scatter'd Body, which the Foe ne'r try'd,
But oftner did among themselves divide,
And some ran ore each night while others sleep
And undescry'd return'd ere Morning peep.
But *Strangeways*, that all night still walkt the round
(For vigilance and Courage both renown'd)
First spy'd the Enemy and gave th' Alarme:
Fighting it single till the rest might arm.
Such *Roman Cocles* strid: before, the Foe;
The falling Bridge behind, the Stream below,   250
Each ran, as Chance him guides, to sev'rall Post,
And all to patern his Example boast.
Their former Trophies they recall to mind,
And to new edge their angry Courage grind.
First enter'd forward *Temple*, Conqueror
Of *Irish* Cattell and *Sollicitor*;
Then daring *Seymor*, that with Spear and Shield
Had stretcht the monster *Patent* on the field;
Keen *Whorwood* next, in aid of Damsell fraile,

---

before all the Country party M.P.s had assembled. On October 12, "The Court party moved for a general excise of all things, which was no way pleasing" (Milward).   236. *Speaker:* Turner.

239. *loose Quarters:* The opposite of close quarters. Loose quarters are indefensible positions.

245. *Strangeways:* Sir John Strangeways, who acted as teller against the government in several divisions on finance during this session.

249. *Cocles:* Publius Horatius Cocles (Macaulay's "Horatius at the Bridge"), who defended single-handed a bridge leading into Rome against the army of Porsena, King of Etruria.

255. *Temple:* Sir Richard Temple, a leader of the Country party who supported the act against the importation of Irish cattle, a major issue in this session. The act passed in January 1667.

256. *Sollicitor:* Sir Heneage Finch (1621-82), Solicitor-General who spoke against the Irish Cattle Bill.

257. *Seymor:* Sir Edward Seymour (1633-1708), later Speaker of the House, who attacked the Canary Patent, a charter for merchants trading with the Canary Islands, as "an illegal patent, a monopoly, and a grievance to the subject."

259. *Whorwood:* Brome Whorwood, M.P. for the city of Oxford, who helped draw up an impeachment against John, Viscount *Mordaunt* (1627-75), constable of

That pierc't the Gyant *Mordant* through his Maile,   260
And surly *Williams*, the Accountants bane,
And *Lovelace* young, of Chimney men the Cane.
Old *Waller*, Trumpet-gen'rall, swore he'd write
This Combat truer than the navall Fight.
Of Birth, State, Wit, Strength, Courage, *How'rd* presumes
And in his Breast wears many *Montezumes*.
These and some more with single Valor stay
The adverse troops and hold them all at bay.
Each thinks his person represents the whole,
And with that thought does multiply his Soule,   270
Believes himself an Army, theirs one Man,
As eas'ly conquer'd, and believing, can;
With Heart of Bees so full, and Head of Mites,
That each, though duelling, a Battell fights.
Such once *Orlando*, famous in Romance,
Broach't whole Brigades like Larks upon his Lance.
    But strength at last still under Number bows,
And the faint sweat trickled down *Temple's* Brows.
Ev'n iron *Strangeways*, chafing yet gave back,
Spent with Fatigue, to breath a while Toback.   280
When, marching in, a seas'nable Recruit

Windsor Castle, who had allegedly imprisoned one William Tayleur because his
daughter would not yield herself to him. On July 8, the King granted Mordaunt a
pardon.
261. *Williams:* A committee to investigate public accounts was appointed
September 26, 1666. Caroline Robbins identifies Williams as Col. Henry Williams
(alias Cromwell), member for Huntingdon.
262. *Lovelace:* John Lovelace (1638?–93), an opponent of the widely-hated hearth
tax.
263–264. *Waller:* Waller was widely criticized as a political turncoat. "As far as his
public utterances went," however, "the second half of his Parliamentary career
was in every way creditable to him. He spoke with great courage against the
dangers of a military despotism, and his voice was constantly raised in appeals for
toleration for Dissenters . . ." (*Dictionary of National Biography*). Compare these lines
with the opening couplet of "Second Advice," p. 117. *Trumpet-gen'rall* may allude
to Waller's position as the poet who celebrates battles but does not participate in
them.
265–266. *How'rd:* Sir Robert Howard (1626–98), M.P. for Stockbridge and
collaborator and brother-in-law of Dryden with whom he wrote *The Indian Queen*
(1665), a drama whose hero is Montezuma. He was prominent in the proceedings
against Clarendon.
275–276: The hero of *Orlando Furioso* spitted six enemies at once on his
lance.   280. *Toback:* Tobacco.   281. *Recruit:* Reinforcements.

Of Citizens and Merchants held dispute;
And, charging all their pikes, a sullen Band
Of *Presbyterian Switzers* made a Stand.
   Nor could all these the Field have long maintain'd
But for th' unknown Reserve that still remain'd:
A grosse of *English* Gentry, nobly born,
Of clear Estates, and to no Faction sworn;
Dear Lovers of their *King*, and Death to meet
For Countryes Cause that glorious think and sweet;   290
To speak not forward, but in Action brave,
In giving gen'rous, but in Counsell grave;
Candidly credulous for once, nay twice,
But sure the *Devill* can not cheat them thrice.
The Van and Battell, though retiring, falls
Without disorder in their Intervalls,
Then, closing all in equall Front, fall on,
Led by great *Garway* and great *Littleton.*
Lee, ready to obey or to command,
Adjutant-Generall was still at hand.   300
The martiall standard, *Sands* displaying, shows
St. Dunstan in it tweaking *Satan's* Nose.
See sudden chance of Warre! To paint or write
Is longer Work and harder than to fight.
At the first Charge the Enemy give out

---

284. *Presbyterian Switzers:* Presumably a faction of Presbyterian members who joined the opposition.
298. *Garway:* William Garraway (Garway or Garroway), M.P. for Chichester, who examined Pepys' accounts October 3, 1666. According to Pepys, Sir William Coventry spoke of him as ill-used by the court but staunchly loyal to the King (October 6, 1666). He seconded Tomkins' motion against the standing army. *Littleton:* Sir Thomas Littleton (d. 1681), second Baronet, member for Great Wenlock, mentioned by Pepys as "one of the greatest speakers in the House" (July 18, 1666).
299. *Lee:* Sir Thomas Lee, member for Aylesbury. Pepys mentions him and Littleton as "professed enemies to us and everybody else," when he was examined by the House, March 5, 1668.
301. *Sands:* Col. Samuel Sandys, M.P. for Worcestershire.
302-303: "In art St. Dunstan is chiefly honoured by a foolish representation of the devil caught by the nose by a pair of blacksmith's pincers. The legend relates that Satan tempted him as he was at work at his forge, by assuming the form of a beautiful girl. Dunstan at once attacked him with his pincers and put him to flight" (S. Baring-Gould, *The Lives of the Saints*). Dunstan (924–88) was Bishop of Worcester, hence the connection with Sandys.

And the *Excise* receives a totall Rout.
   Broken in Courage, yet the Men the same,
Resolve henceforth upon their other Game:
   Where force had fail'd, with Stratagem to play,
And what Haste lost recover by Delay.   310
St. Albans streight is sent to, to forbeare,
Lest the sure Peace forsooth too soon appear.
The Seamen's clamour to three ends they use:
To cheat their Pay, feigne want, the *House* accuse.
Each day they bring the Tale, and that too true,
How strong the *Dutch* their Equipage renew.
Mean time through all the Yards their Orders run
To lay the Ships up, cease the keels begun.
The Timber rots, and uselesse Ax doth rust,
Th' unpractis'd Saw lyes bury'd in its Dust;   320
The busy Hammer sleeps, the Ropes untwine;
The Stores and Wages all are Mine and Thine.
Along the Coast and Harbors they take care
That Money lack, nor Forts be in repaire.
Long thus they could against the *House* conspire,
Load them with Envy, and with Sitting tire:
And the lov'd *King*, and never yet deny'd,
Is brought to beg in publick and to chide.
But when this fail'd, and Months enow were spent,
They with the first dayes proffer seem content: 330
And to Land-tax from the *Excise* turn round,
Bought off with Eighteen-hundred-thousand pound.
Thus like faire Thieves, the *Commons* purse they share,
But all the Members' Lives consulting spare.
   Blither than Hare that hath escap'd the hounds,
The *House* prorogu'd, the *Chancellor* rebounds.

313–314. *Seamen's clamour:* As Pepys reports (December 19, 1666), the seamen were beginning to riot becuase they had not been paid for so long, and because the tickets they received in lieu of cash were not being redeemed by the government.
328: The King addressed an urgent demand for supply to the House on January 18, 1667.
331: The land tax, which was supported by the Country party against the general excise of the Court party, was passed on November 8, 1666.
336. *prorogu'd*: On February 8, 1667 when the land tax bill received the royal assent.

Not so decrepit Æson, hasht and stew'd
With bitter Herbs, rose from the Pot renew'd,
And with fresh Age felt his glad limms unite.
His Gout (yet still he curst) had left him quite.   340
What Frosts to Fruit, what Ars'nick to the Rat,
What to faire *Denham* mortall Chocolat,
What an Account to *Cart'ret*, that, and more,
A *Parliament* is to the *Chancellor*.
So the sad tree shrinks from the Morning's Eye,
But blooms all night and shoots its branches high.
So, at the Sun's recesse, againe returns
The Comet dread, and Earth and Heaven burns.
    Now *Mordant* may within his Castle tow'r
Imprison Parents, and the Child deflowre.   350
The *Irish* herd is now let loose, and comes
By millions over, not by *hecatombs*.
And now, now, the *Canary Patent* may
Be broacht againe for the great Holy-Day.
    See how he reigns in her new Palace culminant,
And sits in state divine like *Jove* the fulminant!
First *Buckingham*, that durst to him rebell,
Blasted with Lightning, struck with Thunder fell.
Next the twelve *Commons* are condemn'd to grone,
And roule in vain at *Sisyphus's* Stone.   360
But still he car'd, while in Revenge he brav'd,
That Peace secur'd and Money might be sav'd;
Gain and Revenge, Revenge and Gain are sweet:
United most, else when by turns they meet.
France had *St. Albans* promis'd (so they sing),
St. Albans promis'd him, and he the *King*.
The Count forthwith is order'd all to close,

337–339: See Ovid, *Metamorphoses*, 7.
345–346. *sad tree: Nyctanthes Arbor-tristis*, Night-Jasmine of India. During the day it
loses its brightness. (Margoliouth)   349: See note on l. 259.
351: See note on l. 255.   357. *to:* against.
357–358: Buckingham had been chief supporter of the Irish Cattle Bill in the
House of Lords, 1666–67, Clarendon opposing. His arrest was ordered February
25, 1667 for treasonable practices, one charge being that he obtained a cast of the
King's horoscope. After some months he gave himself up and was sent to the
Tower.   359–360: Twelve of the eighteen commissioners for the Public
Accounts, appointed March 21, 1667, were members of the House of
Commons.   367. *Count:* That is, the Earl of St. Albans; perhaps with a glance at
his "Frenchiness."

To play for *Flanders* and the stake to lose,
While, chain'd together, two Ambassadors
Like Slaves shall beg for Peace at *Holland's* doores.   370
This done, among his *Cyclopes* he retires
To forge new Thunder and inspect their Fires.
   The *Court*, as once of War, now fond of Peace,
All to new sports their wanton fears release.
From *Greenwich* (where Intelligence they hold)
Comes News of pastime martiall and old:
A Punishment invented first to aw
Masculine Wives, transgressing Natures Law,
Where, when the brawny Female disobeys,
And beats the Husband till for peace he prays,   380
No concern'd Jury for him damage finds,
Nor partiall Justice her Behaviour binds,
But the just Street does the next House invade,
Mounting the neighbor Couple on lean Jade;
The Distaffe knocks, the grains from Kettle fly,
And Boys and Girls in Troops run hooting by.
Prudent Antiquity, that knew by Shame,
Better than Law, domestick Crimes to tame,
And taught Youth by Spectacle innocent!
So thou and I, Dear *Painter*, represent,   390
In quick effigie, others faults, and feigne,
By making them redic'lous, to restraine.
With homely sight, they chose thus to relax
The joys of State for the new Peace and Tax.
So *Holland* with us had the Mast'ry try'd,
And our next neighbors, *France* and *Flanders*, ride.
   But a fresh News, the great designment nips:
Off at the *Isle of Candy, Dutch* and Ships!

368: The French aimed at peace with England in order to be free to carry out their
designs on Flanders.   369: See note on ll. 233-234.
375-396: These lines refer to the "Skimmington Ride," in which aggressive wives
and timid husbands were ridiculed by their neighbors. Here France and Flanders
are the neighbors while Holland is the masterful wife and England the beaten
husband. (Margoliouth)   391. *effigie:* Pronounced as four syllables in the
seventeenth century. Compare "Third Advice," l. 432, p. 143.   398. *Candy:* (1)
Canvey Island, off the Essex coast; (2) Candia – an old name for Crete. Marvell
was probably also referring to the occasion for Busenello's "Prospective of the
Naval Triumph" (tr. Thomas Higgons, 1658) achieved by the Venetian navy over
the Turks near Crete. This poem was Waller's model.

Bab May and *Arlington* did wisely scoffe,
And thought all safe if they were so far off: 400
Modern Geographers, 'twas there, they thought,
Where *Venice* twenty years the *Turk* had fought;
While the first Year our Navy is but shown,
The next divided, and the third we've none.
They, by the Name, mistook it for that Isle
Where *Pilgrim Palmer* travel'd in exile,
With the Bulls horn to measure his own head,
And on *Pasiphäe's* Tombe to drop a Bead.
But *Morrice* learn'd demonstrates, by the Post,
This *Isle of Candy* was on *Essex* Coast.   410
   Fresh Messengers still the sad News assure,
More tim'rous now we are, than first secure.
False terrors our believing Fears devise:
And the *French* Army one from *Calais* spyes.
Bennet and *May* and those of shorter reach
Change all for Guinnies, and a Crown for each;
But wiser Men, and well foreseen in chance,
In *Holland* theirs had lodg'd before, and *France.*
Whitehall's unsafe, the *Court* all meditates
To fly to *Windsor*, and mure up the Gates.   420
Each does the other blame, and all distrust;
But *Mordant*, new oblig'd, would sure be just.
Not such a fatall stupefaction reign'd
At *Londons* Flame, nor so the *Court* complain'd.
The *Bloodworth-Chanc'lor* gives, then does recall,
Orders; amaz'd at last gives none at all.

---

399. *Bab May:* Baptist May, Keeper of the Privy Purse.
406. *Pilgrim Palmer:* A punning reference to Roger Palmer, Earl of Castlemaine, a Roman Catholic. When his wife left him for Charles II he traveled to the Levant in 1664 with the Venetian admiral Andrea Conaro.
408. *Pasiphäe:* Wife of Minos, King of Crete, fell in love with a bull. The product of their union was the Minotaur, which Minos caused Daedalus to imprison in a labyrinth. See Ovid, *Metamorphoses*, especially 8 and 9, and reference to the myth in "Second Advice," ll. 347–354, p. 129.
409. *Morrice:* Sir William Morice (1602–76), joint secretary of state with Arlington. *By the Post:* From his knowledge of postal matters he demonstrates to Arlington, the Postmaster-General, that this Candy is in Essex.
419–420: "The gates of the court were shut up upon the first coming of the Dutch to us" (Pepys, June 17, 1667).   422: See note on l. 260.
425. *Bloodworth:* Sir Thomas Bloodworth was Mayor of London during the Great Fire and was noted for his fecklessness.

   St. Alban's writ to that he may bewaile
To *Master Lewis*, and tell coward tale,
How yet the *Hollanders* do make a noise,
Threaten to beat us, and are naughty Boyes.   430
Now *Doleman's* disobedient, and they still
Uncivill; his unkindnesse would us kill.
Tell him our Ships unrigg'd, our Forts unman'd,
Our Money spent; else 'twere at his command.
Summon him therefore of his Word, and prove
To move him out of Pity, if not Love.
Pray him to make *De Witte* and *Ruyter* cease,
And whip the *Dutch* unlesse they'll hold their peace.
But *Lewis* was of memory but dull,
And to *St. Albans* too undutyfull;   440
Nor Word nor near relation did revere:
But askt him bluntly for his Character.
The Gravell'd *Count* did with the Answer faint
(His Character was that which thou didst paint)
And so inforc'd, like Enemy or Spy,
Trusses his bagage, and the Camp does fly.
Yet *Lewis* writes, and lest our hearts should break,
Consoles us morally out of *Seneque*.
   Two letters next unto *Breda* are sent,
In cipher one to *Harry Excellent*.   450
The first instructs our (verse the Name abhors)
Plenipotentiary Ambassadors
To prove by Scripture, Treaty does imply

427–428: An express with appeals for peace went to St. Albans on June 15.
431. *Doleman's disobedient:* Col. Thomas Dolman, an English officer, commanded the Dutch troops in the invading fleet. An act was passed in October 1665, attainting him if he and others did not surrender by a certain day.
435. *prove:* Attempt.
440: If, as Marvell assumes, St. Albans was secretly married to Henrietta Maria, he would have been Louis XIV's uncle. (Margoliouth)
442. *Character:* Official rank or status.
447–448: This consolatory letter from Louis XIV to Charles is undoubtedly a figment of the poet's imagination. Seneca was one of the classical writers whom Louis, as a young man, was made to read.
451–456: " 'I look upon the peace as made' was the cue taken from St. Albans, and as May passed into June our blind dependence grew more marked" (Feiling, *British Foreign Policy*).   452: Coventry and Holles.

Cessation, as the Look Adultery;
And that, by Law of Arms, in martiall strife,
Who yields his Sword has title to his life.
Presbyter Hollis the first point should cleare;
The second *Coventry* the *Cavalier*.
But would they not be argu'd back from Sea,
Then to return home straight *infectâ re*.   460
But *Harry's* order'd if they won't recall
Their Fleet, to threaten, we will grant them all.
Hide's flippant Stile there pleasantly curvets;
Still his sharp Witt on States and Princes whets
(So *Spain* could not escape his Laughter's spleen:
None but himself must choose the King a Queen),
But, when he came the odious clause to pen
That summons up the *Parliament* agen,
His Writing Master many a time he bann'd,
And wisht himself the Gout to seise his Hand.   470
Never old Leacher more repugnance felt,
Consenting, for his Rupture, to be gelt;
But still in hope he solac't, ere they come,
To work the Peace and so to send them home,
Or in their hasty Fall to find a flaw,
Their Acts to vitiate, and them overaw;
But most rely'd, upon this *Dutch* pretense,
To raise a two edg'd Army for's defense.
    First then he marcht our whole Militia's force
(As if indeed we Ships or *Dutch* had Horse),   480
Then from the usuall commonplace he blames
These, and in standing Army's praise declames,
And the wise *Court*, that always lov'd it deare,
Now thinks all but too little for their Feare.

454: Compare Matthew 5:27–28. "Whosoever looketh on a woman to lust after
her hath committed adultery with her already in his heart."
459. *they:* The Dutch fleet.   460. *infectâ re:* Without having accomplished
anything.   463–466: Clarendon's attitude toward Holland during preliminary
negotiations was unyielding and contemptuous. See Feiling, *British Foreign Policy*,
p. 216.   469. *bann'd:* Cursed.
477–478: After the naval disgrace an army of twelve new regiments under the
command of old Parliamentarians was raised "to conciliate popular opinion ...
But this was only adding fuel to the fire, since it raised the suspicion that a standing
army was intended" (David Ogg, *England in the Reign of Charles II*).
482. *These:* The Dutch.

Hide stamps, and streight upon the ground the swarms
Of currant *Myrmidons* appear in Arms,
And for their Pay he writes, as from the *King*,
With that curs't quill pluckt from a Vultur's wing,
Of the whole *Nation* now to ask a Loan
(The eighteen-hundred-thousand pound was gone).   490
    This done, he pens a Proclamation stout
In rescue of the *Banquiers Banquerouts*,
His minion Imps, that, in his secret part,
Ly nuzling at the sacramentall wart;
Horse-leeches circling at the hem'royd veine:
He sucks the *King*, they him, he them againe.
The Kingdomes Farm he lets to them bid least:
Greater the Bribe, and that's at interest.
Here Men, induc'd by safety, gain, and ease,
Their Money lodge, confiscate when he please.   500
These can at need, at instant, with a scrip,
(This lik'd him best) his Cash beyond Sea whip.
When *Dutch* invade, when *Parliament* prepare,
How can he Engines so convenient spare?
Let no Man touch them or demand his own,
Pain of displeasure of great *Clarindon*.
    The State affaires thus marshal'd, for the rest,
Monk in his shirt against the *Dutch* is prest.
Often, dear *Painter*, have I sat and mus'd
Why he should still be on all adventures us'd: 510
If they for nothing ill, like ashen wood,
Or think him, like herbe John, for nothing good?

---

492. *Banquiers Banquerouts:* Bankrupt bankers, who had lent the King money.
493–496: Compare Cleveland, *Rebel Scot*, ll. 83–85:
    Sure, England hath the hemorrhoids, and these
    On the north postern of the patient seize
    Like leeches . . .
494. *wart:* Nipple.   497. *Kingdomes Farm:* The farming of taxes.
498. *scrip:* Receipt for a portion of a loan subscribed.
511. *ashen wood:* The ash is a tree second in value only to the oak, and its wood has a thousand uses.
512. *herbe John:* Properly St. John's wort applied, in proverbial phrases, to something inert or indifferent.

Whether his Valor they so much admire,
Or that for Cowardise they all retire,
As *Heav'n* in Storms, they call, in gusts of State,
On *Monk* and *Parliament*, yet both do hate.
All Causes sure concurre, but most they think
Under *Herculean* Labors he may sink.
Soon then the independent Troops would close,
And *Hide's* last project would his Place dispose.   520
    Ruyter the while, that had our Ocean curb'd,
Sail'd now among our Rivers undisturb'd:
Survey'd their chrystall Streams and Banks so green
And Beauties ere this never naked seen.
Through the vain Sedge, the bashfull Nymphs he eyd
Bosomes and all which from themselves they hide.
The Sun much brighter, and the Skyes more clear,
He finds the Aire and all things sweeter here.
The sudden change and such a tempting Sight
Swells his old Veins with fresh Blood, fresh Delight.   530
Like am'rous Victors he begins to shave,
And his new Face looks in the *English* wave.
His sporting Navy all about him swim.
And witness their complacence in their Trimme:
Their streaming Silks play through the weather fair
And with inveigling colors court the Aire,
While the red Flaggs breathe on their Top-masts high
Terror and War, but want an Enemy.
Among the Shrowds the Seamen sit and sing,
And wanton Boyes on evry Rope do cling.   540
Old *Neptune* springs the Tides and water lent
(The Gods themselves do help the provident),

519–520: I agree with Margoliouth's suggestion that "independent troops" refers to the projected standing army: "The point may be that, with Monck's death, the obstacles to the consolidation of a standing army under Clarendon's control would disappear."
531–540: This passage seems to show a general indebtedness to Enobarbus' account of the first meeting between Antony and Cleopatra in Shakespeare's play (II, 2, 193–228).
541: Pepys notes (June 14) that the easterly winds and spring tides helped the Dutch to go up the Thames and the Medway and to break the chain at Chatham.

And, where the deep keel on the shallow cleaves,
With Trident's leaver and great shoulder heaves.
Æolus their sailes inspires with Eastern wind,
Puffs them along, and breathes upon them kind.
With pearly Shell the *Tritons* all the while
Sound the Sea-march, and guide to *Sheppy Isle*.

So have I seen, in Aprill's Bud, arise
A Fleet of clouds sailing along the skyes,   550
The liquid Region with their squadrons fill'd,
Their airy Sterns the Sun behind does guild,
And gentle gales them steere, and *Heaven* drives,
When, all on sudden, their calm bosom rives
With Thund'r and Lightning from each armed Clowd:
Shepheards themselves in vain in bushes shrowd;
Such up the Stream the *Belgick* Navy glides,
And at *Sheernesse* unloads its stormy sides.
Sprag there, though practis'd in the Sea-command,
With panting Heart lay like a Fish on Land   560
And quickly judg'd the Fort was not tenable,
Which, if a House, yet were not tenantable.
No man can sit there safe: the Canon pours
Thorow the Walls untight and Bullets show'rs,
The neighb'rhood ill, and an unwholsome Seat,
So at the first Salute resolves Retreat
And swore that he would never more dwell there
Untill the *City* put it in repaire;
So he in front, his Garrison in reare,
March streight to *Chatham* to increase the feare.   570

There our sick Ships unrigg'd in Summer lay,
Like molting Fowle, a weak and easy Prey.
For whose strong bulk Earth scarce could Timber finde,
The Ocean water, or the Heavens wind
Those Oaken Gyants of the ancient race,
That rul'd all Seas and did our *Chanell* grace.
The conscious Stag, so, once the Forrest's dread,
Flyes to the Wood, and hides his armlesse Head.
Ruyter forthwith a Squadron does untack:

---

559. *Sprag:* Sir Edward Spragge (d. 1673), vice-admiral of the Blue, then commanding at Sheerness.

They saile securely through the River's track.   580
An *English* Pilot too, (O shame, O Sin!)
Cheated of Pay, was he that show'd them in.
Our wretched Ships, within, their Fate attend,
And all our hopes now on fraile Chain depend:
Engine so slight to guard us from the Sea,
It fitter seem'd to captivate a Flea.
A Skipper rude shocks it without respect,
Filling his Sailes, more force to recollect.
Th' *English* from Shore the Iron deaf invoke
For its last aid: "Hold Chain, or we are broke!"   590
But with her sailing weight the *Holland* keele,
Snapping the brittle links, does thorough reele
And to the rest the open'd passage shew.
Monke from the bank the dismall Sight does view.
Our feather'd Gallants, which came down that day
To be spectators safe of the new Play,
Leave him alone when first they hear the Gun
(*Cornb'ry* the fleetest) and to *London* run.
Our Seamen, whom no Danger's shape could fright,
Unpaid refuse to mount our Ships for spight,   600
Or to their fellows swim on board the *Dutch*,
Which show the tempting metall in their clutch.
Oft had he sent of *Duncome* and of *Legg*
Canon and Powder, but in vain, to beg:
And *Upnor-Castle's* ill-defended Wall,
Now needfull, does for ammunition call.
He finds, wheres'ere he Succor might expect,
Confusion, Folly, Treach'ry, Feare, Neglect.
But when the *Royal Charles* (what rage, what grief!)
He saw seis'd, and could give her no releif—   610
That sacred Keele, which had, as he, restor'd
His exil'd *Soveraign* on its happy board,
And thence the *Brittish Admirall* became,
Crown'd for that merit with their *Master's* Name,
That Pleasure-boat of War, in whose dear Side

603. *Legg:* William Legge, Lieutenant-General of the Ordnance.
611–612: The *Royal Charles*, formerly the *Naseby*, brought the King to Dover in
1660.

Secure so oft he had his Foe defy'd,
Now a cheap spoyle and the mean Victor's slave,
Taught the *Dutch* Colors from its Top to wave—
Of former gloryes the reproachfull thought,
With present shame compar'd, his Mind distraught.   620
Such, from *Euphrates* bank, a Tygresse fell
After the robber for her Whelps doth Yell;
But sees inrag'd the River flow between;
Frustrate Revenge, and Love, by losse more keen,
At her own Breast her uselesse claws does arme:
She tears her self since him she can not harme.
     The Guards, plac'd for the Chain's and Fleet's defence.
Long since were fled on many a feign'd pretense.
Daniel had there adventur'd, Man of might;
Sweet *Painter*, draw his Picture while I write.   630
Paint him of Person tall, and big of bone,
Large limms, like Ox not to be kill'd but shown.
Scarse can burnt Iv'ry feigne an hair so black,
Or face so red, thine Oker and thy Lack.
Mix a vain terror in his martiall looke,
And all those lines by which men are mistooke;
But when, by Shame constrain'd to goe on board,
He heard how the wild Canon nearer roar'd,
And saw himself confin'd like sheep in pen,
Daniel then thought he was in Lion's den;   640
And when the frightfull fire-ships he saw,
Pregnant with Sulphur, to him nearer draw;
Captain, Lieutenant, Ensigne, all make haste
Ere in the Firy Furnace they be cast:
Three Children tall, unsing'd, away they row
Like *Shadrack, Mesheck,* and *Abednego.*
     Not so brave *Douglas*, on whose lovely chin
The early Down but newly did begin,
And modest Beauty yet his Sex did veile,
While envious Virgins hope he is a Male.   650

---

629. *Daniel:* Probably Sir Thomas Daniel, who commanded a company of foot
guards, who were supposed to defend the *Loyal London* or the *Royal James.*
632. *shown:* Like a prize ox.
634. *Lack:* A crimson pigment.   646. Compare Daniel 3.
647. *Douglas:* Archibald Douglas, who commanded a company of Scottish troops,
died in defending the *Royal Oak*, which was fired by the Dutch.

His yellow Locks curle back themselves to seek,
Nor other Courtship knew but to his Cheek.
Oft as he in chill *Eske* or *Seine* by night
Harden'd and cool'd his limms, so soft, so white,
Among the reeds, to be espy'd by him
The Nymphs would rustle, he would forward swim.
They sigh'd and said, "Fond Boy, why so untame,
That fly'st Loves fires, reserv'd for other Flame?"
Fix'd on his Ship, he fac'd that horrid Day,
And wonder'd much at those that run away;   660
Nor other Fear himself could comprehend
Than lest *Heav'n* fall ere thither he ascend,
But intertains the while his Time too short
With birding at the *Dutch* as if in sport,
Or waves his Sword, and could he then conjure
Within its circle, knows himself secure.
The fatall Bark him boards with grappling fire,
And safely through its Port the *Dutch* retire:
That precious Life he yet disdains to save,
Or with known Art to try the gentle wave.   670
Much him the Honors of his ancient Race
Inspire, nor would he his own Deeds deface,
And secret Joy in his calm Soule does rise
That *Monk* looks on to see how *Douglas* dyes.
Like a glad Lover the fierce Flames he meets,
And tryes his first embraces in their Sheets.
His shape exact, which the bright Flames infold,
Like the Sun's Statue stands of burnisht Gold.
Round the transparent Fire about him glows,
As the clear Ambar on the Bee does close;   680
And as on Angell's heads their Gloryes shine,
His burning Locks adorn his Face divine.
But when in his immortall Mind he felt
His alt'ring Form and soder'd limms to melt,
Down on the Deck he lay'd himself and dy'd,
With his dear Sword reposing by his Side
And, on the flaming plank, so rests his Head
As one that's warm'd himself and gon to bed.
His Ship burns down and with his Reliques sinks,

676: Actually, Douglas left a window, Frances, who petitioned for a prize ship as
compensation.

And the sad stream beneath his Ashes drinks.   690
Fortunate Boy! If either Pencills fame,
Or if my Verse can propagate thy Name,
When *Œta* and *Alcides* are forgot,
Our *English* youth shall sing the valiant *Scott*.
    Each Dolefull Day still with fresh losse returns:
The *Loyall London* now a third time burns,
And the true *Royall Oake* and *Royall James*,
Ally'd in Fate, increase with theirs her Flames.
Of all our Navy none should now survive,
But that the Ships themselves were taught to dive,   700
And the Kind River in its creek them hides,
Fraughting their pierced Keels with oozy tides.
    Up to the *Bridge* contagious Terror strook:
The *Tow'r* it self with the near Danger shook,
And were not *Ruyter's* maw with ravage cloy'd,
Ev'n *London's* ashes had been then destroy'd.
Officious Fear, however, to prevent
Our losse does so much more our losse augment:
The *Dutch* had robb'd those jewells of the *Crowne*;
Our Merchant-men, lest they be burnt, we drown.   710
So when the Fire did not enough devoure,
The Houses were demolish't near the *Tow'r*.
Those Ships that yearly from their teeming Howle
Unloaded here the Birth of either Pole—
Furrs from the North, and silver from the West,
Wines from the South, and spices from the East,
From *Gambo* Gold, and from the *Ganges* Gemms—
Take a short voyadge underneath the *Thames*,
Once a deep River, now with Timber floor'd,
And shrunk, least navigable, to a Ford.   720
    Now (nothing more at *Chatham* left to burn)
The *Holland* squadron leisurely return,
And, spight of *Ruperts* and of *Albermarles*,

693: Hercules (Alcides) was burned to death on Mt. Oeta.
696: The *London* was blown up in March 1665. Then the loyal City of London was burned by the Great Fire. Now the *Loyal London* (compare "Second Advice," ll. 13–24, p. 118) is burned.
700: Some ships were sunk to keep them from being burned.
710: Some merchantmen newly-laden with valuable cargo and newly-commissioned fire ships were sunk in a panic below Woolwich to stop the Dutch.   713. *Howle:* Hold.   720. *least navigable:* At its least navigable point.

To *Ruyter's* Triumph lead the captive *Charles*.
The pleasing Sight he often does prolong:
Her Masts erect, tough Chordage, Timbers strong,
Her moving Shapes, all these he does survey,
And all admires, but most his easy Prey.
The Seamen search her all within, without:
Viewing her strength, they yet their conquest doubt;   730
Then with rude shouts, secure, the Aire they vex,
With gamesome Joy insulting on her Decks.
Such the fear'd *Hebrew*, captive, blinded, shorn,
Was led about in sport, the publick scorn.

  Black Day accurst! on thee let no man hale
Out of the Port, or dare to hoise a saile,
Nor row a boat in thy unlucky houre.
Thee, the years monster, let thy Dam devoure:
And constant Time, to keep his course yet right,
Fill up thy space with a redoubled Night.   740
When aged *Thames* was bound with fetters base,
And Medway chast ravisht before his Face,
And their dear offspring murder'd in their Sight,
Thou and thy fellows held'st the odious Light.
Sad change since first that happy pair was wed,
When all the Rivers grac'd their nuptiall Bed,
And *Father Neptune* promis'd to resigne
His Empire old to their immortall Line!
Now with vain grief their vainer hopes they rue,
Themselves dishonor'd, and the Gods untrue,   750
And to each other, helplesse couple, mone,
As the sad Tortoyse for the Sea does groan.
But most they for their darling *Charles* complain,
And, were it burnt, yet lesse would be their pain.
To see that fatall pledge of Sea-command
Now in the Ravisher *De-Ruyter's* hand,
The *Thames* roar'd, swooning *Medway* turn'd her tide,
And, were they mortall, both for grief had dy'd.

  The *Court* in farthing yet it self does please,
And female *Stuart*, there, rules the foure Seas,   760

733-734. *the fear'd Hebrew:* Samson. See Judges 16.
760: Frances Stuart, on whom Charles had set his eye, married the Duke of
Richmond in 1667. She was the model for Britannia on medals and coins. The
farthings of Charles II bore the legend *Quatuor maria vindico* (I defend the four seas).

But Fate does still accumulate our Woes,
And *Richmond* her commands, as *Ruyter* those.
    After this Losse, to rellish discontent,
Someone must be accus'd by Punishment.
All our miscarriages on *Pett* must fall:
His Name alone seems fit to answer all.
Whose Counsell first did this mad War beget?
Who all Commands sold through the Navy? *Pett.*
Who would not follow when the *Dutch* were bet?
Who treated out the time at *Bergen? Pett.*   770
Who the *Dutch Fleet* with Storms disabled met?
And, rifling Prizes, them neglected? *Pett.*
Who with false news prevented the *Gazette,*
The Fleet divided, writ for *Rupert? Pett.*
Who all our Seamen cheated of their Debt,
And all our Prizes who did swallow? *Pett.*
Who did advise no Navy out to set,
And who the Forts left unrepaired? *Pett.*
Who to supply with Powder did forget
Languard, Sheernesse, Graves-end, and *Upnor? Pett.*   780
Who all our Ships expos'd in *Chatham's* Net?
Who should it be but the *Fanatick Pett.*
Pett, the Sea Architect, in making Ships,

---

763. *relish:* Make pleasant to the taste.

765. *Pett:* Peter Pett (1610-70?) superintended the dockyard at Chatham.
Margoliouth quotes a letter from Henry Savile to his brother, George (June 18):
"Commissioner Pett was sent for from Chatham and sent the last night to the
Tower. He is most undoubtedly to be sacrificed; all that are greater lay the fault
upon him in hopes that he is to bear all the blame; the town has no mind to be so
satisfied." Pett was arraigned October 31, and set free on bail of £5,000. Marvell
spoke that day against sending him to the Tower (Milward, *Diary*). Impeachment
proceedings were begun December 19, but the matter was dropped.

769: On June 3, 1665. It was the Duke of York's flagship that "would not follow."
See "Second Advice," ll. 229-238, p. 125. *Beat* was pronounced *bet.*

770: Compare "Second Advice," ll. 265-288, pp. 126-127.

771-772: Compare "Second Advice," ll. 289-304, pp. 127-128.

773-774: Compare "Third Advice," ll. 283-288, 291-294, p. 139.

777-778: Sir William Coventry seems to have been most culpable for the failure to
send out a fleet in 1667. "It is well known who of the Commissioners of the
Treasury gave advice that the charge of setting forth a fleet this year might be
spared, Sir W.C. by name" (John Evelyn, *Diary*, July 29, 1667).

780. *Languard:* A fort at Harwich attacked by the Dutch in June 1667.

Was the first cause of all these Navall slips:
Had he not built, none of these Faults had bin;
If no Creation, there had been no Sin.
But, his great Crime, one Boat away he sent:
That lost our Fleet, and did our Flight prevent.
    Then, that Reward might in its turn take place,
And march with Punishment in equall pace: 790
Southampton dead, much of the *Treasure's* Care,
And place in Counsell fell to *Duncome's* share.
All men admir'd he to that pitch could fly:
Powder ne'r blew man up so soon so high,
But sure his late good husbandry in Petre
Show'd him to manage the *Exchequer* meeter;
And who the Forts would not vouchsafe a corn,
To lavish the *King's* Money more would scorn.
Who hath no Chimneys, to give all is best;
And ablest Speaker, who of Law has least;   800
Who lesse Estate, for Treasurer most fit,
And for a Couns'lor, he that has least Wit.
But the true Cause was, that, in's Brother *May*,
Th'Exchequer might the Privy-purse obey.
    But now draws near the *Parliament's* return:
Hide and the *Court* again begin to mourn;
Frequent in Counsell, earnest in Debate,
All Arts they try how to prolong its Date.
Grave Primate *Shelden* (much in preaching there)
Blames the last Session and this more does fear: 810

787: The chief charges against Pett were "the not carrying up of the great ships and the using of the boats in carrying away his goods" (Pepys, June 19, 1667).

791. *Southampton*: Thomas Wriothesley, fourth Earl of Southampton (1607-67), Lord High Treasurer, had died in the spring, and the treasury was put in charge of a commission consisting of Albemarle, Ashley, Sir W. Coventry, Sir John Duncombe, and Sir Thomas Clifford. Duncombe was actually appointed to the commission three weeks before the Dutch attack.

793-794: Pepys (May 31, 1667): "I saw Duncombe look as big and take as much state on him as if he had been born a lord."

795. *Petre:* Saltpetre, an ingredient in gunpowder. Duncombe had been Master of the Ordnance, in which capacity he could have made illicit profits.

797. *corn:* A grain of gunpowder.

803. *Brother May:* Baptist May, Keeper of the Privy Purse, Duncombe's brother-in-law.

809. *Shelden:* Gilbert Sheldon (1598-1677), Archbishop of Canterbury, according to Pepys "as very a wencher as can be" (July 29, 1667).

With *Boynton* or with *Middleton* 'twere sweet,
But with a *Parliament* abhors to meet
And thinks 'twill ne'r be well within this Nation
Till it be govern'd by a *Convocation*.
But in the *Thames's* mouth still *Ruyter* laid;
The Peace not sure, new Army must be paid.
Hide saith he hourly waits for a dispatch;
Harry came post just as he shew'd his Watch,
All to agree the Articles were clear,
The *Holland* Fleet and *Parliament* so near;   820
Yet, *Harry* must jobb back, and all mature,
Binding, ere th' *Houses* meet, the *Treaty* sure.
And 'twixt Necessity and Spight, till then,
Let them come up so to goe down agen.
    Up ambles Country Justice on his Pad,
And Vest bespeaks to be more seemly clad.
Plain Gentlemen in Stage-Coach are ore thrown,
And Deputy-Lieutenants in their own.
The portly Burgesse, through the Weather hot,
Does for his Corporation sweat and trott;   830
And all with Sun and Choler come adust
And threaten *Hide* to raise a greater Dust.
But, fresh as from the Mint, the Courtiers fine
Salute them, smiling at their vain designe,
And *Turner* gay up to his Pearch does march
With Face new bleach't, smoothen'd and stiffe with starche;
Tells them he at *Whitehall* had took a turn,
And for three Dayes thence moves them to adjourn.
"Not so!" quoth *Tomkins*, and straight drew his Tongue.

---

811. *Boynton and Middleton:* Katherine Boynton and Mrs. Charles Middleton were
court beauties.   814. *Convocation:* That is, of bishops.
818. *Harry:* Henry Coventry. On July 8 Pepys wrote: "Mr Coventry is come from
Breda, as was expected, but, contrary to expectation, brings with him two or three
articles which do not please the King."
819-824: The idea here seems to be that ambassador Coventry was eager to
believe that the articles implied an early settlement because he was confronted by
the double threat of the Dutch fleet and the approaching session of Parliament in
which the war with Holland would be attacked as a grievance.
824: The House met July 25 and was dismissed July 29.
826. *Vest:* A garment designed by Charles II to make English fashions independent
of France.   831. *adust:* Dried up with heat.

Trusty as steele, that always ready hung;   840
And so, proceeding in his motion warm,
Th' Army soon rais'd he doth as soon disarme.
True Trojan! While this Town can girles afford,
And long as Cider lasts in *Hereford*,
The Girles shall always kisse thee though grown old,
And in eternall Healths thy Name be troll'd.
    Meanwhile the certain News of Peace arrives
At *Court*, and so reprieves their guilty Lives.
Hide orders *Turner* that he should come late,
Lest some new *Tomkins* spring a fresh Debate.   850
The *King* that day rais'd early from his rest,
Expects, as at a Play, till *Turner's* drest.
At last, together *Eaton* come and he:
No Diall more could with the Sun agree.
The *Speaker*, summon'd, to the *Lords* repairs,
Nor gave the *Commons* leave to say their pray'rs,
But like his Pris'ners to the Bar them led,
Where mute they stand to hear their sentence read:
Trembling with Joy and Fear, *Hide* them prorogues,
And had almost mistook and call'd them Rogues.   860
    Dear *Painter*, draw this *Speaker* to the foot:
Where Pencill can not there my Pen shall do't;
That may his Body, this his Mind explain,
Paint him in Golden Gown, with Mace's Brain,
Bright Hair, fair Face, obscure and dull of Head,
Like Knife with Iv'ry haft and edge of Lead.
At Pray'rs, his Eyes turn up the pious white,
But all the while His Private-Bill's in sight.
In Chair, he smoking sits like Master-Cook,
And a Poll-Bill does like his Apron look.   870
Well was he skill'd to season any question,
And made a sawce fit for *Whitehall's* digestion;
Whence ev'ry day, the Palat more to tickle,
Court-mushrumps ready are, sent in in pickle.

---

844. *Hereford:* Tomkins' county.
853. *Eaton*: Sir John Eaton or Ayton, Usher of the Black Rod.
868–870: The Speaker received large fees from the passage of private bills. Turnor
sweats like a cook while the bill is being voted on, and a poll-bill such as that by
which part of the supply was raised in 1666–67 might resemble his spotted apron
because of various amendments attached to it.

When Grievance urg'd, he swells like squatted Toad,
Frisks, like a Frog, to croak a Taxes load;
His patient Pisse he could hold longer then
An Urinall, and sit like any Hen;
At Table jolly as a Country-Host
And soaks his Sack with *Norfolk* like a Toast: 880
At Night than *Chanticleer* more brisk and hot,
And *Sergeant's* Wife serves him for *Pertelott.*
    Paint last the *King* and a dead shade of Night
Only dispers'd by a weak Taper's light,
And those bright gleams that dart along and glare
From his clear Eyes (yet these too dark with Care).
There, as in the calm horror all alone
He wakes and muses of th' uneasy Throne,
Raise up a sudden shape with Virgin's Face:
(Though ill agree her posture, hour, or place)   890
Naked as born, and her round Arms behind
With her own Tresses interwove and twin'd;
Her Mouth lockt up, a blind before her Eyes;
Yet from beneath the Veile her blushes rise,
And silent Tears her secret anguish speak;
Her Heart throbbs and with very shame would break.
The Object strange in him no terror mov'd;
He wonder'd first, then pity'd, then he loved,
And with kind hand does the coy Vision presse,
Whose Beauty greater seem'd by her distresse,   900
But soon shrunk back, chill'd with her touch so cold,
And th' airy Picture vanish't from his hold.
In his deep thoughts the wonder did increase;
And he divin'd, 'twas *England* or the *Peace.*
    Expresse him startling next with listning eare,
As one that some unusuall noyse does hear:
With Canon, Trumpets, Drums, his door surround,
But let some other Painter draw the sound.
Thrice did he rise, thrice the vain Tumult fled,
But again thunders when he lyes in Bed.   910
His mind secure does the known stroke repeat
And finds the Drums *Lewis's* March did beat.

880. *Norfolk:* James Norfolk. Sergeant-at-Arms.
905. *startling:* Starting.   911. *secure:* Careless, overconfident, Now *arch.*

Shake then the room and all his curtains tear
And with blew streaks infect the Taper clear,
While the pale Ghosts his Eye does fixt admire
Of Grandsire *Harry* and of *Charles* his Sire.
Harry sits down, and in his open Side
The grisly Wound reveals of which he dy'd;
And ghastly *Charles*, turning his collar low,
The purple thread about his Neck does show,   920
Then, whisp'ring to his Son in words unheard,
Through the lockt door both of them disappear'd.
The wondrous Night the pensive *King* revolves,
And rising straight on *Hide's* Disgrace resolves.
    At his first step, he *Castlemain* does find,
Bennet and *Coventry*, as 'twere design'd.
And they, not knowing, the same thing propose
Which his hid Mind did in its depths inclose.
Through their feign'd speech their secret Hearts he knew:
To her own Husband, *Castlemain* untrue;   930
False to his Master *Bristoll, Arlington;*
And *Coventry*, falser than any one,
Who to the Brother, Brother would betray,
Nor therefore trusts himself to such as they.
His Father's Ghost too whisper'd him one note,
That who does cut his purse will cut his throat,
But in wise anger he their crimes forbears,
As Thiev's repriev'd for Executioners;
While *Hide*, provok't, his foaming tusk does whet
To prove them Traytors, and himself the *Pett*.   940
    Painter, adieu, how well our Arts agree!
Poetique Picture, painted Poetry!
But this great Worke is for our *Monarch* fit,
And henceforth *Charles* only to *Charles* shall sit.
His master-hand the Ancients shall outdo
Himself the *Painter* and the *Poet* too.

---

916. *Grandsire Harry:* Henry IV of France, father of Henrietta Maria. He was
assassinated by Ravaillac in 1610.
925–926: Lady Castlemaine, Bennet, and Sir William Coventry's position as the
Duke of York's secretary, in which capacity, Marvell implies, he acted against the
King's interests.

To the King

    So his bold Tube Man to the Sun apply'd
And spots unknown to the bright Star descry'd:
Show'd they obscure him while too near they prease,
And seem his Courtiers, are but his disease.   950
Through optick Trunk the Planet seem'd to hear
And hurles them off e'er since in his Careere.
    And you, *Great Sir*, that with him Empire share,
Sun of our World, as he the *Charles* is There:
Blame not the Muse that brought those spots to sight
Which, in your Splendor hid, corrode your Light.
(Kings in the Country oft have gone astray,
Nor of a Peasant scorn'd to learn the Way).
    Would She the unattended Throne reduce,
Banishing Love, Trust, Ornament, and Use,   960
Better it were to live in Cloyster's lock,
Or in faire Fields to rule the easy Flock.
She blames them only who the *Court* restraine,
And, where all *England* serves, themselves would reigne.
    Bold and accurst are they that all this while
Have strove to isle our *Monarch* from his *Isle*,
And to improve themselves, on false pretense,
About the *Common-Prince* have rais'd a Fense;
The *Kingdom* from the *Crown* distinct would see
And peele the Barke to burn at last the Tree.   970
(But *Ceres* Corn, and *Flora* is the Spring,
Bachus is Wine, the *Country* is the *King*).
    Not so does Rust insinuating weare,
Nor Powder so the vaulted Bastion teare,
Nor Earthquake so an hollow Isle o'erwhelm,
As scratching Courtiers undermine a Realme
And through the Palace's Foundations bore,
Burr'wing themselves to hoord their guilty store.
The smallest Vermine make the greatest Waste,
And a poor Warren once a City ras'd.   980
    But they whom, born to Virtue and to Wealth,
Nor Guilt to Flatt'ry binds, nor Want to Stealth;
Whose gen'rous Conscience and whose Courage high

949. *prease:* Press.

Does with clear Counsells their Large Soules supply;
That serve the *King* with their Estates and Care,
And as in Love on *Parliments* can stare,
(Where few the Number, Choice is there lesse hard):
Give us this *Court* and rule without a Guard.

The Vows

When the plate was at pawn and the fob at an eb
And the Spider might weave in our stomack its web
    Our Stomack as empty as braine
      Then *Charles* without Acre
      Made these vows to his *Maker*
    If ere he saw *England* againe.

I will have a Religion then all of mine own
Where *Papist* from *Protestant* shall not be known,
But if it grow troublesome I will have none.

I will have a fine *Parliament* alwayes to freind   10
That shall furnish me Treasure as fast as I spend,
But when they will not they shall be at an end.

I will have as fine Bishops as were e'er made with hands
With consciences flexible to my commands,
But if they displease me I will have all their lands.

I will have my fine *Chancellor* bear all the sway
Yet if men should clamour I'll pack him away
And yet call him home again soon as I may.

I will have a fine Navy to conquer the seas
And the *Dutch* shall give caution for their Provinces,   20
But if they should beat me I will do what they please.

---

1. *fob:* Purse.
17: Clarendon left England on November 29, 1667 for exile in France.
20. *caution:* Security given for the performance of some engagement.

I will have a new *London* instead of the old,
With wide streets and uniforme of mine own mold,
But if they build it too fast, I will soon make them hold.

I will have a fine Son (in making though marr'd)
If not ore a Kingdome to reigne or'e my guard
And Successor, if not to me, to *Gerrard*.

I will have a fine *Court*, with ne're an old face
And alwayes who beards me shall have the next grace,
And I either will vacate or buy him a place.   30

I will have a *Privy Councill* to sit alwayes still,
I will have a fine *Junto* to do what I will,
I will have two fine *Secretaryes* pisse through one quill.

I will have a *Privy-purse* without a controll,
I will wink all the while my Revenue is stole,
And if any be question'd I'll answer the whole.

But whatever it cost I will have a fine whore
As bold as *Alce Pierce* and as faire as *Jane Shore*,
And when I am weary of her I'll have more.

Of my Pimp, I will make my *Ministre premier*,   40
My bawd shall Ambassadors send far and near,
And my Wench shall dispose of the *Congé d'eslire*.

22: The rebuilding of London after the Fire was chiefly due to the energy and imagination of the King.
25-27: The Duke of Monmouth succeeded Lord Gerrard as commander of the King's Lifeguards September 16, 1668. *In making though marr'd* refers to his illegitimacy.   32. *Junto:* The Cabal.
33: There were two secretaries of state from 1660 on.
38: Alice Perrers was mistress of Edward III and Jane Shore of Edward IV.
40. *Pimp:* Probably the Duke of Buckingham, who had formed a plan to make Frances Teresa Stuart Charles' mistress and to govern the King through her. The plan failed (see "Last Instructions," l. 760) but on Clarendon's downfall Buckingham was generally regarded as the King's principal minister.
41. *My bawd:* The Duke of Arlington, a secretary of state who helped to overcome Louise de Kéroualle's resistance to the King in 1670.
42. *Congé d'eslire:* Power of appointment.

If this please not I'll reigne upon any condition,
Miss and I will both learn to live on exhibition,
And I'll first put the *Church* then my *Crown* in Commission.

I will have a fine Tunick, a shash and a Vest
Though not rule like the *Turk* yet I will be so drest
And who knows but the mode may soon bring in the rest?

I will have a fine pond and a pretty Decoy
Where the Ducks and the Drakes may their freedoms enjoy   50
And quack in their language still, *Vive le Roy.*

The Loyall Scott
By Cleveland's *Ghost, upon occasion of the death of Capt.* Douglas, *burnt upon his Ship at* Chatham

Of the old Heroes when the warlike Shades
Saw *Douglas* marching on th' *Elysian* glades,
They streight consulting, gather'd in a ring,

---

44. *on exhibition:* On a fixed allowance.

45: The model for this suggestion seems to have been the putting of the treasury into commission in 1670.

46: In 1666 Charles introduced an eastern mode of dress in reaction against the dominance at court of French fashions.

49–51: The King loved animals and raised many varieties of ducks in St. James's Park. *Decoy:* A pond out of which run narrow arms covered with netting in which waterfowl are captured.

The Loyal Scott: Purports to be John Cleveland's sequel to and recantation of his satirical poem *The Rebel Scot* (written in 1644). In taking as its point of departure Capt. Douglas' heroic death in action against the Dutch, Marvell incorporates with minor changes ll. 647–694 of "Last Instructions."

In almost all previous versions the poem has been hopelessly corrupted by the inclusion of an anti-prelatical tirade of more than one hundred lines whose authenticity Margoliouth first called into question. Margoliouth's suspicions have now been proved by marks indicating most of the corrupt lines in the Bod. MS. A neglected 1694 printing of "The Loyall Scott" provides additional textual authority for removing from the poem pages of dull rhodomontade which have hitherto disfigured it.

Which of their Poets should his welcome sing,
And, as a favourable pennance, chose
Cleveland, on whom that task they would impose.
He understood, but willingly addrest
His ready Muse to court their noble guest.
Much had he cur'd the tumor of his veine:
He judg'd more clearly now and saw more plain,   10
For those soft aires had temper'd every thought,
And of wise *Lethe* he had tooke a draught.
Abruptly he begun, to hide his Art,
As of his Satyre this had been a part—
    Not so brave *Douglas*, on whose lovely chin
The early down but newly did begin,
And modest beauty yet his sex did veile,
While envious virgins hope he is a male.
His shady locks curle back themselves to seek,
Nor other Courtship knew but to his cheek.   20
Oft as he in chill *Esk* or *Seine* by night
Harden'd and cool'd those limms, so soft, so white,
Among the reeds, to be espy'd by him,
The Nymphs would rustle; he would forward swim.
They sigh'd and said, "Fond boy, why so untame,
That fly'st Love's fires, reserv'd for other flame?"
    Fix'd on his ship he fac'd the horrid day,
And wonder'd much at those that run away,
Nor other fear himself could comprehend
Than lest Heav'n fall e'er thither he ascend;   30
But intertains the while his time too short
With birding at the *Dutch*, as if in sport,
Or waves his sword, and could he then conjure
Within its circle, knows himself secure.
    The fatall bark him boards with grapling fire,
And safely through its port the *Dutch* retire.
That precious life he yet disdains to save,

11. *soft aires:* Of Elysium.
14: Cleveland's "Rebel Scot" ends:

> A *Scot* when from the Gallows-tree got loose
> Drops into *Styx*, and turns a Soland Goose.

The recantation begins at this point with

> Not so brave *Douglas* . . .

(Margoliouth)

Or with known art to try the gentle wave.
Much him the honours of his ancient race
Inspire, nor would he his own deeds deface,   40
And secret joy in his calme soule does rise,
That Monk looks on to see how *Douglas* dyes.

    Like a glad Lover the fierce flames he meets,
And tryes his first embraces in their Sheets:
His shape exact, which the bright flames infold,
Like the Sunn's statue stands of burnisht gold.
Round the transparent fire about him glowes,
As the clear Amber of the Bee does close,
And, as on Angells' heads their Gloryes shine,
His burning locks adorn his face divine.   50

    But when in his immortall minde he felt
His alt'ring form and solder'd limms to melt,
Down on the Deck he lay'd himself and dy'd,
With his dear sword reposing by his side;
And on the flaming plank so rests his head
As one that huggs himself in a warm bed.
The ship burns down and with his reliques sinks,
And the sad stream beneath his ashes drinks.

    Fortunate Boy, if e'er my verse may claime
That matchlesse grace to propagate thy name,   60
When *Œta* and *Alcides* are forgot,
Our English youth shall sing the valiant *Scott*.

    Shall not a death so gen'rous now when told
Unite the distance, fill the breaches old?
Such in the *Roman Forum Curtius* brave,
Galloping down, clos'd up the gaping cave.
No more discourse of *Scotch* or *English* race,
Nor chaunt the fabulous hunt of *Chevy-Chase*:
Mix'd in *Corinthian* metall at thy flame,
Our Nations melting thy *Colossus* frame.   70

    Prick down the point, whoever has the art,
Where Nature *Scotland* does from *England* part.
Anatomists may sooner fix the cells

---

68. *Chevy-Chase:* A famous old English ballad describing the warfare between the Douglas and Percy families on the Anglo-Scottish border.
69. *Corinthian metall:* Bronze, of which the Colossus of Rhodes was cast. The constituent metals would represent England and Scotland, now alloyed symbolically in the contemplated union.

Where Life resides, or Understanding dwells.
But this we know, though that exceeds our skill,
That whosoever sep'rates them does kill.

  Will you the *Tweed* that sudden bounder call
Of soyle, of witt, of manners, and of all?
Why draw we not as well the thrifty line
From *Thames, Trent, Humber*, or at least the *Tyne*?   80
So may we the State corpulence redresse,
And little *England* when we please make lesse.

  What Ethick river is this wondrous *Tweed*,
Whose one bank virtue, other vice does breed?
Or what new Perpendicular does rise
Up from her stream continu'd to the Skyes,
That between us the common aire should bar
And split the influence of every starre?
But who considers right will find indeed
'Tis *Holy-Island* parts us, not the *Tweed*.   90
Though Kingdomes joyn, yet *Church* will *Kirk* oppose:
The *Mitre* still divides, the *Crown* does close;
As in *Rogation Week*, they whip us round
To keep in mind the *Scotch* and *English* bound.

  Had it not been for such a Bias strong,
Two Nations ne'er had miss'd the mark so long.
The world in all does but two nations beare:
The good, the bad, and those mix'd everywhere.
Under each *Pole* place either of the two,
The bad will basely, good will bravely do,   100
And few indeed can parallel our climes
For worth heroick, or heroick crimes.
The tryall would, however, be too nice
Which stronger were, a *Scotch* or *English* vice,
Or whether the same virtue would reflect
From *Scotch* or *English* heart the same effect.

  Nation is all but Name: a *Shibboleth*
Where a mistaken accent causes death.
In *Paradise* names only nature show'd;
At *Babel* names from pride and discord flow'd,   110

90. *Holy-Island:* Lindisfarne, off the coast of Northumberland, site of the first Celtic
Christian establishment in England.
93: In the Rogation Week ceremonies parish boundaries were fixed in the minds of
parishioners by token whippings.

And ever since Men, with a female spight,
First call each other Names and then they fight.
Scotland and *England!* cause of just uproare:
Do Man and Wife signifie Rogue and Whore?
Say but a *Scot*, and streight we fall to sides:
That Syllable like a *Picts* wall divides.
Rationall Man! Words, pledges all of peace,
Perverted serve dissention to increase.
For shame extirpate from each loyall breast
That senseless rancour against interest.   120
One *King*, one *Faith*, one *Language*, and one *Isle*,
English or *Scotch*, 'tis all but crosse and pile.

    Charles, our great soule, this only understands:
He our Affections both and Will commands,
And, where twin-sympathyes can not attone,
Knows the last secret how to make us one.
Just so the prudent husband-man, who sees
The idle tumult of his factious bees,
The morning dews and flowr's neglected grown,
The Hive a Combe-case, every Bee a Drone,   130
Powders them o'er, till none discern his foes,
And all themselves in meale and freindship lose:
The Insect Kingdome streight begins to thrive,
And each work hony for the common Hive.

    Pardon, young *Heroe*, this so long transport:
(Thy death more nobly did the same exhort).
My former Satyre for this verse forget:
My fault against my Recantation set.
I single did against a nation write:
Against a nation thou didst single fight.   140
My diff'ring crime does more thy virtue raise,
And such my Rashness best thy valour praise.

    Here *Douglas*, smiling, said he did intend,
After such franknesse shown, to be his freind:
Forwarn'd him therefore, lest in time he were
Metempsychos'd in some *Scotch Presbyter*.

---

116. *Picts wall:* One of the walls built in Roman times to exclude marauders.
122. *crosse and pile:* Heads and tails (of the same coin).

Epigramme Upon Blood's *attempt to steale the Crown*

When daring *Blood*, his rents to have regain'd,
Upon the *English* Diadem distrain'd,
He chose the Cassock, surcingle, and Gown
(No mask so fit for one that robbs a Crown);
But his lay-pity underneath prevayl'd
And while he spar'd the *Keeper's* life, he fail'd.
With the Priests Vestments had he but put on
A Bishops cruelty, the Crown was gone.

Upon Sir Robert Vyner's *setting up the Kings-statue in* Wool-church *Market*

i

As Cityes that to the Fierce Conqueror yield
Do at their own charges their Cittadells build,
So *Sir Robert* advanc'd the *Kings* statue, in token
Of Bankers defeated, and *Lumbardstreet* broken.

Epigramme. Upon Blood's attempt to steale the Crown: Colonel Thomas Blood (1618?–1680?), a daring adventurer, was rewarded for his activities on the Parliamentary side in the Civil Wars with lands in Ireland which were confiscated after the Restoration. He twice attempted to kidnap the Duke of Ormonde, whom, as Lord-Lieutenant, Blood held responsible for the confiscation. In May 1671 Blood, disguised as a parson, nearly succeeded in an attempt to make off with the crown jewels. He was captured, but refusing to talk to an examining magistrate, was brought before the King, who pardoned him, restored his lands, and employed him as an intelligence agent.

Upon Sir Robert Vyner's setting up the Kings-statue in Wool-church Market: On May 29, 1672, Sir Robert Viner, a rich goldsmith who, with other bankers, had suffered losses when Charles closed the Exchequer earlier in the year, unveiled an equestrian statue of the King in Stocks Market. The statue had originally represented a King of Poland with a Turk beneath his horse's feet, but Viner had the horseman changed into Charles and the prostrate figure into Cromwell. The conversion was so badly done that Viner covered it up for further alterations, hence the plea of l. 57: "restore us our King."

3. *advanc'd:* (1) erected; (2) promoted, that is, from King of Poland to King of England; and (3), loaned on security.

4. *Lumbardstreet:* The center of banking in the City.

ii

Some thought it a knightly, and generous deed,
Obliging the City with a King and a Steed,
When with honour he might from his word have gone back:
He that vowes for a Calme is absolv'd by a wrack.

iii

But now it appeares from the first to the last
To be all a revenge and Malice forecast,   10
Upon the *Kings* birth day to set up a thing
That showes him a Monster more like than a King.

iv

When each one that passes findes fault with the Horse,
Yet all do affirme the *King* is much worse,
And some by the likeness *Sir Robert* suspect
That he did for the *Kings* his owne Statue erect.

v

To see him so disfigur'd the herbe-women chide,
Who upon their pannyers more decently ride,
And so loose is his seat that all men agree
Even *Sir William Peak* sits much firmer than he.   20

vi

But a Market, they say, does suite the *King* well,
Who the *Parliament* buys and Revenue does sell,
And others, to make the similitude hold,
Say *his Majesty* himself is bought too and sold.

vii

This Statue is surely more scandalous farr
Than all the *Dutch* pictures that caused the War,

17-18: Herbwomen sold their produce in the Stocks Market and rode to market seated on the panniers of their horses.
20. *Sir William Peak:* Lord Mayor in 1667.
24: An allusion to Charles' subventions from Louis XIV under the secret treaty of Dover.
26: One of Charles' pretexts for declaring war on the Dutch in 1672 was the alleged circulation of abusive pictures in Holland.

And what the *Exchequer* for that took on trust
May be henceforth confiscate for Reason more just.

   viii
But *Sir Robert*, to take the Scandall away,
Does the fault upon the Artificer lay   30
And alledges the workmanship was not his owne,
For he counterfeits onely in Gold, not in Stone.

   ix
But, *Sir Knight of the Vine*, how came't in your thought
That when to the scaffold your Liege you had brought,
With Canvas and deale you e'er since do him cloud,
As if you it meant for his Coffin and shrowd?

   x
Has *Blood* him away, as his Crowne once, convey'd,
Or is he to *Clayton's* gone in Masquerade,
Or is he in Caball in this Cabinet sett,
Or have you to the *Counter* remov'd him for debt?   40

   xi
Methinks by the Equipage of this vile scene
That to change him into a Jackpudding you mean,
Or else thus expose him to popular flouts
As if we'd as good have a King made of Clouts.

   xii
Or do you his beames out of modesty veile
With three shatter'd planks and the Ragg of a Saile,
To express how his navy was tatter'd and torn,
The day that he was both restored and born?

37: See the epigram on Blood, p. 193.
38: Charles liked to make impromptu visits masked, and Sir Robert Clayton was
one of the richest men in London.
40. *Counter*: A debtor's prison.   42. *Jackpudding:* A mountebank.
47-48: An allusion to the Battle of Sole Bay, May 28, 1672, when the *Royal James*
blew up with the Earl of Sandwich on board.

xiii

Sure the *King* will ne'er think of repaying his bankers,
Whose loyalty all expires with his Spankers,   50
Now the *Indies* or *Smirna* do not him inrich,
They'll scarcely afford a ragg to his Breech.

xiv

But Sir Robert affirmes that we do him much wrong
For the Graver's at work to reform him thus long
But alas! he will never arrive at his end,
For 'tis such a *King* as no chisel can mend.

xv

But with all his faults pray restore us our *King*,
As ever you hope in December for Spring;
For though the whole world can not shew such another,
Yet we'd better by far have him than his Brother.   60

Upon the Citye's going in a body to Whitehall to present his Majesty with the Instrument of his Freedome in a golden box of £1000 set with Diamonds; as a Comittee to the Duke his in a box of £500 or thereabouts.

i

> The *Londoners* gent
> To the *King* do present

---

50. *Spankers:* Gold coins.
51: In March 1672, before war was declared, an attack on the Dutch Smyrna fleet failed ignominiously.
Upon the Citye's going in a body to Whitehall: On October 29, 1674, Charles II attended the installation of Sir Robert Viner as Lord Mayor of London. In token of their gratitude for this favor, the Lord Mayor and aldermen presented the King with a gold box containing the freedom of the City on December 18. Marvell's poem parodies the doggerel stanza used in songs for the Lord Mayor's show.
1. *gent:* Well-bred.

In a box the City-Maggot:
           'Tis a thing sure of weight,
           That requires the might
Of the whole *Guildhall-team* to drag it.

    ii

          While their Churches unbuilt
          And their houses undwelt
And their Orphans want bread to feed'm
          In a golden Box   10
          Set with stones of both Rocks
They in chaines offer up their Freedome.

    iii

          O yee addle-braind Citts,
          Who henceforth in their wits
Would intrust their youth to your heeding,
          Who in Di'monds and Gold
          Have him thus inroll'd
Yet knew both his freinds and his breeding?

    iv

          Beyond sea he began,
          And such riot there ran   20
Till all the world there did leave him;
          And then he came o'er
          Ten times worse than before:
O what fools were you to receive him!

    v

          He ne'er knew, not he,
          How to serve, or be free,
Though he past through so many adventures:
          But e'er since he was bound
          ('Tis the same to be crown'd)
He has ev'ry day broke his Indentures.   30

---

11. *both Rocks:* Two qualities of precious stones.
12: The Lord Mayors, present and past, wore gold chains with their ceremonial
robes.   19-72: Charles is depicted as an unruly City apprentice.

vi

He spends all his dayes
In running to playes,
When he should on his bookes be poring;
And he wasts all the nights
In the constant delights
Of revelling, drinking, and whoring.

vii

Though oft bound to the Peace,
He never would cease,
But molested the Neighbors with quarrells:
And when he was beat,   40
Still he made his retreat
To his *Clevelands*, his *Nells*, and his *Karwells*.

viii

When his Masters too rash
Him intrusted with Cash,
He us'd as his own to spend on't;
And among his wilde Crew
The money he threw,
As if he should ne'er see an end on't.

ix

Throughout *Lumbardstreet*
With each man he could meet   50
He would run on the Score and Borrow:
But when they askt for their own,
He was broken and gone
And his Creditors left all to sorrow.

x

Nay, his Company lewd
Were twice grown so rude
(But he chanc't to have more sobriety,

42: The Duchess of Cleveland, Nell Gwynne, and Louise de Kéroualle were
Charles' mistresses.
43-48: An allusion to Charles' borrowings from City goldsmiths and to his closing
of the Exchequer in 1672.
49. *Lumbardstreet:* The center of banking in the City.

And the *House* was well barr'd)
Else with Guard upon Guard
He had burglar'd all our Propriety.   60

xi

The Plot was soe laid,
Had it not been betrayd,
As had cancell'd all former disasters:
All *Cheapside* had been Strumpets
To *his Highness's* Trumpets,
And the Soldiers had been all your Masters.

xii

His Word nor his Oath
Can not bind him to troth,
He neglects both Credit and History;
And though he has now   70
Serv'd two Prentiships through,
He knows not his Trade nor his Mistery.

xiii

So many are his Debts
And the Bastards he gets,
Which must all be defray'd by *London*,
That, notwithstanding the care
Of *Sir Thomas Playre*,
The *Chamber* must needs be undone.

xiv

Then, *London*, rejoyce
In thy fortunate choice,   80
To have made this freeman of Spices;
Yet I do not mistrust
But he may grow more just,
For his Virtues exceed still his Vices.

---

60. *Propriety:* Property.
71. *two Prentiships:* Twice seven years, 1660–1674.
77–78: Sir Thomas Player, chamberlain of the City, presented the freedom to
Charles. He was in charge of the Chamber, the Corporation treasury.
81. *Spices:* Charles was an honorary member of the company of Grocers.

xv

But what little thing
Is this that they bring
To the *Duke*, the *Kingdome's* darling?
Yet they hug it and draw
Like Ants at a straw,
Though too small for the gristle of *Starling*.   90

xvi

If a Box of Pills
To cure the *Duke's* ills,
He is too far gone to begin it:
Or does your grave show
In Processioning go
With a Pyx and the Host within it?

xvii

You durst not, I finde,
Leave his Freedome behinde,
And in this Box you have sent it:
But if ever he get   100
For himself up to set,
The whole Nation may live to repent it.

xviii

And yet if your toy
You would wisely imploy,
'Tmight deserve a Box and a gold one;
In Balloting it use
A new *Duke* to chuse,
For we've had too much of the old one.

xix

The very first Head
Of the Oath you him read   110
Shows how fit you are to govern;
When in heart you all knew

91–93: The Duke had syphilis.   94–96: The Duke was a Roman Catholic.

He could never be true
To *Charles* our *King and Sover'n.*

xx

And how could he sweare
That he would forebeare
To Colour the goods of an Alien,
Who still does advance
The government of *France*
With a Wife and Religion *Italian?*   120

xxi

But all ye blind Apes
Led in *Hell* by the Papes,
Never hope in *England* to swagger;
He'll finde, who 't unlocks,
In the bottom of the Box
London bears the Cross with a Dagger.

xxii

And now, *Worshipfull Sirs,*
Go and fold up your Furrs,
And turne againe, *Viner* turne againe:
I see, whoe'er's freed,   130
You for Slaves are decreed
Untill you all burne againe, burne againe.

The Statue at Charing Crosse

i

What can be the mystery why Charing Crosse
This five months continues still buffled with Board?

117: To enter an alien's goods at the custom-house under a citizen's name.
120: The Duke took Maria d'Este as his second wife in 1673.
126. *Crosse with a Dagger:* The arms of London.
The Statue at Charing Crosse: As part of a program to appeal to popular sentiment, the Lord Treasurer Danby in 1675 erected at Charing Cross a bronze equestrian statue of Charles I cast in 1633, but the long delay in carrying out the project laid it open to ridicule.

Dear *Wheeler*, impart; we're all at a losse,
Unlesse we must have *Punchinello* restor'd.

ii

'Twere to *Scaramuccio* too great disrespect
To limit his Troop to this Theater small,
Beside the injustice it were to eject
The Mimick so legally seis'd of *Whitehall*.

iii

For a Diall the place is too unsecure,
Since the Privy garden could not it defend: 10
And so near to the *Court* they will never indure
Any monument how their time they misspend.

iv

Where these deals yet in store for sheathing our Fleet,
When the *King* in Armada to *Portsmouth* should saile,
Or the *Bishops* and *Treasurer* did they agree't
To repaire with such riff-raffe our *Churches* old Pale?

v

No; to comfort the hearts of the poore *Cavalier*,
The late *King* on horseback is here to be shown.
What adoo with your Kings and your statues is here:
Have we not had enough already of one?   20

3. *Wheeler:* Sir Charles Wheeler, close friend and supporter of Danby.
4. *Punchinello:* Puppet shows had been presented in a booth in Charing Cross in the
1660s, but in 1675 the *Commedia dell' arte*, in which Punchinello and Scaramuccio
are important characters, was being performed by living actors at Whitehall.
9. *Diall:* An elaborate sundial of glass in the privy garden at Whitehall destroyed
one June night in 1675 by a gang of riotous courtiers.
14: In July 1675 the King sailed from Gravesend to Portsmouth and back in very
bad weather and was feared lost.
15-16: An allusion to Danby's scheme for an alliance of Anglicans and Royalists
against Catholics, Nonconformists, and all opponents of the prerogative.
20. *one:* Viner's statue of Charles II at Woolchurch.

vi

Does the *Treasurer* think men so loyally tame,
When their pensions are stopt, to be fool'd with a sight?
And 'tis forty to one if he play the old game
He'll reduce us ere long too to forty and eight.

vii

The *Trojan horse* so, not of brasse but of wood,
Had within it an Army that burnt up the Town,
And however, 'tis ominous, if understood,
For the old *King* on Horse back is but an Half-crown.

viii

Yet his *Broth'r-in-law's* Horse had gain'd such repute
That the *Treas'rer* thought prudent to try it againe: 30
And instead of that Market of herbes and of fruite
He will here keep a Market of *Parliament men*.

ix

But why is the work then so long at a stand?
Such things you should never or suddenly do:
As the *Parliament* twice was prorogu'd by your hand,
Will you venture so far to prorogue the King too?

x

Let's have a *King*, *Sir*, be he new, be he old;
Not *Viner* delay'd us so, though he were broken.
Though the *King* be of Copper and *Danby* of Gold,
Shall a *Treas'rer* of Guinny a Prince grudge of Token?   40

22: In 1674 Danby put a temporary stop on salaries, pensions, and secret service
money in order to pay off the fleet at the end of the war.
24. *forty and eight:* The year in which the Second Civil War began.
25-26: An oblique suggestion that Catholics set the Great Fire of 1666.
29. *Broth'r-in-law:* Viner.
40: An allusion to Danby's wealth and the King's property: shall a treasurer
grudge a Prince a token of Guinea?

xi

The huswifely *Tresuresse* sure is grown nice,
And so liberally treated the *Members* at Supper,
She thinks not convenient to go to the price,
And we've lost both our *King* and our Horse and our Crupper.

xii

Where so many *Bartys* there are to provide,
To buy a *King* is not so wise as to sell:
And however she said, it could not be deny'd
That a Monarch of Gingerbread would do as well;

xiii

But the *Treasurer* told her he thought she was mad
And his *Parliament-list* withall did produce,   50
Where he show'd her that so many Voters he had
As would the next Tax reimburse them with use.

xiv

So the Statue will up after all his delay;
But to turne the face to *Whitehall* you must shun:
Though of Brasse yet with grief it would melt him away
To behold ev'ry day such a *Court*, such a *Son*.

41–42: See *The Checker-Inn.*   44. *Crupper:* Buttocks.
45. *Bartys:* Danby's wife was the former Bridget Bertie.
50: Danby introduced systematic bribing of members of the Commons and kept
lists of supporters.

Poets and Heroes

Fleckno, *an English Priest at* Rome

Oblig'd by frequent visits of this man,
Whom as Priest, Poet, and Musician,
I for some branch of *Melchizedeck* took,
(Though he derives himself from *my Lord Brooke*)
I sought his Lodging; which is at the Sign
Of the sad *Pelican*; Subject divine
For Poetry: There three Stair-Cases high,
Which signifies his triple property,
I found at last a Chamber, as 'twas said,
But seem'd a Coffin set on the Stairs head,   10
Not higher than Seav'n, nor larger than three feet;
Only there was nor Seeling, nor a Sheet,
Save that th' ingenious Door did as you come
Turn in, and shew to Wainscot half the Room.
Yet of his State no man could have complain'd;
There being no Bed where he entertain'd:
And though within one Cell so narrow pent,
He'd *Stanzas* for a whole Appartement.
    Straight, without further information,
In hideous verse, he, and a dismal tone,   20
Begins to exorcise, as if I were
Possest, and sure the *Devil* brought me there.
But I, who now imagin'd my self brought
To my last Tryal, in a serious thought
Calm'd the disorders of my youthful Breast,

Fleckno, an English Priest at Rome: Richard Flecknoe was a poetaster and Roman Catholic priest whom Marvell encountered in Rome in 1645 or 1646. Dryden immortalized him in *Mac Flecknoe* as one who
    In prose and verse was owned, without dispute,
    Through all the realms of nonsense, absolute.
Marvell's satire is an extravaganza in the manner of Donne.
3. *Melchizedeck:* A prophet, priest, and king (Genesis 14:18).
4: Flecknoe had dedicated a religious tract to Lady Neville Brook in 1640.
12. *Seeling ... Sheet:* Black hangings and winding-sheets used at funerals.
18. *Stanzas:* Rooms (Italian).

And to my Martyrdom prepared Rest.
Only this frail Ambition did remain,
The last distemper of the sober Brain,
That there had been some present to assure
The future Ages how I did indure: 30
And how I, silent, turn'd my burning Ear
Towards the Verse: and when that could not hear,
Held him the other; and unchanged yet,
Ask'd still for more, and pray'd him to repeat:
Till the Tyrant, weary to persecute,
Left off, and try'd t' allure me with his Lute.
    Now as two Instruments, to the same key
Being tun'd by Art, if the one touched be
The other opposite as soon replies,
Mov'd by the Air and hidden Sympathies;   40
So while he with his gouty Fingers craules
Over the Lute, his murmuring Belly calls,
Whose hungry Guts to the same streightness twin'd
In Echo to the trembling Strings repin'd.
    I, that perceiv'd now what his Musick ment,
Ask'd civilly if he had eat this Lent.
He answered yes, with such, and such an one;
For he has this of gen'rous, that alone
He never feeds, save only when he tryes
With gristly Tongue to dart the passing Flyes.   50
I ask'd if he eat flesh. And he, that was
So hungry that though ready to say *Mass*
Would break his fast before, said he was Sick,
And th' *Ordinance* was only Politick.
Nor was I longer to invite him: Scant
Happy at once to make him Protestant,
And Silent. Nothing now Dinner stay'd
But till he had himself a Body made.
I mean till he were drest: for else so thin
He stands, as if he only fed had been   60
With consecrated Wafers: and the *Host*
Hath sure more flesh and blood than he can boast.
This *Basso Relievo* of a Man,
Who as a Camel tall, yet easly can
The Needle's Eye thread without any stich,

63. *Basso Relievo:* Bas-relief (Italian).

(His only impossible is to be rich)
Lest his too suttle Body, growing rare,
Should leave his Soul to wander in the Air,
He therefore circumscribes himself in rimes;
And swaddled in's own papers seaven times,   70
Wears a close Jacket of poetick Buff,
With which he doth his third Dimension Stuff.
Thus armed underneath, he over all
Does make a primitive *Sotana* fall;
And above that yet casts an antick Cloak,
Worn at the first Counsel of *Antioch*;
Which by the *Jews* long hid, and Disesteem'd,
He heard of by Tradition, and redeem'd.
But were he not in this black habit deck't,
This half transparent Man would soon reflect   80
Each colour that he past by; and be seen,
As the *Chamelion*, yellow, blew, or green.
     He drest, and ready to disfurnish now
His Chamber, whose compactness did allow
No empty place for complimenting doubt,
But who came last is forc'd first to go out;
I meet one on the Stairs who made me stand,
Stopping the passage, and did him demand:
I answer'd he is here *Sir*; but you see
You cannot pass to him but thorow me.   90
He thought himself affronted; and reply'd,
I whom the Pallace never has deny'd
Wil make the way here; I said *Sir* you'l do
Me a great favour, for I seek to go.
He gath'ring fury still made sign to draw;
But himself there clos'd in a Scabbard saw
As narrow as his Sword's; and I, that was
Delightful, said there can no Body pass
Except by penetration hither, where
Two make a crowd, nor can three Persons here   100

74. *Sotana:* Cassock.
76. *Worn:* As in Folio; Bod. MS. reads *Torn*. *Antioch*: The site of many theological councils, the first of which was held in 264.
85. *Complimenting doubt:* As to who should leave first.
99. *penetration:* Supposed occupation by two or more bodies of the same space at the same time.
100–101: An allusion to the doctrine of the Trinity.

Consist but in one substance, Then, to fit
Our peace, the Priest said I too had some wit:
To prov't, I said, the place doth us invite
By its own narrowness, Sir, to unite.
He ask'd me pardon; and to make me way
Went down, as I him follow'd to obey.
But the propitiatory Priest had straight
Oblig'd us, when below, to celebrate
Together our attonement: so increas'd
Betwixt us two the Dinner to a Feast.   110

    Let it suffice that we could eat in peace;
And that both Poems did and Quarrels cease
During the Table; though my new made Friend
Did, as he threatned, ere 'twere long, intend
To be both witty and valiant: I loth,
Said 'twas too late, he was already both.

    But now, Alas, my first Tormentor came,
Who satisfy'd with eating, but not tame,
Turns to recite; though Judges most severe
After th' Assizes dinner mild appear,   120
And on full stomach do condemn but few:
Yet he more strict my sentence doth renew,
And draws out of the black box of his Breast
Ten quire of paper in which he was drest.
Yet that which was a greater cruelty
Than *Nero's* Poem he calls charity,
And so the *Pelican* at his door hung
Picks out the tender bosome to its young.

    Of all his Poems there he stands ungirt
Save only two foul copies for his shirt: 130
Yet these he promises as soon as clean.
But how I loath'd to see my Neighbour glean
Those papers, which he pilled from within
Like white fleaks rising from a Leper's skin!
More odious than those raggs which the *French* youth
At ordinaries after dinner show'th,
When they compare their *Chancres* and *Poulains*.

104. *By:* As in Bod. MS.; Folio reads *But*.
126: When Nero was singing no one was permitted to leave the theatre.
133. *pilled:* Peeled.

Yet he first kist them, and after takes pains
To read; and then, because he understood
Not one Word, thought and swore that they were good.   140
But all his praises could not now appease
The provok't Author, whom it did displease
To hear his Verses, by so just a curse,
That were ill made, condemn'd to be read worse:
And how (impossible) he made yet more
Absurdityes in them than were before.
For he his untun'd voice did fall or raise
As a deaf Man upon a Viol playes,
Making the half points and the periods run
Confus'der than the atoms in the Sun.   150
Thereat the Poet swell'd, with anger full,
And roar'd out, like *Perillus* in's own *Bull*;
Sir you read false. That any one but you
Should know the contrary. Whereat, I, now
Made Mediator, in my room, said, Why?
To say that you read false *Sir* is no Lye.
Thereat the waxen Youth relented straight;
But saw with sad dispair that 'twas too late.
For the disdainful Poet was retir'd
Home, his most furious Satyr to have fir'd   160
Against the Rebel; who, at this struck dead,
Wept bitterly as disinherited.
Who should commend his Mistress now? Or who
Praise him? both difficult indeed to do
With truth. I counsell'd him to go in time,
Ere the fierce Poet's anger turn'd to rime.
   He hasted; and I, finding my self free,
As one scap't strangely from Captivity,
Have made the Chance be painted; and go now
To hang it in *Saint Peter's* for a Vow.   170

152: The tyrant Phalaris had a bronze bull made by the sculptor Perillus.
158. '*twas:* Bod. MS.; Folio reads *was*.

To his Noble Friend Mr. Richard Lovelace, *upon his Poems*

    Sir,
Our times are much degenerate from those
Which your sweet Muse, which your fair Fortune chose,
And as complexions alter with the Climes,
Our wits have drawne th' infections of our times.
That candid Age no other way could tell
To be ingenious, but by speaking well.
Who best could prayse, had then the greatest prayse,
'Twas more esteemed to give, than weare the Bayes:
Modest ambition studi'd only then,
To honor not her selfe, but worthy men.   10
These vertues now are banisht out of Towne,
Our Civill Wars have lost the Civicke crowne.
He highest builds, who with most Art destroys,
And against others Fame his owne employs.
I see the envious Caterpillar sit
On the faire blossome of each growing wit.
    The Ayre's already tainted with the swarms
Of Insects which against you rise in arms.
Word-peckers, Paper-rats, Book-scorpions,
Of wit corrupted, the unfashion'd Sons.   20
The barbed Censurers begin to looke
Like the grim consistory on thy Booke:
And on each line cast a reforming eye,
Severer than the yong Presbytery.
Till when in vaine they have thee all perus'd,
You shall for being faultless be accus'd.
Some reading your *Lucasta*, will alledge

To his Noble Friend Mr. Richard Lovelace: Marvell's was one of many commendatory
poems included in the first edition of Richard Lovelace's *Lucasta* (1649). Lovelace
was a Cavalier, and the Parliamentary censorship seems to have delayed the
book's publication for political reasons (ll. 21–24).
22. *consistory:* Presbyterian court.

You wrong'd in her the Houses Priviledge.
Some that you under sequestration are,
Because you write when going to the Warre,   30
And one the book prohibits, because *Kent*
Their first Petition by the Authour sent.
    But when the beauteous Ladies came to know
That their deare *Lovelace* was endanger'd so:
Lovelace that thaw'd the most congealed brest,
He who lov'd best and them defended best.
Whose hand so rudely grasps the steely brand,
Whose hand so gently melts the Ladies hand.
They all in mutiny though yet undrest
Sally'd, and would in his defence contest.   40
And one the loveliest that was yet e're seen,
Thinking that I too of the rout had been.
Mine eyes invaded with a female spight,
(She knew what pain 'twould be to lose that sight.)
O no, mistake not, I reply'd, for I
In your defence, or in his cause would dy.
But he secure of glory and of time
Above their envy or mine aid doth clime.
Him, valiant men, and fairest Nymphs approve,
His Booke in them finds Judgement, with you Love.   50

Upon the death of the Lord Hastings

    Go, intercept some Fountain in the Vein,
Whose Virgin-Source yet never steept the Plain.
Hastings is dead, and we must finde a Store
Of Tears untoucht, and never wept before.
Go, stand betwixt the *Morning* and the *Flowers*;

28. *Houses Priviledge:* Parliamentary privilege, which included freedom of speech.
wrong'd: Abused.
29-30: An allusion to Lovelace's famous poem, "To Lucasta, on Going to the
Wars." The estates of royalists were confiscated by Parliament.
31-32: Lovelace had presented in 1642 a Kentish petition on the King's behalf and
was imprisoned in consequence.
39. *undrest*: (1) *En déshabillé* (2) unarmed.
Upon the Death of the Lord Hastings: Henry, Lord Hastings, died of smallpox in June
1649 at the age of nineteen. Marvell's elegy was one of many published in a volume
called *Lachrymae Musarum*.

And, ere they fall, arrest the early *Showers*.
Hastings is dead; and we, disconsolate,
With early *Tears* must mourn his early *Fate*.
　　Alas, his *Vertues* did his *Death* presage:
Needs must he die, that doth out-run his *Age*.   10
The Phlegmatick and Slowe prolongs his day,
And on Times Wheel sticks like a *Remora*.
What man is he, that hath no *Heaven* beguil'd,
And is not thence mistaken for a *Childe?*
While those of growth more sudden, and more bold,
Are hurried hence, as if already old.
For, there above, They number not as here,
But weigh to Man the *Geometrick* yeer.
　　Had he but at this Measure still increast,
And on *the Tree of Life* once made a Feast,   20
As that of *Knowledge*; what Loves had he given
To Earth, and then what Jealousies to Heaven!
But 'tis a *Maxime* of that State, That none,
Lest He becomes like Them, taste more than one.
Therefore the *Democratick* Stars did rise,
And all that Worth from hence did *Ostracize*.
　　Yet as some *Prince*, that, for State-Jealousie,
Secures his neerest and most lov'd *Ally*;
His Thought with richest Triumphs entertains,
And in the choicest Pleasures charms his Pains: 30
So he, not banisht hence, but there confin'd,
There better recreates his active Minde.
　　Before the *Chrystal Palace* where he dwells,
The armed *Angels* hold their *Carouzels*;
And underneath, he views the *Turnaments*
Of all these Sublunary *Elements*.
But most he doth th' *Eternal Book* behold,
On which the *happie Names* do stand enroll'd;
And gladly there can all his Kindred claim,
But most rejoyces at his *Mothers* name.   40
　　The gods themselves cannot their Joy conceal,
But draw their Veils, and their pure Beams reveal:

12. *Remora:* A sucking-fish which attaches itself to the hulls of ships.
18. *Geometrick yeer:* A measure of actual growth, as distinguished from age.

Onely they drooping *Hymeneus* note,
Who for sad *Purple*, tears his *Saffron*-coat;
And trails his Torches th'row the Starry Hall
Reversed, at his *Darlings* Funeral.
    And *Æsculapius*, who, asham'd and stern,
Himself at once condemneth, and *Mayern*;
Like some sad *Chymist*, who prepar'd to reap
The *Golden Harvest*, sees his Glasses leap.   50
For, how Immortal must their Race have stood,
Had *Mayern* once been mixt wth *Hastings* blood!
How Sweet and Verdant would these *Lawrels* be,
Had they been planted on that *Balsam*-tree!
    But what could he, good man, although he bruis'd
All Herbs, and them a thousand ways infus'd?
All he had try'd, but all in vain, he saw,
And wept, as we, without Redress or Law.
For *Man* (alas) is but the *Heavens* sport;
And *Art* indeed is Long, but *Life* is Short.   60

To his worthy Friend Doctor Witty *upon his Translation of the Popular Errors*

    Sit further, and make room for thine own fame,
Where just desert enrolles thy honour'd Name
The good Interpreter. Some in this task
Take off the Cypress vail, but leave a mask,
Changing the Latine, but do more obscure
That sence in *English*, which was bright and pure.
So of Translators they are Authors grown,
For ill Translators make the Book their own.

43–46: Hastings died the day before he was to marry the daughter of Sir Theodore Turquet de Mayerne, Charles I's physician.
49. *Chymist:* Alchemist.   50. *leap:* Crack.
To his worthy Friend Doctor Witty: This poem together with one by Marvell in Latin appeared as commendatory verses to Robert Witty's translation of Robert Primrose's treatise, *De Vulgi in Medicinâ Erroribus Libri quatuor.* Witty's version, *Popular Errors ... in Physick,* was published in 1651.
4. *Cypress vail:* Light transparent material, alluding to the language of the original.
mask: The obscurities introduced by a bad translator.

Others do strive with words and forced phrase
To add such lustre, and so many rayes,   10
That but to make the Vessel shining, they
Much of the precious Metal rub away.
He is Translation's thief that addeth more,
As much as he that taketh from the Store
Of the First Author. Here he maketh blots
That mends; and added beauties are but spots.
    Celia whose English doth more richly flow
Than *Tagus*, purer than dissolved snow.
And sweet as are her lips that speak it, she
Now learns the tongues of *France* and *Italy*;   20
But she is *Celia* still: no other grace
But her own smiles commend that lovely face;
Her native beauty's not Italianated,
Nor her chaste mind into the *French* translated:
Her thoughts are *English*, though her sparkling wit
With other Language doth them fitly fit.
    Translators learn of her: but stay, I slide
Down into Error with the Vulgar tide;
Women must not teach here: the Doctor doth
Stint them to Cawdles, Almond-milk, and Broth.   30
Now I reform, and surely so will all
Whose happy Eyes on thy Translation fall,
I see the people hastning to thy Book,
Liking themselves the worse the more they look,
And so disliking, that they nothing see
Now worth the liking, but thy Book and thee.
And (if I Judgment have) I censure right;
For something guides, my hand that I must write.
You have Translations statutes best fulfil'd.
That handling neither sully nor would guild.   40

18. *Tagus:* Portuguese river.

On Mr. Milton's *Paradise Lost*

When I behold the Poet blind, yet bold,
In slender Book his vast Design unfold,
Messiah Crown'd, *Gods* Reconcil'd Decree,
Rebelling *Angels*, the Forbidden Tree,
Heav'n, Hell, Earth, Chaos, All; the Argument
Held me a while, misdoubting his Intent,
That he would ruine (for I saw him strong)
The sacred Truths to Fable and old Song,
(So *Sampson* groap'd the Temples Posts in spight)
The World o'rewhelming to revenge his Sight.   10

Yet as I read, soon growing less severe,
I lik'd his Project, the success did fear;
Through that wide Field how he his way should find
O're which lame Faith leads Understanding blind;
Lest he perplext the things he would explain,
And what was easie he should render vain.

Or if a Work so infinite he spann'd,
Jealous I was that some less skilful hand
(Such as disquiet alwayes what is well,
And by ill imitating would excell)   20
Might hence presume the whole Creations day
To change in Scenes, and show it in a Play.

Pardon me, *mighty Poet*, nor despise
My causeless, yet not impious, surmise.
But I am now convinc'd and none will dare
Within thy Labours to pretend a Share.
Thou hast not miss'd one thought that could be fit,
And all that was improper dost omit:
So that no room is here for Writers left,
But to detect their Ignorance or Theft.   30

On Mr. Milton's Paradise Lost: This poem is prefixed to the second edition of *Paradise Lost* (1674) where it immediately precedes Milton's foreword discussing his use of blank verse.   17. *spann'd:* Encompassed.
19-20: Here, as in ll. 47-48, an allusion to Dryden, who "tagged" (added rhymes to) Milton's epic in an operatic version, *The State of Innocence and the Fall of Man.*
30. *detect:* Expose.

That Majesty which through thy Work doth Reign
Draws the Devout, deterring the Profane.
And things divine thou treatst of in such state
As them preserves, and Thee, inviolate.
At once delight and horrour on us seize,
Thou singst with so much gravity and ease;
And above humane flight dost soar aloft,
With Plume so strong, so equal, and so soft.
The *Bird* nam'd from that *Paradise* you sing
So never Flags, but alwaies keeps on Wing.   40
     Where couldst thou Words of such a compass find?
Whence furnish such a vast expense of Mind?
Just Heav'n Thee, like *Tiresias*, to requite,
Rewards with *Prophesie* thy loss of Sight.
     Well might thou scorn thy Readers to allure
With tinkling Rhime, of thy own Sense secure;
While the *Town-Bays* writes all the while and spells,
And like a Pack-Horse tires without his Bells.
Their Fancies like our bushy Points appear,
The Poets tag them; we for fashion wear.   50
I, too, transported by the *Mode* offend,
And while I meant to *Praise* thee, must Commend.
Thy verse created like thy *Theme* sublime,
In Number, Weight, and Measure, needs not *Rhime*.

An Epitaph upon ⸺

Enough: and leave the rest to Fame.
'Tis to commend her but to name.
Courtship, which living she declin'd,
When dead to offer were unkind.
Where never any could speak ill,
Who would officious Praises spill?

39–40: An allusion to the popular error that birds of paradise had no feet and were
therefore always in flight.
49. *bushy Points:* Tasselled laces for fastening stockings.

Nor can the truest Wit or Friend,
Without Detracting, her commend.
To say she liv'd a *Virgin* chaste,
In this Age loose and all unlac't;   10
Nor was, when Vice is so allow'd,
Of *Virtue* or asham'd, or proud;
That her Soul was on Heav'en so bent
No Minute but it came and went;
That ready her last Debt to pay
She summ'd her Life up ev'ry day;
Modest as Morn; as Mid-day bright;
Gentle as Ev'ning; cool as Night;
'Tis true: but all so weakly said:
'Twere more Significant, *She's Dead*.   20

Poems in Latin and Greek

Ad Regem Carolum *Parodia*

Jam satis pestis, satis atque diri
Fulminis misit pater, et rubenti
Dexterâ nostras jaculatus arces
  Terruit urbem.

Terruit cives, grave nè rediret
Pristinum seclum nova monstra questum,
Omne cùm pestis pecus egit altos
  Visere montes;

Cùm scholae latis genus haesit agris,
Nota quae sedes fuerat bubulcis;   10
Cùm togâ abjectâ pavidus reliquit
  Oppida doctus.

Vidimus *Chamum* fluvium retortis
Littore à dextro violenter undis
Ire plorantem monumenta pestis,
  Templáque clausa.

Granta dum semet nimiùm querenti
Miscet uxorem, vagus et sinistrâ
Labitur ripâ, *Jove* comprobante,
  Tristior amnis.   20

Audiit coelos acuisse ferrum,
Quo graves *Turcae* meliùs perirent;
Audiit mortes vitio parentum
  Rara juvéntus.

Ad Regem Carolum Parodia: This poem and the one which follows appeared in a Cambridge volume of Latin and Greek verses on the birth of Princess Anne, March 17, 1637. The "*Parodia*" is a close adaptation of Horace's *Odes*, I.2.
  The translation is by A. B. Grosart.

Quem vocet divûm populus ruentis
Imperî rebus? prece quâ fatigent
Doctior coetus minùs audientes
    Carmina coelos?

Cui dabit partes luis expiandae
Jupiter, tandem venias, precamur,   30
Nube candentes humeros amictus
    Auxiliator.

Sive tu mavis, *Erycina* nostra,
Quam jocus circumvolat et *Cupido*,
Túque neglectum genus et nepotes
    Auxeris ipsa.

Sola tam longam removere pestem,
Quam juvat luctus faciésque tristis,
Prolis optatâ reparare mole
    Sola potésque.   40

Sive felici *Carolum* figurâ
Parvulus Princeps imitetur, almae
Sive *Mariae* decoret puellam
    Dulcis imago.

Serus in coelum redeas, diúque
Laetus intersis populo *Britanno*,
Néve te nostris vitiis iniquum
    Ocyor aura

Tollat. Hîc magnos potiùs triumphos,
Hîc ames dici pater atque princeps,   50
Et novâ mortes reparato prole
    Te patre, Caesar.

TRANSLATION

To King Charles. *An Imitation*

Enough by this of plague and lightning pale
    Our Sire has sent his way, who from his red
Right hand our hallow'd turrets did assail,
    And thrill'd the town with dread:

With dread the people thrill'd, lest the dire age
    Return, which mourn'd unwonted horrid sights,
When the dire Plague sent every flock to graze
    The lofty mountain-heights:

When the broad meadows felt the scholars' tread,
    Where once the simple herd in peace lay down,   10
When, casting off his robes, the doctor fled
    From the deserted town.

We saw the muddi'd *Camus* vehement,
    With waves driven backward on Midsummer Plain,
Rush, mourning many a plague-built monument
    And shut-up college fane;

While *Granta* with his much complaining mate
    Is huddled close, and on the nearer shore,
As *Jove* looks on indifferent to their fate,
    Glides chafing more and more.   20

The scatter'd youth are told how angry *Heaven*
    Whetteth his sword, more meet for heathen *Turks*;
Are told of hapless crowds to slaughter driven
    By their own fathers' works.

1: The university was closed in 1636 on account of the plague.
13–17: *Camus* and *Granta* are the branches which form the Cambridge river.
22. *Turks:* An allusion to the Sallee pirates.

What God, I marvel, will the people cite
    To prop their falling State? How many times
Must our thrice-learned crowds the gods invite
    To listen to their rhymes?

To whom will *Jupiter* assign the task
    To expiate our blot? Come then, we pray,   30
Hiding thy features in cloudy mask,
    Be thou our help this day.

Or wouldst thou rather, *Erycina* fair,
    Round whom young *Sport* and *Cupid* gambol free,
Help thy neglected race, and watch with care
    Thy own posterity?

Thou only mayst remove this Plague malign,
    Whom nothing but sad looks and grief delight;
Thou only canst repair our failing line,
    And fairer hopes excite.   40

Whether some little *Charles* his father's grace
    With happy imitation wear anew,
Or the sweet image of *Maria's* face
    Blush with a maiden hue,

Late be thy journey to the lucent star,
    Long mayst thou tarry here in *English* clime;
Nor any wind pernicious waft thee far,
    Sick of thy people's crime.

Here rather triumph largely, and aspire
    To be thy people's father as their king;   50
That from thy death-invaded race, O Sire,
    A second stock may spring.

33. *Erycina:* Venus.

Πρὸς Κάρολον τὸν βασιλέα

"Ω Δυσαριστοτόκος, Πέντ' ὦ δυσποτμος ἀριθμός!　　5. Novemb.
　"Ω Πέντε στυγερὸν, Πέντ', ἀΐδαο πύλαι!　　　　5. Aug.
'Αγγλῶν ὦ μέγ' ὄνειδος , ὦ οὐρανίοισιν ἀπεχθές!
　'Αλλ' ἀπελύμαινες Κάρρολε τοῦτον ἄνα.
Πέμπτον τέκνον ἔδωκε μογοστόκος Εἰλείθυια,
　Πέντε δὲ Πένταθλον τέκνα καλοῦσι τεόν.
Εἰ δὲ θέλεις βίβλόις ταῖς ὀψιγόνοισι τίεσθαι,
　Πεντήτενχου ἔχεις παιδια διογενῆ.
"Η ὅτι θεσπεσίης φιλέεις μήστωρας ἀοιδῆς,
　'Αρμονίην ποιεῖς τὴν Διὰ πέντε Πάτερ.　　　　　　　10

'Ανδρέας ὁ Μαρβέλλου, ἐκ τοῦ τῆς Τριαδος

TRANSLATION

To King Charles

O figure FIVE, presaging evil fate
T' Earth's best! O hated Hades' five-fold gate!
O England's scandal, and abhorr'd of Heaven!
To purge its stain, O *Charles*, to thee is given.
Since kind *Lucina* give thee a FIFTH child,
Pentathlon shall thy children five be styled.
Wouldst thou be famous in many an after-book,
In thy fair children see a Pentateuch;
And since thou lovest poesy divine,
In Harmony's five notes, O Father shine.　　　　　　10

Andrew Marvell, Trinity College

Πρὸς Κάρολον: The rather labored wit of this poem celebrating the birth of the
Princess Anne, Charles' fifth child, plays on the number five with allusions to the
date of two plots against the life of James I (August 5, 1600, and November 5,
1605).
　I have reprinted A. B. Grosart's translation with minor alterations.

ROS

Cernis ut *Eoi* descendat Gemmula Roris,
  Inque Rosas roseo transfluat orta sinu.
Sollicitâ Flores stant ambitione supini,
  Et certant foliis pellicuisse suis.
Illa tamen patriae lustrans fastigia Sphaerae,
  Negligit hospitii limina picta novi.
Inque sui nitido conclusa voluminis orbe,
  Exprimit aetherei quâ licet Orbis aquas.
En ut odoratum spernat generosior *Ostrum*,
  Vixque premat casto mollia strata pede.   10
Suspicit at longis distantem obtutibus Axem,
  Inde et languenti lumine pendet amans,
Tristis, et in liquidum mutata dolore dolorem,
  Marcet, uti roseis Lachryma fusa Genis.
Ut pavet, et motum tremit irrequieta Cubile,
  Et quoties *Zephryo* fluctuat Aura, fugit.
Qualis inexpertam subeat formido Puellam,
  Sicubi nocte redit incomitata domum.
Sic et in horridulas agitatur Gutta procellas,
  Dum prae virgineo cuncta Pudore timet.   20
Donec oberrantem Radio clemente vaporet,
  Inque jubar reducem Sol genitale trahat.
Talis, in humano si possit flore videri,
  Exul ubi longas Mens agit usque moras;
Hace quoque natalis meditans convivia Coeli,
  Evertit Calices, purpureosque Thoros.
Fontis stilla sacri, Lucis scintilla perennis,
  Non capitur *Tyriâ* veste, vapore *Sabae*.
Tota sed in proprii secedens luminis Arcem,
  Colligit in Gyros se sinuosa breves.   30
Magnorumque sequens Animo convexa Deorum,
  Sydereum parvo fingit in Orbe Globum.

Ros: This is the Latin counterpart of "On a Drop of Dew," which it probably
preceded. Although the two poems are at times quite close to each other in thought
and expression, each is an independent poem in its own right.

  The translation is from *The Latin Poetry of Andrew Marvell* by William McQueen
and Kiffin Rockwell. Reprinted by permission of the University of North Carolina
Studies in Comparative Literature.

Quàm bene in aversae modulum contracta figurae
    Oppositum Mundo claudit ubique latus.
Sed bibit in speculum radios ornata rotundum;
    Et circumfuso splendet aperta Die.
Quâ Superos spectat rutilans, obscurior infra;
    Caetera dedignans, ardet amore Poli.
Subsilit, hinc agili Poscens discedere motu,
    Undique coelesti cincta soluta Viae.   40
Totaque in aereos extenditur orbita cursus;
    Hinc punctim carpens, mobile stringit iter.
Haud aliter Mensis exundans Manna beatis
    Deserto jacuit Stilla gelata solo:
Stilla gelata solo, sed Solibus hausta benignis,
    Ad sua quâ cecidit purior Astra redit.

TRANSLATION

Dew

See how a little jewel of Orient dew descends
And, sprung from the rosy breast to Dawn, flows onto the
        roses.
The flowers stand, opened in solicitous desire,
And strive to entice with their leaves.
Yet that drop, surveying the heights of its native sphere,
Disdains the painted threshold of its new dwelling.
And enclosed within its shining globe,
It shapes the waters of the ethereal sphere as it can.
See how it, more noble, scorns the odorous purple,
And scarcely presses the soft resting place with its pure foot.   10
It looks up at the distant heavens with a long gaze,
And, desiring that place, hangs with a faint glow,
Sad, changed by sorrow into liquid sorrow,
It is spent, like a tear upon a rosy cheek.
Restless, how it trembles and quivers on its troubled couch,
And, as often as the air stirs with a breeze, rolls about.

Just as fear seizes a naive girl
If she returns home at night alone.
Thus the drop, shaken in tiny storms,
Now in its virginal shyness fears everything,   20
Until the engendering sun warms its hovering form
With gentle rays and draws it back to splendor.
Such, if it could be seen in the human flower,
Is the exiled soul, constantly aware of long delays;
It too, thinking of the feasts of its native heaven,
Overturns the drinking cups and purple banquet couches.
A drop of the sacred fountain, a glimmer of eternal light,
It is not caught in Tyrian robe or scent of Saba,
But withdrawing completely into the fortress of its own light,
It draws inward, closing upon itself.   30
Conforming in its nature with the arching heaven of the
        great gods,
It builds a starry heaven in its small sphere.
How well contracted into a little image of the heavens,
It shuts up everywhere its side opposed to the world.
But, ornate, it drinks the rays of the sun into its rounded
        mirror,
And shines, open to the surrounding light.
Glowing where it faces the gods, but darker below;
Scorning all else, it burns with love of the heavens.
It leaps up, desiring to depart quickly,
Fully ready, freed for its heavenly journey.   40
And, its whole surface stretched in aerial course,
Leaving in an instant, it speeds to its goal.
Not otherwise did manna, overflowing with blessed
        nourishment,
Lie, a frozen drop, on the desert soil:
A frozen drop on the ground, but drawn by propitious suns,
It returns, purer, to the stars whence it fell.

Magdala, *lascivos sic quum dimisit Amantes*

Magdala, lascivos sic quum dimisit Amantes,
  Fervidaque in castas lumina solvit aquas;
Haesit in irriguo lachrymarum compede *Christus*,
  Et tenuit sacros uda Catena pedes.

Hortus

Quisnam adeo, mortale genus, praecordia versat?
Heu Palmae, Laurique furor, vel simplicis Herbae!
Arbor ut indomitos ornet vix una labores;
Tempora nec foliis praecingat tota malignis.
Dum simul implexi, tranquillae ad serta Quietis,
Omnigeni coeunt Flores, integraque Sylva.
  Alma Quies, teneo te! et te Germana Quietis
Simplicitas! Vos ergo diu per Templa, per urbes,
Quaesivi, Regum perque alta Palatia frustra.
Sed vos Hortorum per opaca silentia longe   10
Celarant Plantae virides, et concolor Umbra.
  O! mihi si vestros liceat violasse recessus,
Erranti, lasso, et vitae melioris anhelo,
Municipem servate novum, votoque potitum,
Frondosae Cives optate in florea Regna.
  Me quoque, vos *Musae*, et te conscie testor *Apollo*,
Non Armenta juvant hominum, *Circique* boatus,

Magdala: Marvell's English version of this epigram is stanza viii of "Eyes and Tears," p. 9.
Hortus has the same theme as Marvell's "Garden." In the Folio the printer inserted *Desunt multa* ("many lines are missing") after l. 48, assuming that "*Hortus*" must originally have had a passage corresponding to stanzas v–viii of "The Garden." Neither poem, however, can be regarded as a close version of the other, and since "*Hortus*" has no counterpart to the most interesting stanzas of "The Garden," it is reasonable to assume tht the Latin poem was written first.
  The translation is from *The Latin Poetry of Andrew Marvell* by William McQueen and Kiffin Rockwell. Reprinted by permission of the University of North Carolina Studies in Comparative Literature.
10. *Hortorum:* As in Cooke; *Hotrorum* in the Folio.

Mugitusve Fori; sed me Penetralia veris,
Horroresque trahunt muti, et Consortia sola.
   Virgineae quem non suspendit Gratia formae?   20
Quam candore Nives vincentem, Ostrumque rubore,
Vestra tamen viridis superet (me judice) Virtus.
Nec foliis certare Comae, nec Brachia ramis,
Nec possint tremulos voces aequare susurros.
   Ah quoties saevos vidi (quis credat?) Amantes
Sculpentes Dominae potiori in cortice nomen?
Nec puduit truncis inscribere vulnera sacris.
Ast Ego, si vertras unquam temeravero stirpes,
Nulla *Neaera, Chloe, Faustina, Corynna,* legetur:
In proprio sed quaeque libro signabitur Arbos.   30
O charae *Platanus, Cyparissus, Populus, Ulmus*!
   Nec *Veneris Mavors* meminit si *Fraxinus* adsit.
Formosae pressit *Daphnes* vestigia *Phoebus*
Invertitque faces, nec se cupit usque timeri;
Aut exporrectus jacet, indormitque pharetrae;
Non auditurus quanquam Cytherea vocarit;
Nequitias referunt nec somnia vana priores.
   Laetantur *Superi*, defervescente Tyranno,
Et licet experti toties *Nymphasque Deasque,*
Arbore nunc melius potiuntur quisque cupitâ.   40
Jupiter annosam, neglectâ conjuge, *Quercum*
Deperit; haud aliâ doluit sic pellice *Juno*.
Lemniacum temerant vestigia nulla Cubile,
   Nec *Veneris Mavors* meminit si *Fraxinus* adsit.
Formosae pressit *Daphnes* vestigia *Phoebus*
Ut fieret *Laurus*; sed nil quaesiverat ultra.
Capripes et peteret quòd *Pan Syringa* fugacem,
Hoc erat ut *Calamum* posset reperire Sonorum.

Desunt multa
Nec tu, Opifex horti, grato sine carmine abibis:
Qui brevibus plantis, et laeto flore, notasti   50
Crescentes horas, atque intervalla diei.

---

35. *exporrectus:* As in Cooke; *experrectus* in the Folio.
37. *referunt:* As in Cooke; *referuut* in the Folio.
44: As in the Folio; the Bod. MS. reads: Dum *Veneri Myrtus Marti* dum *Fraxinus*
adsit.

Sol ibi candidior fragrantia Signa pererrat;
Proque truci *Tauro*, stricto pro forcipe *Cancri*,
Securis violaeque rosaeque allabitur umbris.
Sedula quin et Apis, mellito intenta labori,
Horologo sua pensa thymo Signare videtur.
Temporis O suaves lapsus! O Otia sana!
    O Herbis dignae numerari et Floribus Horae!

TRANSLATION

The Garden

    What madness so stirs the heart of man?
Alas, madness for the Palm and the Laurel, or for the simple
    grass!
So that one tree will scarcely crown his curbless efforts,
Nor wholly circle his temples with its scanty leaves.
While at the same time, entwined in garlands of tranquil
    Quiet,
All flowers meet, and the virgin woods.
    Fair Quiet, I hold you! And you, sister of Quiet,
Innocence! You a long time in temples, in cities
I sought in vain, and in the palaces of kings.
But you in the shaded silences of gardens, far off,   10
The green plants and like-colored shadow hide.
    Oh, if I am ever allowed to profane your retreats,
Wandering about, faint, and panting for a better life,
Preserve your new citizen, and me, having attained my wish,
Leafy citizens, accept in the flowery kingdom.
    Me also, you *Muses*—and I call you, omniscient *Apollo*, as
    witness—
Herds of men do not please, nor the roaring of the *Circus*,
Nor the bellowing of the Forum; but me the sanctuaries of
    spring,
And silent veneration draw, and solitary communion.

Whom does the grace of maidenly beauty not arrest?   20
Which, although it excels snows in whiteness and purple in
    redness,
Yet your green force (in my opinion) surpasses.
Hair cannot compete with leaves, nor arms with branches,
Nor are tremulous voices able to equal your whisperings.
    Ah, how often have I seen (Who would believe it?) cruel
      lovers
Carving the name of their mistress on bark, which is more
    worthy of love.
Nor was there a sense of shame for inscribing wounds on
    sacred trunks.
But I, if ever I shall have profaned your stocks,
No *Neaera, Chloe, Faustina, Corynna* shall be read:
But the name of each tree shall be written on its own bark.   30
O dear *plane tree, cypress, poplar, elm*!
    Here Love, his wings cast aside, walks about in sandals,
Laying aside his nerveless bows and hissing arrows,
And inverts his torches, nor does he wish to be feared;
Or he lies stretched out and sleeps on his quiver;
Nor will he hear, although Cytherea call;
Nor do idle dreams report previous iniquities.
    The Gods rejoice, the Tyrant ceasing to rage,
And although they have known *nymphs* and *goddesses* many
    times,
Each one achieves his desires better now in a *tree*.   40
Jupiter, forgetful of his wife, languishes for the aged oak;
Juno has not suffered thus for another rival.
No traces dishonor the bed of *Vulcan*,
Nor is *Mars* mindful of *Venus* if the *ash* be present.
Apollo pursued beautiful *Daphne*
That she might become a *laurel*; but he had sought nothing
    more.
And though goat-footed *Pan* fell upon fleeing *Syrinx*,
This was that he might procure a sounding reed.

Desunt multa
And you, maker of the garden, shall not depart without a
    grateful song:
You who in the brief plants and joyous flowers have   50
    indicated
The growing hours and intervals of the day.
There the sun more bright passes through the fragrant signs;
And fleeing the fierce *Bull*, the *Crab's* threatening claw,
Glides toward the safe shadows of roses and violets.
And the sedulous bee, intent on its sweet labor,
Seems to mark its duties with the thyme as horologe.
O sweet lapse of time! O healthful ease!
    O hours worthy to be numbered in herbs and flowers!

Epigramma in Duos montes
Amosclivum *Et* Bilboreum

Farfacio

Cernis ut ingenti distinguant limite campum
    Montis Amosclivi Bilbore que juga!
Ille stat indomitus turritis undique saxis:
    Cingit huic laetum Fraxinus alta Caput.
Illi petra minax rigidis cervicibus horret:
    Huic quatiunt virides lenia colla jubas.
Fulcit *Atlanteo* Rupes ea vertice coelos:
    Collis at hic humeros subjicit *Herculeos*.
Hic ceu carceribus visum sylvâque coercet:
    Ille Oculos alter dum quasi meta trahit.   10
Ille Giganteum surgit ceu *Pelion Ossa*:
    Hic agit ut *Pindi* culmine *Nympha* choros.
Erectus, praeceps, salebrosus, et arduus ille:
    Acclivis, placidus, mollis, amoenus hic est.

Epigramma in Duos Montes Amosclivum et Bilboreum: In this poem, as in its
companion-piece, "On the Hill and Grove at Bilborough," Marvell employs the
topography of the Yorkshire country to pay tribute to the great Fairfax family.
    The translation is based on that of the Rev. J. H. Clark.

Dissimilis Domino coiit Natura sub uno;
   Farfaciâque tremunt sub ditione pares.
Dumque triumphanti terras perlabitur Axe,
   Praeteriens aequâ stringit utrumque Rotâ.
Asper in adversos, facilis cedentibus idem;
   Ut credas Montes extimulasse suos.   20
Hi sunt *Alcidae Borealis* nempe Columnae,
   Quos medio scindit vallis opaca freto.
An potius, longe sic prona cacumina nutant,
   Parnassus cupiant esse *Maria* tuus.

TRANSLATION

Epigram on the two Mountains *of* Amos-Cliff *and* Bilborough

To Fairfax

Behold how Almias-cliff and Bilborough's brow
Mark with huge bounds the spacious plain below!
Dauntless, on that, the rocky turrets frown,
This the tall ash adorns with cheerful crown;
There the rough rocks in terrors grim are dress'd,
Here the smooth hill displays a verdant crest;
That height, like *Atlas*, seems to prop the skies,
But this beneath *Herculean* shoulders lies;
This, as a cell or grove, contracts the gaze,
That, as a goal, his head from far displays;   10
There *Pelion* on *Ossa* heaves amain,
Here some sweet nymph of *Pindus* leads her train.
The steep, the rough, the difficult, are there;
Here all is sloping, gentle, soft and fair.
But Nature doth both characters display
In *Fairfax*, whom with awe they both obey,
And, as his car rolls by, alike do feel
The impartial touch of his triumphant wheel.
Stern to the foe, and mild to him that yields,
His habits drawn from his paternal fields;   20

Here, with a woody strait between, one sees
The Pillars (in the North) of *Hercules*;
Or rather, since their bow'd tops thus agree,
Let them, *Maria*, thy *Parnassus* be!

Dignissimo suo Amico Doctori Wittie *De Translatione Vulgi Errorum* D. Primrosii

Nempe sic innumero succrescunt agmine libri,
    Saepia vix toto ut jam natet una mari.
Fortius assidui surgunt a vulnere proeli:
    Quoque magis pressa est, auctior Hydra redit.
Heu quibus Anticyris, quibus est sanabilis herbis
    Improba scribendi pestis, avarus amor!
India sola tenet tanti medicamina morbi,
    Dicitur et nostris ingemuisse malis.
Utile Tabacci dedit illa miserta venenum,
    Acri veratro quod meliora potest.   10
Jamque vides olidas libris fumare popinas:
    Naribus O doctis quam pretiosus odor!
Hâc ego praecipua credo herbam dote placere,
    Hinc tuus has nebulas Doctor in astra vehit.
Ah mea quid tandem facies timidissima charta?
    Exequias Siticen jam parat usque tuas.
Hunc subeas librum Sancti ceu limen asyli,
    Quem neque delebit flamma, nec ira Jovis.

Dignissimo suo Amico Doctori Wittie: See notes on the companion-piece, "To his worthy Friend Doctor Witty."
    The translation is by A. B. Grosart.
10. *Acri:* As in Cooke; *Acci* in the Folio.

TRANSLATION

To my Honoured Friend Dr. Witty, Concerning his Translation of the Popular Errors of Dr. Primrose

Our books in growing ranks so numerous be,
That scarce one cuttle-fish swims i' the sea.
Sturdier they rise from printing-press's blows:
The more 'tis press'd, this *Hydra* bulkier grows.
Can aconite or plant else known to men
Expel this cacoëthes of the pen?
Ind only on our sorrows taking pity
Provides an antidote, dear Dr. *Wittie*.
Tobacco, useful poison, Ind bestows,
Which more than hellebore extirpates our woes,   10
See the rank clouds above the pages steam,
Than which learn'd noses nought more luscious deem.
Methinks this herb my choicest gift will prove;
From this thy doctor wafts his clouds above.
Ah, what, my timid verse, mayst thou avail?
He'll plot thy ruin, and thy loss bewail.
Hide 'neath this book—a sacred refuge given—
Which neither flame shall blast nor wrath of Heaven.

In Legationem Domini Oliveri St. John ad Provincias Foederatas

Ingeniosa Viris contingunt Nomina magnis,
    Ut dubites Casu, vel Ratione data.
Nam *Sors*, caeca licet, tamen est praesaga *futuri;*
    Et sub *fatidico Nomine* vera premit.
Et Tu, cui soli voluit *Respublica* credi,

In Legationem Domini Oliveri St. John ad Provincias Foederatas: In 1651 Oliver St. John
was chosen by Parliament to negotiate an alliance with the United Provinces. The
negotiations failed.
    The translation is by A. B. Grosart.

Foedera seu *Belgis*, seu nova Bella feras;
Haud frustra cecidit tibi Compellatio fallax,
    Ast scriptum *ancipiti Nomine* Munus erat;
Scilicet hoc *Martis*, sed *Pacis* Nuntius illo:
    Clavibus his *Jani* ferrea Claustra regis.   10
Non opus Arcanos Chartis committere Sensus,
    Et variâ licitos condere Fraude Dolos.
Tu quoque si taceas tamen est *Legatio Nomen*
    Et velut in *Scytale* publica verba refert.
Vultis *Oliverum, Batavi, Sanctumve Johannem?*
Antiochus gyro non breviore stetit.

TRANSLATION

On the Embassy of Lord Oliver St. John to the United Provinces

Apt names to great men oft we see are given,
Whether by accident, or will of Heaven:
For Chance, though blind, looks through the future ages,
And in a pregnant NAME the truth presages.
So thou, to whom the State commits her voice,
Whether fresh War or Treaties be thy choice,
Not idly thou a doubtful style dost bear,
Whose double meaning will thy part declare.
This threatens War, the other breathes of Peace;
Of *Janus'* iron locks thou hast the keys.   10
What need our will on parchment to indite,
And frame accustom'd guille with cunning sleight?
Thy NAME's an embassy, though void of speech,
As by a secret scroll our terms to teach.
Say, *Dutchmen*, is it Oliver or St. John?
Jerusalem's fate had naught less fine to hinge on.

15. *Oliver or St. John:* A man of peace (whose emblem is the olive, with a glance at Cromwell), or one calling his hearers to repentance (like John the Baptist).

A Letter to Doctor Ingelo, *then with my Lord* Whitlock, *Ambassador from the Protector* to the Queen of Sweden

Quid facis *Arctoi* charissime transfuga coeli,
    Ingele, proh serò cognite, rapte citò?
Num satis Hybernum defendis pellibus Astrum,
    Qui modo tam mollis nec bene firmus eras?
Quae Gentes Hominum, quae sit Natura Locorum,
    Sint Homines potius dic ibi sintne Loca?
Num gravis horrisono *Polus* obruit omnia lapsu,
    Jungitur et praeceps Mundus utrâque nive?
An melius canis horrescit Campus Aristis,
    Annuus Agricolis et redit Orbe labor?   10
Incolit, ut fertur, saevam Gens mitior Oram,
    Pace vigil, Bello strenua, justa Foro.
Quin ibi sunt *Urbes*, atque alta *Palatia Regum*,
    Musarumque domus, et sua *Templa Deo*.
Nam regit Imperio populum *Christina* ferocem,
    Et dare jura potest *regia Virgo* viris.
Utque trahit rigidum *Magnes* Aquilone Metallum,
    Gaudet eam Soboles ferrea sponte sequi.
Dic quantum liceat fallaci credere Famae,
    Invida num taceat plura, sonetve loquax.   20
At, si vera fides, Mundi melioris ab ortu,
    Saecula *Christinae* nulla tulere parem.
Ipsa licet redeat (nostri decus orbis) *Eliza*,
    Qualis nostra tamen quantaque *Eliza* fuit.
Vidimus Effigiem, mistasque Coloribus Umbras:
    Sic quoque *Sceptripotens*, sic quoque visa *Dea*.
Augustam decorant (raro concordia) frontem
    Majestas et Amor, Forma Pudorque simul.
Ingens Virgineo spirat *Gustavus* in ore:
    Agnoscas animos, fulmineumque Patrem.   30
Nulla suo nituit tam lucida Stella sub Axe;

A Letter to Dr. Ingelo: Nathaniel Ingelo went to Sweden in 1653 as chaplain of an
embassy from Oliver Cromwell to the young Queen Christina. Marvell's letter to
Ingelo contains an encomium obviously intended for her eyes.
    The translation is by A. B. Grosart.

Non Ea quae meruit Crimine *Nympha* Polum.
Ah quoties pavidum demisit conscia Lumen,
  Utque suae timuit *Parrhasis* Ora *Deae!*
Et, simulet falsâ ni Pictor imagine Vultus,
  Delia tam similis nec fuit ipsa sibi.
Ni quod inornati *Triviae* sint forte Capilli,
  Sollicitâ sed huic distribuantur Acu.
Scilicet ut nemo est illâ reverentior aequi;
  Haud ipsas igitur fert sine Lege Comas.   40
Gloria sylvarum pariter communis utrique
  Est, et perpetuae Virginitatis Honos.
Sic quoque *Nympharum* supereminet Agmina collo,
  Fertque *Choros Cynthi* per Juga, perque Nives.
Haud aliter pariles Ciliorum contrahit Arcus
  Acribus ast Oculis tela subesse putes.
Luminibus dubites an straverit illa Sagittis
  Quae fovet exuviis ardua colla Feram.
Alcides humeros coopertus *pelle Nemaeâ*
  Haud ita labentis sustulit Orbis Onus.   50
Heu quae Cervices subnectunt Pectora tales,
  Frigidiora Gelu, candidiora Nive.
Caetera non licuit, sed vix et tota, videre;
  Nam clausi rigido stant *Adamante* Sinus.
Seu Chlamys Artifici nimium succurrerit auso,
  Sicque imperfectum fugerit impar Opus:
Sive tribus spernat Victrix certare *Deabus*,
Et pretium formae nec spoliata ferat.
Junonis properans et clara Trophaea *Minervae;*
  Mollia nam *Veneris* praemia nosse piget.   60
Hinc neque consuluit fugitivae prodiga Formoe,
  Nec timuit seris invigilasse Libris.
Insomnem quoties *Nymphae* monuere sequaces
  Decedet roseis heu color ille Genis.
Jamque vigil leni cessit *Philomela* sopori,
  Omnibus et Sylvis conticuere Ferae.
Acrior illa tamen pergit, Curasque fatigat:
  Tanti est doctorum volvere scripta Virum.
Et liciti quae sint moderamina discere Regni,

44. *perque:* As in Cooke; *per* in the Folio.
48. *fovet:* As in Grosart; *foret* in the Folio.

Quid fuerit, quid sit, noscere quicquid erit.   70
Sic quod in ingenuas *Gothus* peccaverit Artes
   Vindicat, et studiis expiat *Una* suis.
Exemplum dociles imitantur nobile Gentes,
   Et geminis Infans imbuit Ora sonis.
Transpositos *Suecis* credas migrasse *Latinos*,
   Carmine Romuleo sic strepit omne Nemus.
Upsala nec priscis impar memoratur *Athenis*,
   Aegidaque et *Currus* hic sua *Pallas* habet.
Illinc O quales liceat sperasse Liquores,
   Quum *Dea* praesideat fontibus ipsa sacris!   80
Illic Lacte ruant illic et flumina Melle,
   Fulvaque inauratam tingat Arena *Salam.*
Upsalides Musae nunc et majora canemus,
   Quaeque mihi Famae non levis Aura tulit.
Creditur haud ulli *Christus signasse suorum*
   Occultam gemma de meliore Notam.
Quemque tenet charo descriptum *Nomine* semper,
   Non minus exculptum Pectore fida refert.
Sola haec virgineas depascit Flamma Medullas,
   Et licito pergit solvere corda foco.   90
Tu quoque Sanctorum fastos *Christina* sacrabis,
   Unica nec *Virgo Volsiniensis* erit.
Discite nunc *Reges* (*Majestas proxima caelo*)
   Discite proh magnos hinc coluisse *Deos.*
Ah pudeat Tantos puerilia fingers coepta,
   Nugas nescio quas, et male quaerere Opes.
Acer *Equo* cunctos dum praeterit ille *Britanno*,
   Et pecoris spolium nescit inerme sequi.
Ast *Aquilam* poscit *Germano* pellere *Nido*,
   Deque *Palatino* Monte fugare *Lupam.*   100
Vos etiam latos in praedam jungite *Campos*,
   Impiaque arctatis cingite Lustra Plagis.
Victor Oliverus nudum Caput exerit Armis,
   Ducere sive sequi nobile laetus Iter.
Qualis jam *Senior* Solymae *Godfredus* ad Arces,
   Spina cui canis floruit alba Comis.
Et *Lappos Christina* potest et solvere *Finnos*,
   Ultima quos *Boreae* carcere Claustra premunt.
Aeoliis quales Venti fremuere sub antris,

97. *ille:* As in Cooke; *illa* in the Folio.

Et tentant Montis corripuisse moras.   110
Hanc *Dea* si summa demiserit Arce procellam
    Quam gravis *Austriacis Hesperiisque* cadat!
Omnia sed rediens olim narraveris Ipse;
    Nec reditus spero tempora longa petit.
Non ibi lenta pigro stringuntur frigore Verba,
    Solibus, et tandem Vere liquanda nove.
Sed radiis hyemem *Regina* potentior urit;
    Haecque magis solvit, quam ligat illa Polum.
Dicitur et nostros moerens audisse Labores,
    Fortis et ingenuam Gentis amasse Fidem.   120
Oblatae *Batavam* nec paci commodat *Aurem*;
    Nec versat *Danos* insidiosa *dolos*.
Sed pia festinat mutatis Foedera rebus,
    Et *Libertatem* quae dominatur amat.
Digna cui *Salomon* meritos retulisset honores,
    Et *Saba* concretum Thure cremasset Iter.
Hanc tua, sed melius, celebraverit, *Ingele, Musa*;
    Et labor est vertrae debitus ille Lyrae.
Nos sine te frustra *Thamisis* saliceta subimus,
    Sparsaque per steriles Turba vagamur Agros.   130
Et male tentanti querulum respondet Avena:
    Quin et *Rogerio* dissiluere fides.
Haec tamen absenti memores dictamus *Amico*,
    Grataque speramus qualiacumque fore.

TRANSLATION

How now, dear exile to the northern zone,
Too late known *Ingelo*, too early gone?
Canst thou with furs the wintry star defy—
So infirm here, so weak beneath our sky?
What race of men, what scen'ry do you share?
Or are there men, or is there scen'ry there?
Does the vast pole, harsh-wheeling, waste the land?
Does snow the swift world bind on either hand?
Or better, does the plain with whitening ears
Bristle, and Labour crown the circling years?   10
A milder race, they say, holds these stern plains;
Industrious peace, stout arms, just judgment reigns;
There too are cities and a regal seat,

Haunts of the Muses, and God's temples meet:
For great *Christina* rules the stalwart race—
A virgin queen o'er men the sceptre sways;
And as the magnet draws the rigid stone,
That iron race delights her force to own.
Is't so: are we to trust deceitful Fame?
Brags she, or envious hints her silent blame?   20
If all be true, then since the world was young,
No equal to *Christina* has been sung;
Though our own boast, *Eliza*, came again,
She were her match, and might her meed attain.
I saw her limn'd, with chequer'd light and shade—
E'en in her picture seem'd she goddess-maid!
Upon her brow (rare harmony!) there move
Modesty, Beauty, Majesty and Love;
Gustavus breathes from out her maiden face,
You mark his dash and spirit in her grace.   30
No star so bright upon its axis burn'd—
Not she who by her crime such prison earn'd:
Conscious, how oft her tearful light she veil'd,
As *Parrhasis* before the goddess quail'd!
And if the painter drew not from his mind,
Delia herself was not of rarer kind;
Except that *Trivia's* hair was unbedeck'd,
While hers is comb'd in fashion circumspect:
Forsooth, none lives so reverent of the right,
And e'en her locks must by fix'd laws be dight;   40
Alike the glory of the woods is she,
And flower of aye-inviolate Chastity.
So o'er her virgin bands tall *Cynthia* shows,
And leads her troop athwart the rocks and snows;
E'en so she bends her eyebrows' double bow,
As though keen arrows from her eyes she'd throw.
One doubts if with her eyes the beast she slew
Whose fur around her neck and breast we view.
Alcides' self girt with a lion's hide,
Bearing the wheeling globe, scarce with her vied.   50

34. *Parrhasis* is an Arcadian epithet for Callisto, a nymph of Diana seduced by
Zeus, and changed into Ursa Major, the brightest Northern constellation. (Carl E.
Bain)   36. *Delia:* Diana.   37. *Trivia:* Diana of the crossways.
50: Hercules for a time took Atlas' place as upholder of the heavens.

And her fair throat, as white as northern snow,
But not as white as breasts half glimps'd below!
No more—scarce even this might there be seen:
Stern steel encas'd the bosom of my *Queen*.
Or did her mantle aid imperfect art,
Which then retired, unequal to its part?
Or with those three to vie does she disdain,
And Beauty's palm, though ne'er disrobed, would gain?—
Eager for *Juno's, Pallas'* glorious spoils.
Shrinking from *Venus'* captivating toils,   60
She reck'd no more the fleeting fame of looks,
But nightly gave her studious mind to books.
How oft her maids that sleepless soul would warn,
"Alas, the bloom once gone will ne'er return."
Now *Philomel* her labour lulls in sleep,
And all the woods a restful silence keep,
More ardent still her busy care she plies,
And makes each learned work her welcome prize:
To know and keep within her sovereignty,
To learn what is, what was, and what shall be;   70
Avenging thus the rude *Goth's* barbarous fires,
She expiates the fury of her sires.
From her the docile tribes example take,
And into two-voiced speech their infants break;
the *Latins* yield themselves to *Swedish* bounds,
And every grove with *Roman* song resounds.
Upsala now with ancient *Athens* vies;
Here *Pallas'* shield, and here her chariot lies.
Ah, what clear stream shall hence our hopes fulfill,
When our *Athene* guards the sacred rill!   80
Their happy streams with milk and honey flow,
And *Saal* is ting'd with *Issell's* golden glow.—
Upsalian Muses, take a loftier flight,
And sing of matters none may rank too light.
'Tis said that *Christ* not even to His own
Reveal'd the mystery of that "white stone";
And Him, *Christina*, whose blest name thou wearest
Graven within thy faithful heart thou bearest.
On this pure flame her virgin soul is fed,

---

82. *Saal ... Issell:* Swedish rivers.

Before this fire her inmost heart outspread.   90
Thou too, *Christina*, hast thy saintship won;
Bolsena's maid bears not the palm alone.
Learn then, ye kings, whom Heav'n has raised on high,
From this example, *God* to glorify:
Blush, being great, to compass childish things,
Vain trifles, and the wealth which sorrow brings;
See our brave *British* horseman pass them all,
No spoils of unarm'd flock before him fall,—
Fluttering the eagle in his *German* pine,
Driving the she-wolf from the *Palatine*.   100
Ye too combine your camps, and seek your prey:
Hedge-in with narrowing bonds this evil day;
Triumphant *Cromwell* lifts his helmless head.
Ready to lead, or follow nobly led.
Like *Godfrey* at the citadel of old,
Adown whose back the white locks thickly roll'd,
Christina can let loose the *Finns* and *Lapps*,
Whom *Boreas* in his prison close enwraps;
As fret the winds in their *Æolian* cave,
And strain to burst their narrow mountain-grave.   110
If SHE their veh'ment fury should unchain,
What storm would break on *Austria* and *Spain*!
But thou returning shalt account for all—
And speedy be the time of thy recall!
No longer then our tardy speech shall freeze;
Loos'd by the glowing sun and Spring's fresh breeze,
A *Queen* more powerful thaws the wintry ground,
And trebly frees the Pole which th' other bound.
They say she heard and piti'd our sad case,
Praising the clear faith of a sturdy race;   120
Refus'd the wily *Dutchman's* proffer'd pact,
And spurn'd to use insidious thought or act;
Eager a mutual treaty to ordain,
And loves the liberty which marks her reign.
Worthy that *Solomon* his praise should pay,

92: St. Christina drowned in the Lake of Bolsena.   97: Cromwell.
99: The Holy Roman Empire.   100: The Catholic Church.
105. *Godfrey:* Godfrey of Bulloigne, a heroic crusader, who put on a crown of thorns
before entering Jerusalem.

And *Sheba's* queen burn incense in her way.
Thou, *Ingelo*, wilt better chant her fame;
Thy lyre more sweetly may the honour claim.
Without thee listless on *Thames'* banks we rove,
And o'er the barren plains disbanded move.   130
The pipe discordant mocks our awkward throat,
And *Roger's* cithern will not yield a note.
Still, mindful, to our absent friend we sing;
And may our strains, though light, some pleasure bring!

In Effigiem Oliveri Cromwell

Haec est quae toties *Inimicos* Umbra fugavit,
At sub quâ *Cives* Otia lenta terunt.

TRANSLATION

On the Portrait of Oliver Cromwell

Before this shadow oft his en'mies fled;
Beneath it lives secure the people led.

In eandem Reginae Sueciae *transmissam*

Bellipotens Virgo, septem Regina Trionum.
    Christina, Arctoi lucida stella Poli;
Cernis quas merui dura sub Casside Rugas;
    Sicque *Senex* Armis impiger Ora fero;
Invia Factorum dum per Vestigia nitor,
    Exequor et Populi fortia Jussa Manu.
At tibi submittit frontem reverentior *Umbra*,
    Nes sunt *hi Vultus* Regibus usque truces.

132. *Roger:* Benjamin Rogers, a composer whose music Ingelo had performed
before Queen Christina.   The translation is by A. B. Grosart.

On the same being sent to the Queen of Sweden

O virgin Queen of the North, expert in war,
Christina, th' Arctic heaven's fair-shining star,
See the hard helmet's furrows on my brow—
Though old, not sluggard, yet in arms I go.
Whilst in Fate's pathless toils I struggle still,
And work the mandates of the people's will,
To you this shade its reverent forehead bends,
My looks not always stern to royal friends.

Upon an Eunuch; a Poet
Fragment

Nec sterilem te crede; licet, mulieribus exul,
Falcem virginiae nequeas immittere messi,
Et nostro peccare modo. Tibi Fama perennè
Proegnabit; rapiesque novem de monte Sorores;
Et pariet modulos *Echo* repetita Nepotes.

TRANSLATION

Deem not that thou art barren, though, forlorn,
Thou plunge no sickle in the virgin corn,
And, mateless, hast no part in our sweet curse.
Fame shall be ever pregnant by thy verse;
The vocal Sisters nine thou shalt embrace,
And *Echo* nurse thy words, a tuneful race.

The translation is by A. B. Grosart.

In the French translation of Lucan, by Monsieur De Brebeuf are these Verses

C'est de luy que nous vient cet Art ingenieux
De peindre la Parole, et de parler aux Yeux;
Et, par les traits divers des figures tracées,
Donner de la couleur et du corps aux pensées.

TRANSLATION

Facundis dedit ille notis, interprete plumâ
Insinuare sonos oculis, et pingere voces,
Et mentem chartis, oculis impertiit aurem.

Epigramme. Upon Blood's attempt to steal the Crown

Bludius, ut ruris damnum repararet aviti,
    Addicit fisco dum Diadema suo;
Egregium Sacro facinus velavit Amictu:
    (Larva solet Reges fallere nulla magis).
Excidit ast ausis tactus pietate profanâ,
    Custodem ut servet, maluit ipse capi.
Si modo Saevitiam texisset Pontificalem,
    Veste Sacerdotis, rapta Corona foret.

In the French translation of Lucan: Marvell shared a contemporary interest in analogies between poetry and painting derived from Horace's *Ars Poetica*, and he employed the *ut pictura poesis* idea in "The Gallery" and the satirical painter poems. The French version corresponds to Lucan's *Pharsalia*, III, 200–221. The Latin is Marvell's.

    In Lucan: "*Phoenices primi, famae si creditur, ausi/Mansuram rudibus vocem signare figuris.*" Translation (by George de F. Lord): "The Phoenicians were the first, if we can believe reports, who were so bold as to figure forth speech in rude characters for future time." 1. *luy*: Refers to the Phoenicians, who invented the alphabet. 3: The Bod. MS. substitutes for the following line:
    Conspicuamque levi mentem transmittere chartâ
    (And transpose the mind before one's eyes on light paper).
Epigramme. Upon Blood's attempt to steal the Crown: See note on Marvell's English version, p. 193.

Inscribenda Luparae

Consurgit *Luparae* Dum non imitabile culmen,
   Escuriale ingens uritur invidia.

Aliter

Regibus haec posuit *Ludovicus* Templa futuris;
   Gratior ast ipsi *Castra* fuere Domus.

Aliter

Hanc sibi Sydeream *Ludovicus* condidit Aulam;
   Nec se propterea credidit esse *Deum*.

Aliter

Atria miraris, summotumque Aethera tecto;
   Nec tamen in toto est arctior Orbe Casa.

Aliter

Instutuente domum *Ludovice*, prodiit Orbis;
   Sic tamen angustos incolit ille Lares.

Aliter

Sunt geminae *Jani* Portae, sunt Tecta *Tonantis*;
   Nec deerit *Numen* dum *Ludovicus* adest.

Inscribenda Luparae: Mrs. E. E. Duncan Jones has recently shown that Marvell wrote these Latin couplets on the Louvre in 1671 or 1672 in response to Louis XIV's offer of a prize for the best distich on its façade. Marvell was shortly to regard Louis as England's most dangerous enemey.

   The translation By William McQueen and Kiffin Rockwell. Reprinted by permission of the University of North Carolina Studies in Comparative Literature.

TRANSLATION

To be Inscribed on the Louvre

While the inimitable roof of the *Louvre* rises,
　　The huge *Escorial* burns with envy.

An Alternate
Louis built this temple for future kings,
　　But the camp was a more pleasing home to him.

Another
Louis built this starry palace for himself,
　　Nor did he believe on that account that he was a god.

Another
You marvel at the halls, and the sky pushed up by the roof;
　　Yet there is not in the whole world a less roomy house.

Another
Louis founding his house, the world came forth;
　　Yet thus he inhabits a cramped household.

Another
These are the double gates of *Janus*, these are the roofs of the
　　　　Thunderer;
　　Nor is divinity lacking while *Louis* is present.

To a Gentleman that only upon the sight of the Author's writing, had given a Character of his Person and Judgment of his Fortune

Illustrissimo Viro
Domino Lanceloto Josepho de Maniban
Grammatomanti

Quis posthac chartae committat sensa loquaci,
    Si sua crediderit Fata subesse stylo?
Conscia si prodat Scribentis Litera sortem,
    Quicquid et in vita plus latuisse velit?
Flexibus in calami tamen omnia sponte leguntur:
    Quod non significant Verba, Figura notat.
Bellerophonteas signat sibi quisque Tabellas;
    Ignaramque Manum Spiritus intus agit.
Nil praeter solitum sapiebat Epistola nostra,
    Exemplumque meae Simplicitatis erat.   10
Fabula jucundos qualis delectat Amicos;
    Urbe, lepore, novis, carmine tota scatens.
Hic tamen interpres quo non securior alter,
    (Non res, non voces, non ego notus ei)
Rimatur fibras notularum cautus Aruspex,
    Scripturaeque inhians consulit exta meae.
Inde statim vitae casus, animique recessus
    Explicat; (haud *Genio* plura liquere putem.)
Distribuit totum nostris eventibus orbem,
    Et quo me rapiat cardine *Sphaera* docet.   20
Quae *Sol* oppositus, quae *Mars* adversa minetur,
    Jupiter aut ubi me, *Luna, Venusque* juvent.
Ut trucis intentet mihi vulnera *Cauda Draconis*;
    Vipereo levet ut vulnera more Caput.

To a Gentleman: Maniban was an abbot whose skill in divination from letters Marvell had heard of through his nephew William Popple. Marvell wrote this poem in 1676 and sent it to Maniban as a skeptic's challenge. Some of the laudatory phrases are ambiguous.
    The translation is by A. B. Grosart.
    Grammatomanti: As in Cooke; *Grammatomantis* in Folio.

Hinc mihi praeteriti rationes atque futuri
   Elicit, *Astrologus* certior *Astronomo.*
Ut conjecturas nequeam discernere vero,
   Historiae superet sed Genitura fidem.
Usque adeo caeli respondet pagina nostrae,
   Astrorum et nexus syllaba scripta refert.   30
Scilicet et toti subsunt Oracula mundo,
   Dummodo tot foliis una *Sibylla* foret.
Partum, Fortunae mater Natura, propinquum
   Mille modis monstrat mille per indicia:
Ingentemque Uterum quâ mole Puerpera solvat;
   Vivit at in praesens maxima pars hominum.
Ast Tu sorte tuâ gaude Celeberrime Vatum;
   Scribe, sed haud superest qui tua fata legat.
Nostra tamen si fas praesagia jungere vestris,
   Quo magis inspexti sydera spernis humum.   40
Et, nisi stellarum fueris divina propago,
   Naupliadâ credam te *Palamede* satum.
Qui dedit ex avium scriptoria signa volatu,
   Sydereâque idem nobilis arte fuit.
Hinc utriusque tibi cognata scientia crevit,
   Nec minus augurium Litera quam dat Avis.

TRANSLATION

To the Illustrious Dr. Lancelot. Joseph de Maniban, *Seer*

Who now to paper would his thoughts commit,
Knowing his very fate depends on it,
And that the writing blabs the writer's lot,
And whatso'er in life he'd wish forgot?
In the pen's curves all things at once are read,
The writing's form shows what the words ne'er said.
Each bears, like *Glaucus'* son, his fatal letter,
And the mind drives the hand that knows no better.

7. *Glaucus' son:* Bellerophon, who unwittingly carried a letter to his host, Iobates, king of Lycia, saying that the bearer should be killed.

My letter smack'd of naught obscure that day,
It was but written in my simple way;   10
A gossip, such as friends jocose would choose,
"Doing" the town, amusement, music, news.
Yet, lo! th' Interpreter, impartial wight,
Who knows me not, nor in what vein I write,
Observes my writing as a soothsayer wise,
And like a victim's entrails closely spies.
He shows my way of life, my mental store—
My guardian-angel scarce could tell you more;
Designs the map of all my devious mood,
And gives my latitude and longitude.   20
Shows what *Mars* adverse, what the sun portends,
How *Venus*, *Jupiter*, the *Moon*, befriends.
How *Dragon's-tail* bespeaks me many a wound,
And snake-like lifts his bruis'd head from the ground.
He reads the Past, foretells the Future's hopes,
And beats astrologers at horoscopes.
Guesses from truth, lest I perchance discern
From page more true than history I shall learn—
From heaven's own page, accordant with my own,
My written syllables by star-plot known.   30
An oracle the whole world underlies—
Give but a *Sibyl* fit for such emprise.
A speedy birth, Luck's mother, Nature, bodes,
Foretells by thousand hints, in thousand modes,
How grandly she will ease her mighty womb:
Yet men still live for this side o' the tomb.
But thou, great *Seer*, be happy in thy lot,
Write, though none other glean thy story's plot.
Yet, might I dare my prescient soul to trust,
The more thou readst the stars thou spurn'st the dust.   40
And if thou be not of the stars divine,
I hold thee sprung of *Nauplius's* line,
Who sent his letters by the feather'd post,
And won his laurels from the starry host.
From him each science grew, reveal'd by thee;
Both bird and letter give their augury.

Poems of Doubtful Authorship

An Elegy upon the Death of my
Lord Francis Villiers

Tis true that he is dead: but yet to chuse,
Methinkes thou Fame should not have brought the news
Thou canst discourse at will and speak at large:
But wast not in the fight nor durst thou charge.
While he transported all with valiant rage
His Name eternizd, but cut short his age;
On the safe battlements of Richmonds bowers
Thou wast espyd, and from the guilded Towers
Thy silver Trumpets sounded a Retreat,
Farre from the dust and battails sulphry heat.   10
Yet what couldst thou have done? 'tis alwayes late
To struggle with inevitable fate.
Much rather thou I know expectst to tell
How heavy *Cromwell* gnasht the earth and fell.
Or how slow Death farre from the sight of day
The long-deceived *Fairfax* bore away.
But untill then, let us young *Francis* praise:
And plant upon his hearse the bloody bayes,
Which we will water with our welling eyes.
Teares spring not still from spungy Cowardize.   20
The purer fountaines from the Rocks more steep
Destill and stony valour best doth weep.

An Elegy upon the Death of my Lord Francis Villiers: Lord Francis Villiers, posthumous son of the first Duke of Buckingham, was killed in battle near Richmond in July 1648. A unique copy of this poem in the library of Worcester College, Oxford, carries an ascription to Marvell by George Clarke (1660–1736), a literary scholar and statesman. The reliability of his ascription is carefully assessed in Margoliouth's edition. Suffice it to say here that the circumstantial evidence leaves considerable room for doubt as to the poem's authenticity.

  Two small additional indications in favor of Marvell's authorship are his well-known attachment to the Buckingham line and his detailed allusion to the manufacture of Chinese porcelain in "The First Anniversary," ll. 19-20, p. 93, and here in ll. 31-36.

Besides Revenge, if often quencht in teares,
Hardens like Steele and daily keener weares.
    Great *Buckingham*, whose death doth freshly strike
Our memoryes, because to this so like;
Ere than in the Eternall Court he shone,
And here a Favorite there found a throne;
The fatall night before he hence did bleed,
Left to his *Princess* this immortall seed.   30
As the wise *Chinese* in the fertile wombe
Of Earth doth a more precious clay entombe,
Which dying by his will he leaves consignd:
Til by mature delay of time refind
The christall metall fit to be releast
Is taken forth to crowne each royall feast;
Such was the fate by which this Postume breathd,
Who scarcely seems begotten but bequeathd.
    Never was any humane plant that grew
More faire than this and acceptably new.   40
'Tis truth that beauty doth most men dispraise:
Prudence and valour their esteeme do raise.
But he that hath already these in store,
Can not be poorer sure for having more.
And his unimitable handsomenesse
Made him indeed be more than man, not lesse.
We do but faintly Gods resemblance beare
And like rough coyns of carelesse mints appeare:
But he of purpose made, did represent
In a rich Medall every lineament.   50
    Lovely and admirable as he was,
Yet was his Sword or Armour all his Glasse.
Nor in his Mistris eyes that joy he tooke,
As in an Enemies himselfe to looke.
I know how well he did, with what delight
Those serious imitations of fight.
Still in the trialls of strong exercise
His was the first, and his the second prize.
    Bright Lady, thou that rulest from above
The last and greatest Monarchy of Love: 60
Faire *Richmond* hold thy Brother or he goes.
Try if the Jasmin of thy hand or Rose

Of thy red Lip can keep him alwayes here.
For he loves danger and doth never feare.
Or may thy tears prevaile with him to stay?
    But he resolv'd breaks carelesly away.
Onely one argument could now prolong
His stay and that most faire and so most strong:
The matchlesse *Chlora* whose pure fires did warm
His soule and only could his passions charme.   70
    You might with much more reason go reprove
The amorous Magnet which the North doth love.
Or preach divorce and say it is amisse
That with tall Elms the twining Vines should kisse
Then chide two such so fit, so equall faire
That in the world they have no other paire.
Whom it might seeme that Heaven did create
To restore man unto his first estate.
Yet she for honours tyrannous respect
Her own desires did and his neglect.   80
And like the Modest Plant at every touch
Shrunk in her leaves and feared it was too much.
    But who can paint the torments and that pain
Which he profest and now she could not faigne?
He like the Sun but overcast and pale:
Shee like a Rainbow, that ere long must faile,
Whose rosiall cheek where Heaven it selfe did view
Begins to separate and dissolve to dew.
    At last he leave obtaines though sad and slow,
First of her and then of himselfe to goe.   90
How comely and how terrible he sits
At once and Warre as well as Love befits!
Ride where thou wilt and bold adventures find;
But all the Ladies are got up behind.
Guard them, though not they selfe: for in thy death
Th' Eleven thousand Virgins lose their breath.
    So *Hector* issuing from the Trojan wall
The sad *Iliades* to the Gods did call
With hands displayed and with dishevell'd haire
That they the Empire in his life would spare.   100
While he secure through all the field doth spy
Achilles, for *Achilles* only cry.

Ah ignorant that yet e'er night he must
Be drawn by him inglorious through the dust.
   Such fell young *Villiers* in the chearfull heat
Of youth: his locks intangled all with sweat
And those eyes which the Sentinell did keep
Of love closed up in an eternall sleep.
While *Venus* of *Adonis* thinks no more
Slaine by the harsh tuske of the Savage Boare.   110
Hither she runns and hath him hurried farre
Out of the noise and blood, and killing warre:
Where in her Gardens of Sweet myrtle laid
Shee kisses him in the immortall shade,
   Yet dyed he not revengelesse: Much he did
Ere he could suffer. A whole Pyramid
Of Vulgar bodies he erected high:
Scorning without a Sepulcher to dye.
And with his steele which did whole troopes divide
He cut his Epitaph on either Side.   120
Till finding nothing to his courage fit
He rid up last to death and conquer'd it.
   Such are the Obsequies to *Francis* own:
He best the pompe of his owne death hath showne.
And we hereafter to his honour will
Not write so many, but so many kill.
Till the whole Army by just vengeance come
To be at once his Trophee and his Tombe.

A Dialogue between
Thyrsis *and* Dorinda

Dorinda.   When Death shall part us from these Kids,
             And shut up our divided Lids,
             Tell me, *Thyrsis*, prethee do,
             Whither thou and I must go.

Thyrsis.   To the Elizium: (*Dorinda*) oh, where is't?

Thyrsis.   A Chaste Soul can never mis't.

Dorinda.   I know no way, but one, our home;
             Is our Cell Elizium?

Thyrsis.   Turn thine Eye to yonder Skie,
             There the milky way doth lye;   10
             'Tis a sure but rugged way,
             That leads to Everlasting day.

Dorinda.   There Birds may nest, but how can I,
             That have no wings and cannot fly?

Thyrsis.   Do not sigh (fair Nimph) for fire
             Hath no wings, yet doth aspire
             Till it hit against the Pole:
             Heaven's the Center of the Soul.

Dorinda.   But in Elizium how do they
             Pass Eternity away?   20

A Dialogue between Thyrsis and Dorinda: This poem was removed from the Bod. MS.
A musical setting for it has been found in a manuscript of Henry Lawes, who was
killed at the Battle of Chester in September 1645. This would suggest a very early
date of composition if the poem is indeed Marvell's. Further doubt as to its
authenticity arises from the concluding speech of Dorinda where the advocacy of
suicide is completely unlike anything in Marvell's other verse.

In the Folio the poem appears between "On the Victory obtained by Blake"
and "The Character of Holland"; I have emended the defective text from other
versions.

Thyrsis.   Oh, ther's neither hope nor fear,
Ther's no Wolf, no Fox, no Bear,
No need of Dog to fetch our stray,
Our Lightfoot we may give away;
No Oat-pipe's needfull, there thine Ears
May feast with Musick of the Spheres.

Dorinda.   Oh sweet! oh sweet! How I my future
    state
By silent thinking Antidate:
I prethee let us spend our time to come
In talking of *Elizium*.   30

Thyrsis.   Then I'le go on: There, sheep are full
Of sweetest grass, and softest wooll;
There, birds sing Consorts, garlands grow,
Cool winds do whisper, springs do flow.
There, alwayes is a rising Sun,
And day is ever but begun.
Shepheards there bear equal sway,
And every Nimph's a Queen of *May*.

Dorinda.   Ah me, ah me. (*Thyrsis.*) *Dorinda*, why
    do'st Cry?
Dorinda.   I'm sick, I'm sick, and fain would dye: 40
Convince me now that this is true
By bidding, with mee, all adieu.
Thyrsis.   I cannot live without thee: I
Will for thee, much more with thee, dye.

Dorinda.   Then let us give *Carillo* charge o'th'Sheep,
And thou and I'le pick poppies and them
    steep
In wine, and drink on't till we weep;
So shall we smoothly pass away in sleep.

Tom May's *Death*

As one put drunk into the Packet-boat,
Tom May was hurry'd hence and did not know't.
But was amaz'd on the Elysian side,
And with an Eye uncertain, gazing wide,
Could not determine in what place he was,
For whence in Stevens ally Trees or Grass.
Nor where the Popes head, nor the Mitre lay,
Signs by which still he found and lost his way.
At last while doubtfully he all compares,
He saw near hand, as he imagin'd *Ares*.   10
Such did he seem for corpulence and port,
But 'twas a man much of another sort;
'Twas *Ben* that in the dusky Laurel shade
Amongst the Chorus of old Poets laid,
Sounding of ancient Heroes, such as were
The Subjects Safety, and the Rebel's Fear,
But how a double headed Vulture Eats
Brutus and *Cassius*, the Peoples cheats.
But seeing *May* he varied streight his Song,
Gently to signifie that he was wrong.   20
Cups more than civil of *Emathian* wine,
I sing (said he) and the *Pharsalian* Sign,
Where the Historian of the Common-wealth
In his own Bowels sheath'd the conquering health.
By this *May* to himself and them was come,
He found he was translated, and by whom.

Tom May's Death: May (1595–1650) translated Lucan's *Pharsalia* (1627) and published a continuation in Latin and English, which carried the story down to the death of Caesar. Despite many favors from Charles I, May went over to the Parliamentary side in the Civil Wars, perhaps out of disappointment at not receiving the laureateship. In 1680 May's remains were exhumed from Westminister Abbey.
7. *Popes head . . . Mitre:* Taverns frequented by the bibulous poet.
10. *Ares:* Unidentified.   13: Ben Jonson in fact admired May's Lucan.
21–24: May's translation of Lucan's *Pharsalia* begins:
    Warres more than civill on Æmathian plaines
    We sing; rage licensd; where great Rome distaines
    In her owne bowels her victorious swords; . . .
26. *translated:* Death has "translated" him as Jonson has just "translated" the opening lines of May's Lucan.

Yet then with foot as stumbling as his tongue
Prest for his place among the Learned throng.
But *Ben*, who knew not neither foe nor friend,
Sworn Enemy to all that do pretend,   30
Rose more than ever he was seen severe,
Shook his gray locks, and his own Bayes did tear
At this intrusion. Then with Laurel wand,
The awful Sign of his supream command,
At whose dread Whisk *Virgil* himself does quake,
And *Horace* patiently its stroke does take,
As he crowds in he whipt him ore the pate
Like *Pembroke* at the Masque, and then did rate:
  "Far from these blessed shades tread back agen
Most servil wit, and Mercenary Pen.   40
Polydore, Lucan, Allan, Vandale, Goth,
Malignant Poet and Historian both.
Go seek the novice Statesmen, and obtrude
On them some Romane cast similitude,
Tell them of Liberty, the Stories fine,
Until you all grow Consuls in your wine.
Or thou *Dictator* of the glass bestow
On him the *Cato*, this the *Cicero*.
Transferring old *Rome* hither in your talk,
As *Bethlem's* House did to *Loretto* walk.   50
Foul Architect that hadst not Eye to see
How ill the measures of these States agree.
And who by *Romes* example *England* lay,
Those but to *Lucan* do continue *May*.
But thee nor Ignorance nor seeming good
Misled, but malice fixt and understood.
Because some one than thee more worthy weares
The sacred Laurel, hence are all these tears?
Must therefore all the World be set on flame,
Because a Gazet writer mist his aim?   60

38: During a masque at Whitehall in 1634 the Earl of Pembroke, Lord
Chamberlain, broke his staff over May's shoulders and was required by the King
to apologize and make amends.
41. *Polydore:* Polydore Virgil (1470?–1555?) wrote a history of England and was
subsequently imprisoned for an attack on Henry VIII and Wolsey. *Allan:* One of
the Alani, a Scythian people whose reputation was like the Vandals' and the Goths'.
50: The *Santa Casa* of Loreto, venerated as the house of the Virgin Mary, was
miraculously conveyed there from Nazareth.

And for a Tankard-bearing Muse must we
As for the Basket *Guelphs* and *Gibellines* be?
When the Sword glitters ore the Judges head,
And fear has Coward Churchmen silenced,
Then is the Poets time, 'tis then he drawes,
And single fights forsaken Vertues cause.
He, when the wheel of Empire, whirleth back,
And though the World's disjointed Axel crack,
Sings still of ancient Rights and better Times,
Seeks wretched good, arraigns successful Crimes.   70
But thou base man first prostituted hast
Our spotless knowledge and the studies chaste,
Apostatizing from our Arts and us,
To turn the Chronicler to *Spartacus*.
Yet wast thou taken hence with equal fate,
Before thou couldst great *Charles* his death relate.
But what will deeper wound thy little mind,
Hast left surviving *Davenant* still behind
Who laughs to see in this thy death renew'd,
Right Romane poverty and gratitude.   80
Poor Poet thou, and grateful Senate they,
Who thy last Reckoning did so largely pay.
And with the publick gravity would come,
When thou hadst drunk thy last to lead thee home.
If that can be thy home where *Spencer* lyes
And reverend *Chaucer*, but their dust does rise
Against thee, and expels thee from their side,
As th' Eagles Plumes from other birds divide.
Nor here thy shade must dwell; Return, Return,
Where Sulphrey *Phlegeton* does ever burn.   90
Thee *Cerberus* with all his Jawes shall gnash,
Megæra thee with all her Serpents lash.
Thou rivited unto *Ixion's* wheel

---

62. *Basket:* Perhaps the *borsa* which received the votes in Florentine elections, frequently contested by the rival Guelphs and Ghibellines. (Margoliouth).

74. *Spartacus:* The Earl of Essex, a Parliamentary leader praised in May's *Breviary of the History of the Parliament of England* (1650).

76: May abruptly concludes his *Breviary*, which omits the trial, condemnation, and execution of Charles I, with the observation that "so great a business would make an History by itself."

78. *Davenant:* Sir William Davenant, poet-laureate.

92. *Megæra:* A Greek goddess of vengeance.

Shalt break, and the perpetual Vulture feel.
'Tis just what Torments Poets ere did feign,
Thou first Historically shouldst sustain."
   Thus by irrevocable Sentence cast,
   May only Master of these Revels past.
   And streight he vanisht in a Cloud of pitch,
   Such as unto the Sabboth bears the Witch.   100

On the Victory obtained by Blake *over the* Spaniards, *in the Bay of* Sanctacruze, *in the Island of* Teneriff 1657

Now does *Spains* Fleet her spatious wings unfold,
Leaves the new World and hastens for the old:
But though the wind was fair, they slowly swoome
Frayted with acted Guilt, and Guilt to come:
For this rich load, of which so proud they are,
Was rais'd by Tyranny, and rais'd for War;
Every capatious Gallions womb was fill'd,
With what the Womb of wealthy Kingdomes yield,
The new Worlds wounded Intrails they had tore,
For wealth wherewith to wound the old once more.   10
Wealth which all others Avarice might cloy,
But yet in them caus'd as much fear, as Joy.
For now upon the Main, themselves they saw,
That boundless Empire, where you give the Law,
Of winds and waters rage, they fearful be,
But much more fearful are your Flags to see.
Day, that to those who sail upon the deep,
More wish't for, and more welcome is than sleep,
They dreaded to behold, Least the Sun's light,
With *English* Streamers, should salute their sight: 20
In thickest darkness they would choose to steer,

On the Victory obtained by Blake: Admiral Robert Blake destroyed a fleet of sixteen Spanish treasure ships in the Bay of Santa Cruz, Teneriffe, on April 20, 1657. The victory was celebrated with a day of thanksgiving in London. The poem was published in 1674 with the tributes to Cromwell excised. The fact that it does not appear in the Bod. MS. casts some doubt on its authenticity.

So that such darkness might suppress their fear;
At length theirs vanishes, and fortune smiles;
For they behold the sweet Canary Isles;
One of which doubtless is by Nature blest
Above both Worlds, since 'tis above the rest.
For least some Gloominess might stain her sky,
Trees there the duty of the Clouds supply;
O noble Trust which Heaven on this Isle poures,
Fertile to be, yet never need her showres.   30
A happy People, which at once do gain
The benefits without the ills of rain.
Both health and profit Fate cannot deny;
Where still the Earth is moist, the Air still dry;
The jarring Elements no discord know,
Fewel and Rain together kindly grow;
And coolness there, with heat doth never fight,
This only rules by day, and that by Night.
Your worth to all these Isles a just right brings,
The best of Lands should have the best of Kings.   40
And these want nothing Heaven can afford,
Unless it be the having you their Lord;
But this great want will not a long one prove,
Your Conquering Sword will soon that want remove.
For *Spain* had better, Shee'l ere long confess,
Have broken all her Swords, than this one Peace,
Casting that League off, which she held so long,
She cast off that which only made her strong.
Forces and art, she soon will feel, are vain,
Peace, against you, was the sole strength of Spain.   50
By that alone those Islands she secures,
Peace made them hers, but War will make them yours.
There the indulgent Soil that rich Grape breeds,
Which of the Gods the fancied drink exceeds;
They still do yield, such is their pretious mould,
All that is good, and are not curst with Gold.
With fatal Gold, for still where that does grow,
Neither the Soyl, nor People quiet know.
Which troubles men to raise it when 'tis Oar,

47: England and Spain had been at peace since the treaty of 1630.

And when 'tis raised, does trouble them much more.   60
Ah, why was thither brought that cause of War,
Kind Nature had from thence remov'd so far?
In vain doth she those Islands free from Ill,
If fortune can make guilty what she will.
But whilst I draw that Scene, where you ere long,
Shall conquests act, your present are unsung,
  For *Sanctacruze* the glad Fleet takes her way,
And safely there casts Anchor in the Bay.
Never so many with one joyful cry
That place saluted, where they all must dye.   70
Deluded men! Fate with you did but sport,
You scap't the Sea, to perish in your Port.
'Twas more for *Englands* fame you should dye there,
Where you had most of strength, and least of fear.
  The Peek's proud height the *Spaniards* all admire,
Yet in their brests carry a pride much higher.
Onely to this vast hill a power is given,
At once both to Inhabit Earth and Heaven.
But this stupendious Prospect did not neer
Make them admire so much as they did fear.   80
  For here they met with news, which did produce
A grief above the cure of Grapes best juice.
They learn'd with Terrour that nor Summers heat,
Nor Winters storms, had made your Fleet retreat.
To fight against such Foes was vain, they knew,
Which did the rage of Elements subdue,
Who on the Ocean, that does horror give
To all besides, triumphantly do live.
  With haste they therefore all their Gallions moar,
And flank with Cannon from the Neighbouring shore.   90
Forts, Lines, and Sconces all the Bay along
They build and act all that can make them strong.
  Fond men who know not whilst such works they raise,
They only Labour to exalt your praise.
Yet they by restless toyl, became at Length
So proud and confident of their made strength

That they with joy their boasting General heard
Wish then for that assault he lately fear'd.
His wish he has, for now undaunted *Blake,*
With winged speed, for *Sanctacruze* does make.   100
For your renown, his conquering Fleet does ride
Ore Seas as vast as is the *Spaniards* pride,
Whose Fleet and Trenches view'd, he soon did say,
We to their Strength are more oblig'd than they.
Wer't not for that, they from their Fate would run,
And a third World seek out our Armes to shun.
Those Forts, which there so high and strong appear,
Do not so much suppress, as shew their fear.
Of Speedy Victory let no man doubt,
Our worst works past, now we have found them out.   110
Behold their Navy does at Anchor lye,
And they are ours, for now they cannot fly.
    This said, the whole Fleet gave it their applause,
And all assumes your courage, in your cause.
That Bay they enter, which unto them owes
The noblest wreaths that Victory bestows.
Bold *Stainer* Leads: this Fleets design'd by fate
To give him Lawrel, as the Last did Plate.
    The Thund'ring Cannon now begins the Fight,
And though it be at Noon, creates a Night.   120
The Air was soon after the fight begun
Far more enflam'd by it than by the Sun.
Never so burning was that Climate known:
War turn'd the temperate to the Torrid Zone.
    Fate these two Fleets between both Worlds had brought.
Who fight, as if for both those Worlds they fought.
Thousands of wayes Thousands of men there dye;
Some Ships are sunk, some blown up in the skie.
Nature never made Cedars so high aspire
As Oakes did then, Urg'd by the active fire,   130
Which by quick powders force so high was sent,
That it return'd to its own Element.
Torn Limbs some leagues into the Island fly,

117. *Stainer:* A subordinate of Blake's, who had captured or destroyed most of the Spanish treasure fleet in September 1656.
132: *its:* Fire's.

Whilst others lower, in the Sea do lye.
Scarce souls from bodies sever'd are so far
By death, as bodies there were by the War.
Th' all-seeing Sun, neer gaz'd on such a sight,
Two dreadful Navies there at Anchor Fight.
And neither have, or power, or will to fly;
There one must Conquer, or there both must dye.   140
Far different Motives yet engag'd them thus;
Necessity did them, but Choice did us.

    A choice which did the highest worth express,
And was attended by as high success.
For your resistless genious there did Raign,
By which we Laurels reapt ev'n on the Mayn.
So prosperous Stars, though absent to the sence,
Bless those they shine for, by their Influence.

    Our Cannon now tears every Ship and Sconce,
And o're two Elements Triumphs at once.   150
Their Gallions sunk, their wealth the Sea does fill,
The only place where it can cause no Ill.

    Ah would those Treasures which both Indies have
Were buryed in as large, and deep a grave;
Wars chief support with them would buried be,
And the Land owe her peace unto the Sea.
Ages to come your conquering Arms will bless;
There they destroy what had destroy'd their Peace.
And in one War the present age may boast
The certain seeds of many Wars are lost.   160

    All the Foes Ships destroy'd, by Sea or fire,
Victorious *Blake* does from the Bay retire;
His Seige of *Spain* he then again pursues,
And there first brings of his success the news;
The saddest news that ere to *Spain* was brought.
Their rich Fleet sunk, and ours with Lawrel fraught.
Whilst fame in every place, her Trumpet blowes,
And tells the World how much to you it owes.

Index of First Lines

273

Index of Poem Titles

ABOUT THE EDITOR

GEORGE deFOREST LORD is George Bodman Professor Emeritus at Yale University, where he has taught from 1947, specializing in seventeenth-century literature, epic and satire. He is General Editor of the Yale edition of *Poems on Affairs of State*, and first produced his highly respected edition of Marvell's poetry in 1968.

ABOUT THE INTRODUCER

A. ALVAREZ has edited anthologies of twentieth-century verse, and is the author of *The Savage God*.

This book is set in BASKERVILLE. John
Baskerville of Birmingham formed his
ideas of letter-design during his
early career as a writing-master
and engraver of inscriptions.
He retired in middle age,
set up a press of his
own and produced
his first book
in 1757.